HOME AND OFFICE DESK REFERENCE

Mary A. De Vries

PRENTICE HALL
Paramus, New Jersey 07652

Library of Congress Cataloging-in-Publication Data

De Vries, Mary Ann.
    Home and Office Desk Reference.
    Includes index.
    ISBN 0-13-619073-1
    1. Office practice—Handbooks, manuals, etc. 2. Secretaries—
Handbooks, manuals, etc. I. Title.
HF5547.5.D39   1989   89-31209
651.3—dc20   CIP

Printed in the United States of America

10 9 8 7 6 5 4 3

ISBN 0-13-619073-1

Originally published as *The Office Source Book* ISBN 0-13-798430-8

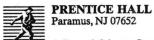 **PRENTICE HALL**
Paramus, NJ 07652

A Simon & Schuster Company

On the World Wide Web at http://www.phdirect.com

Prentice-Hall International (UK) Limited, *London*
Prentice-Hall of Australia Pty. Limited, *Sydney*
Prentice-Hall Canada Inc., *Toronto*
Prentice-Hall Hispanoamericana, S.A., *Mexico*
Prentice-Hall of India Private Limited, *New Delhi*
Prentice-Hall of Japan, Inc., *Tokyo*
Simon & Schuster Asia Pte. Ltd., *Singapore*
Editora Prentice-Hall do Brasil, Ltda., *Rio de Janeiro*

**In Memory of
Anna Kool De Vries**

What You Need to Know: Special Features of the *Home and Office Desk Reference*

Remember when you got your first electric typewriter? You wondered how you ever managed with that old manual. Now everyone is asking how a busy office could possibly function without a word processor, personal computer, or at least an electronic typewriter. When something comes along that makes your job easier and improves your productivity, you can't imagine how you got along before.

But the rapid technological advances that govern so much of modern business activity have also forced us continually to reconsider the problem of handling massive amounts of information. We need to know *so much* nowadays. To prepare ourselves and to be knowledgeable in a multitude of areas, we read handbooks and rely on dictionaries, business encyclopedias, and miscellaneous books and magazines for ongoing, daily reference.

The difficulty in trying to fit the extensive collection of data that we need into the limited space of a traditional office handbook has frustrated writers and publishers for decades. The *Home and Office Desk Reference* is the first practical solution to this puzzle. The almanac-fact book format is the best—perhaps the only—format that enables us to condense substantial amounts of material into one book by distilling the information into quick-scan lists, tables, charts, and diagrams.

Although the *Home and Office Desk Reference* is not intended to replace your favorite handbook or textbook—it *is* specifically designed to be the single most important addition to basic desk books that you will find available today. Because so much resource material has been recycled to fit the almanac-fact book format, the coverage in the *Home and Office Desk Reference* very comprehensive. Nine chapters cover essential office practices and important related matters, including the facts and reference material regularly needed to perform the varied tasks germane to modern business activity.

1. "Office Practices" deals with numerous basic office skills and procedures such as filing, typing, dictation, time management, records retention, employee performance, and reproduction processes.

2. "Postal and Telecommunications Services" presents important regulations, rules, and procedures concerning matters such as postal service, envelope addressing, air and ground transport services, mail rooms and mailing practices, and telecommunications.

3. "Meetings and Travel" includes key topics such as meeting preparation, agendas, meeting minutes, railroad accommodations, major airports, travel expense reports, and passport agencies.

4. "Grammar and Composition" covers a wide range of language and composition concerns such as rules of grammar and parts of speech, abbreviations, correct word use, punctuation, capitalization, spelling, and word division.

5. "Correspondence" offers a variety of material about written communication such as letter formats; forms of address; model letters, memos, and invitations; form-letter guidelines; and letter-writing techniques.

6. "Report Preparation and Production" illustrates the many aspects of report writing such as styles of reports, editing techniques, tabular format, copyright guidelines, and principal reference sources.

7. "Data Processing and Finance" provides numerous lists of technical facts and figures such as mathematical, computer, and other symbols; interest tables; bookkeeping and accounting guidelines; tax information; and banking services.

8. "Weights, Measures, and Values" consists of miscellaneous tables and lists such as standard measures, the metric system, measurement conversions, and land measurements.

9. "Glossaries" defines fundamental terms in the fields of accounting and book-keeping, statistics, banking, investments, credit and collection, data processing, business management, business law, real estate, insurance, and printing and publishing.

Almanac-fact books are noted for providing both an extensive amount of information and a wide variety of information. Typically, an almanac-fact book reports statistical, tabular, and general information. Since the *Home and Office Desk Reference* is a specialized book—that is, compiled for anyone who runs an office at home or at work—it contains *specific* statistical, tabular, and other information *selected especially for these persons.* The purpose of this almanac-fact book, then, is not to report the population of Chile or tell you who won the World Series last year; it is to offer important facts and figures that you can use *daily* in your *work.* For instance, in this book you can find answers to questions such as:

How long should I keep old correspondence and other records?

What steps should I follow in training an assistant?

Can I insure a priority-mail package?

What supplies should I keep in the mail room?

What is the proper way to address an envelope for the post office's optical character reader?

How should I type a meeting notice?

In which states and cities are the major U.S. airports located?

What does the computer abbreviation *RAM* mean?

Should I hyphenate a compound adjective such as *well known*?

When should I use a numeral or spell out a number under 100?

Should I use *that* or *which* to introduce a clause set off with commas?

Where should I divide the word *telecommunications* at the end of a line?

How do I type the signature line in a business letter using the simplified format?

What is the proper way to edit manuscript copy?

What does the flowchart symbol for *input/output* look like?

How can I compute interest at 10 percent using the 6 percent/60-day method?

What is a *credit entry* in bookkeeping?

Must left and right columns in a balance sheet be typed equal length?

What is the metric equivalent of 1 yard?

To locate the information you need to answer your question, either check the detailed alphabetical index in the back of the book or check the chronological listing of entries in the table of contents. To help you further, tables and lists include numerous cross-references to other items where applicable.

The *Home and Office Desk Reference* fills a void that has been particularly conspicuous in the past decade as people have had to find and absorb more and more information to keep pace with advancing technology. Use it as an easy-access, quick-reference source of time-saving, practical tips—something to help you work faster and better every day.

Mary A. De Vries

Acknowledgments

The *Home and Office Desk Reference* could not have been compiled without a generous supply of information from individuals, companies, educational facilities, U.S. governmental agencies and departments, and other organizations. Some of those who responded to my requests for information and materials were particularly helpful, and I want to thank all of them for their time and for sharing their expertise: Morris Golde, Electric Wastebasket Corporation; Clare Gorman, MCI International; Jerry Heitman, Professional Secretaries International; Donna Kelly, Official Airline Guides; Tom Miller, RCA Global Communications; Doris Griffin, U.S. Postal Service; and Trudy Prall, American Automobile Association. I also greatly appreciated the valuable material and cooperation of A. G. Edwards and Sons, Federal Express Corporation, International Paper Company, National Railroad Passenger Corporation, Southwestern Bell, United Parcel Service, and Western Union.

Mary A. De Vries

Contents

Office Practice (cont.)

CHAPTER 2

Postal and Telecommunications Services   47

CHAPTER 3

Meetings and Travel   83

Meetings and Travel (cont.)

CHAPTER 4

Grammar and Composition 97

CHAPTER 5

Correspondence 183

Correspondence (cont.)

Report Preparation and Production (cont.)

Data Processing and Finance 273

Data Processing and Finance (cont.)

CHAPTER 8

Weights, Measures, and Values 307

Glossaries 321

Index 383

CHAPTER 1

Office
Practices

GENERAL AND SPECIALIZED OFFICE DUTIES

General Duties	Specialized Duties
Receiving-screening telephone calls and office visitors	Composing and/or taking and transcribing complex correspondence
Placing telephone calls	Researching and preparing reports and special material
Sending telex and various electronic messages	Editing and rewriting special material (e.g., proposals, sales brochures)
Processing traditional incoming-outgoing mail	Preparing company publications (e.g., newsletter)
Filing and follow-up—general office	Taking and preparing conference and meeting minutes
Word processing—general office	
Taking routine dictation	Taking and transcribing dictation in a second language
Transcribing telephone and office dictation	Handling various advertising and public relations duties
Composing letters or memos	Word processing—technical or statistical
Maintaining office mailing lists	
Making and canceling appointments	Handling special filing (e.g., microfilm, automated data storage and retrieval)
Maintaining calendars	
Making travel arrangements and preparing itineraries	Handling conference and meeting arrangements (e.g., registration duties)
Operating basic office machines (e.g., mimeograph, postage meter, facsimile, copier)	Addressing groups and introducing speakers
Assisting in equipment and office furnishings selection	Coordinating and managing special-project work
Finding, hiring, and supervising assistants	Using specialized office equipment (e.g., typesetting) and software
Handling petty cash fund	Handling bookkeeping and accounting functions
Making bank deposits and reconciling bank statements	Preparing budgets, payrolls, and expense reports
Requisitioning-purchasing and storing supplies	Handling billing, credit, and collection duties
Maintaining inventories	

General Duties	Specialized Duties
Arranging dinner, theater, and other social-business engagements	Preparing and running computer programs
Developing and maintaining harmonious working relationships	Setting up and maintaining an office or company library
Taking authorized action when employer is away	Preparing training manuals and job specifications
Assisting employer with miscellaneous tasks (e.g., collecting material for a meeting)	Making time and work analyses
	Developing time-saving forms and procedures
Implementing and maintaining other general office practices and procedures	Handling other special duties, projects, and assignments.

SELF-RATING CHECKLIST OF OFFICE SKILLS AND ABILITIES

Skills/Abilities	Good	Average	Poor
Word processing (general office)	( )	( )	( )
Filing (general office)	( )	( )	( )
Electronic filing background	( )	( )	( )
Dictation (taking and transcribing notes)	( )	( )	( )
Dictation (transcribing from machines)	( )	( )	( )
Telephone communication	( )	( )	( )
Telex and electronic messaging	( )	( )	( )
Knowledge of basic office machines (e.g., typewriter, copier, facsimile, postage meter)	( )	( )	( )
Knowledge of special office machines (e.g., typesetting, data processing)	( )	( )	( )
Education and/or experience in data processing	( )	( )	( )
Writing (routine office correspondence)	( )	( )	( )
Writing (e.g., special publications, reports, proposals, publicity material)	( )	( )	( )
Knowledge of spelling, grammar, and punctuation rules	( )	( )	( )
Knowledge of business English	( )	( )	( )

Skills/Abilities	Good	Average	Poor
Working knowledge of second language	( )	( )	( )
Administrative skill	( )	( )	( )
Clerical skill	( )	( )	( )
Supervisory/leadership ability	( )	( )	( )
Decision-making ability	( )	( )	( )
Initiative	( )	( )	( )
Organizational ability	( )	( )	( )
Success with interpersonal relations	( )	( )	( )
Personality and temperament	( )	( )	( )
Trustworthiness	( )	( )	( )
Businesslike appearance	( )	( )	( )
Health	( )	( )	( )
Memory/retention ability	( )	( )	( )
Listening ability	( )	( )	( )
Reading comprehension	( )	( )	( )
Interest in details	( )	( )	( )
Accuracy	( )	( )	( )
Speed (most secretarial tasks)	( )	( )	( )
Arithmetic/math ability	( )	( )	( )
Bookkeeping/record-keeping ability	( )	( )	( )
Knowledge of company policies and procedures	( )	( )	( )
Special field/subject (e.g., retailing) knowledge	( )	( )	( )
Technical subject (e.g., engineering) knowledge	( )	( )	( )

STUDY OUTLINE FOR CERTIFIED PROFESSIONAL SECRETARY (CPS) EXAM

Subject	Examination Content
I. Behavioral Science in Business	Tests the principles of human relations and your understanding of self, peers, subordinates, and superiors. Focuses on the fundamentals of one's own needs and motivations, nature of conflict, problem-solving techniques, essentials of supervision and communication, leadership styles, and understanding of the informal organization. Multiple-choice questions.

Subject	Examination Content
II. Business Law	Measures your knowledge of the principles of business law as they may operate (not merely knowledge of definitions) in the working world and your knowledge of the content and implications of the operation of governmental controls on business. Understanding of the historical setting in which these controls developed should be emphasized in preference to names and dates. Multiple-choice questions.
III. Economics and Management	Covers economics (35 percent) and management (65 percent). Emphasis on understanding the basic concepts underlying Canada-Jamaica-United States business operations. To prepare, you should read current periodicals to keep informed about the latest government regulations in business. Multiple-choice questions.
IV. Accounting	Attempts to measure knowledge of the elements of the accounting cycle, ability to analyze financial statements, ability to perform arithmetical operations associated with accounting and computing interest and discounts, and ability to summarize and interpret financial data. Multiple-choice questions.
V. Communication Applications	Measures your proficiency in preparing communications. Consists of (60 percent) composing communications from directions given orally at approximately 70 to 80 wpm and (40 percent) editing, abstracting, and preparing communications in final format. Subjective evaluations.
VI. Office Administration and Technology	Covers subject matter unique to secretary's position. Includes traditional and contemporary responsibilities created by data processing, communications media, advances in office management, records management, and office systems. Multiple-choice questions.

Source: Adapted from *Capstone*, 1983. Published by Professional Secretaries International, Institute for Certifying Secretaries, 301 East Armour Boulevard, Kansas City, MO 64111.

STANDARD CHRONOLOGICAL RESUME FORMAT

	Name
	Street
JOB TITLE (Desired position)	City/State/Zip Code
	Telephone

OBJECTIVE

(One-paragraph summary of type of position you want, location desired, willingness to travel, and willingness to relocate.)

EMPLOYMENT

19XX–Present　　(Job title; company; city/state; type of firm; and brief summary of your responsibilities and any accomplishments.)

19XX–19XX　　(Same data.)

EDUCATION

19XX–19XX　　(School; city/state; degree or certificate of completion; summary of program, courses, or type of study; and any academic honors or achievements.)

19XX–19XX　　(Same data.)

LICENSES

(Type of license and any associated qualifications or restrictions; authorizing agency; license number and expiration date.)

MILITARY RECORD

19XX–19XX　　(Branch; rank; responsibilities; tours of duty; if honorably discharged; if in reserve; and any special recognition or honor.)

OTHER ACCOMPLISHMENTS (AND QUALIFICATIONS)

(Summary of additional achievements and activity such as special-project work, creative endeavors, awards received, fluency in another language, and special skills and abilities not mentioned above.)

MEMBERSHIPS

(List of organizations and any associated data such as offices held with dates.)

PERSONAL DATA

(Age; marital status; children; height; weight; citizenship status; state of health.)

SALARY DESIRED

(State an expectation or that you will negotiate.)

REFERENCES

(State that references will be furnished on request or at the interview.)

AVAILABILITY

(Date you can begin work or "immediately.")

TIME-MANAGEMENT TECHNIQUES

Technique	Strategy
Set objectives	Define each objective in writing (e.g., to reorganize the files). Make your goals realistic and set a deadline for each task.
Establish priorities	Arrange your tasks in the order of their importance, so that urgent matters are handled first.
Organize and plan your work	Develop an overall work plan and define the steps in each task. Have all supplies available before you begin work and keep material properly filed and easy to locate. Evaluate time requirements for various tasks. Allow time for necessary interruptions but avoid giving yourself more time than is needed for a job. Schedule involved work during periods of few or no interruptions. Break large jobs into a group of smaller steps and schedule difficult tasks first or when you feel the most energetic. Handle material (e.g., mail) once or as few times as possible. Use calendars and other scheduling aids and devise checklists with deadlines for multistep jobs, checking off each step as it is completed.
Delegate work	Delegate tasks that others can handle to give you more free time for essential priority work. Review assignments carefully with assistants to avoid errors and misunderstandings that would waste time.
Make time studies	Keep time charts to determine how you are using your time. Evaluate the charts to see whether too much valuable time is being devoted to low-priority matters.

Technique	Strategy
Evaluate your output cost	Determine what your time is worth and what it costs to do each task. If it is costing too much for some tasks, find more efficient, less costly procedures.
Control interruptions	Let people know when you are busy. Arrange specific meetings with assistants and other coworkers at a convenient time to avoid continual interruptions during the day. Do not initiate nonbusiness conversations or encourage social visiting. When you must ask someone to telephone, give a time that best suits your work plan.
Say no	Study your list of priorities and know your limits in time and energy. Say no to outside impositions on your time that involve low-priority and nonessential tasks. Be a cooperative coworker but not a patsy.
Cooperate with others	Legitimate cooperation with coworkers can pay dividends. When you need assistance or information, you can often save time and energy by calling on others.
Develop effective communications	State your business clearly to avoid later misunderstandings and interruptions. Listen carefully when you are the receiver of a message, and if possible, pose all questions you have in a single contact.
Simplify tasks	Handle each task in as few steps as possible (e.g., avoid making unnecessary file copies that involve extra handling time). Make a telephone call instead of a trip if possible and shop by phone or mail when you can. Ask people to come to you. Look for steps in each job that can be eliminated or combined. Use time-saving forms to record information.
Group similar activities	To increase your efficiency, handle similar activities together. If you have to go to the office supply store and look up something in the library, do both while you're out.
Avoid procrastination	Do not waste time on unnecessary chores simply to avoid difficult or unpleasant tasks. Avoid scheduling jobs you dislike during hours when you are tired or may find an excuse to interrupt your work. Try handling difficult jobs first unless your easier work is among the high-priority material. Divide difficult jobs into several, less formidable stages.

Technique	Strategy
Use down time productively	During moments when you must wait for something such as a return phone call, make it a point to accomplish something: review dictation, make up a list of work to do, or open the mail.
Pace yourself	Schedule important work for times of high energy. Pace yourself so you do not drain your energy reserve early in the day. Plan your workload to carry you to the end of the day and to make maximum use of your periods of peak energy and creativity. Pressure, and hence stress, increases when you modify your most effective pace, which leads to errors that must be corrected later.

COMMON FILING SYSTEMS

System	Chief Characteristics
Alphabetical	*One of the simplest and one of the two most common filing systems, where material is filed and indexed alphabetically. Sometimes used in combination with other filing systems.*
	Name file: Material filed alphabetically according to correspondent or name. (See *Indexing* and *Alphabetizing Rules,* p. 15.) No cross-index or list of files is required.
	Subject file: Material filed alphabetically according to subject (preferably a noun). Main subjects may be expanded to include folders with subject subheadings. Subheading folders are filed alphabetically behind the appropriate subject headings. Subject files may also be arranged numerically or in some other way.
	Name and subject file: Material for both subject and name filed together, alphabetically. This procedure is common when one has primarily subjects with an occasional name or primarily names with an occasional subject

System	Chief Characteristics
Numerical	*One of the two most common filing systems, where material is filed in some logical numerical order. Well suited for material with identification numbers, for rapidly expanding files, and in conjunction with data-processing systems.* *Subject-duplex file:* Material filed numerically by subject, with base numbers for subjects (100, 101, 102, . . .) and auxiliary numbers or letters for subheadings (100.1, 100.2, . . .). An auxiliary alphabetical cross-index is required. *Consecutive-number file:* Material filed numerically in ascending order (200, 201, 202, . . .). An auxiliary alphabetical cross-index is required. *Terminal-digit file:* Material filed numerically by units or digits (768342 = 76–83–42) to facilitate location. The units on the right might refer to the file drawer ; those in the center, to the folder; and those on the left, to the placement of papers within a folder. An auxiliary alphabetical cross-index is required. *Coded-number file:* Material filed numerically by identification number, such as insurance policy number. An auxiliary alphabetical cross-index is required.
Geographic	*A system commonly used by sales and marketing personnel and others who are concerned with the location of companies and individuals.* *Geographical-location file:* Material filed alphabetically, or in some logical pattern, by state. Subheadings such as county are filed alphabetically, or in some other logical pattern, behind the appropriate major heading. Subheadings in turn might have sub-subheadings such as city. An auxiliary alphabetical cross-index is required.
Decimal	*Based on the Dewey decimal system, which is found in some libraries and specialized businesses.* *Decimal file:* Material classified under headings numbered 000 to 900, with subheadings numbered 10 to 90 (200.10, 200.20, . . .), and sub-subheadings numbered 1 to 9 (200.10.1, 200.10.2, . . .),, and so on. An auxiliary alphabetical cross-index is required.

System	Chief Characteristics
Chronological	*An auxiliary file of carbon copies and photocopies arranged by date.* *Chronological file:* A common means of arranging copies of outgoing letters and other material in a file folder with the most recent date on top. New folders are opened as needed—daily, weekly, monthly, annually. Supplements the regular files.

BASIC FILING EQUIPMENT AND SUPPLIES

Equipment	Principal Features	Basic Supplies
Standard office file	Commonly, letter- and legal-size cabinets with drawers, often with key locks, sometimes insulated; vertical and lateral styles, with or without suspension system.	File folders and other document holders; hanging frames and folders for suspension systems; guides, tabs, and labels.
Rollaway file	File cabinet on casters to permit easy movement; sometimes with lower or upper shelf; often with lid on the file section, rather than pull-out drawer.	Same supplies specified above for standard office files and below for EDP files.
Combination-unit file	Equipment designed to serve multiple purposes; various storage and filing compartments within a single unit, such as file drawers, storage shelves with doors, card trays with doors or drawers, and a wide top shelf to serve as an equipment stand or minidesk.	Same supplies specified above for standard office files and below for open-shelf files and various card files.

Equipment	Principal Features	Basic Supplies
Open-shelf file	Bookcase-style units with shelves and no doors; various sizes and uses.	Usually, letter- and legal size file folders; other folders or containers for odd-size materials; guides, tabs, and labels.
Reference-shelf file	Bookcase-style units with doors on the shelves that will lower like a counter-top in front of each shelf.	Usually letter- and legal size file folders; other folders or containers for odd-size material; guides, tabs, and labels.
Safety file	Floor and shelf- or desk-top containers; often fire and humidity proof with combination locks.	Any desired folder, box, or other container for storing documents and valuables; miscellaneous labeling materials for contents.
Office storage cabinet	Various sizes and styles of cabinets with doors; sometimes a combination unit with rod in one section for hanging clothes and storage shelves in the other section.	Any type of envelope, folder, or container that will fit on the shelf; traditional labels for shelves, doors, and contents.
Data storage and retrieval center	Electronically controlled central filing center, where file containers are transported in and out by operator-activated (push-button) equipment.	Storage containers; traditional file folders or other document folders; guides, tabs, labels.
Terminal-digit file	Often large, motorized equipment with open-shelf, hanging-folder design; may be circular (i.e., rotary) style, with numerous floor-to-ceiling shelves.	File folders and other document holders; guides, tabs, and labels.
Vertical card file	Anything from a small cardboard box to a multiple-drawer cabinet.	File cards, often 3 × 5 inches; also 4 × 6 inches and 5 × 8 inches; guides, tabs, and labels.

Equipment	Principal Features	Basic Supplies
Visible card file	Generally, trays, narrow flat drawers, or books designed for quick access and easy viewing of contents.	Cards or sheets in pockets on horizontal trays, transparent inserts for books, or other visible holders; guides, tabs, and labels, also small metal or plastic signals.
Elevator file	Power-driven, multiple-card unit with trays on shelves that can be elevated or lowered to the level of the operator.	Cards, usually 3 × 5 inches; guides, tabs, and labels.
Rotary wheel file	Small, desk-top wheel, often used for a desk telephone-address list; or large, motorized, carousel-style equipment. (See also *Terminal-digit file*.)	Cards, often with notches to attach to the wheel; standard file folders; guides, tabs, and labels.
Random file	Keyboard-activated card file; often consisting of drawers equipped with magnetic rods.	Cards with typed or printed data and metal teeth that are activated by the magnetic rods in the equipment; guides, tabs, and labels.
EDP file	Electronic data-processing file; specifically designed tabulating card file, vertical file, removable tray file, or regular filing cabinet with drawers.	Miscellaneous holders for magnetic tapes and discs, punched cards and tapes: EDP binders, racks, drum libraries, folders, pockets, special trays, metal reel containers, disk books and packs; guides, tabs, and labels.
Printout storage file	Storage rack with shelf-style pockets for storing binders and loose sheets, with or without doors; mobile and stationary	Binders and EDP folders; guides, tabs, and labels.

Equipment	Principal Features	Basic Supplies
	vertical and lateral print-out files with drawers; or hanging binder racks.	
Microfilm storage file	Photographic equipment that copies material for storage in greatly reduced form; reader-printer equipment magnifies a document on a television screen for reading or prints it out as hard copy (i.e., a photocopy of the document).	Specially designed folders or pockets; acetate jacket cards; guides, tabs, and labels.
Art and blue-print file	Equipment designed to accommodate large, odd-size drawings, blue-prints, and miscellaneous artwork; open-shelf, vertical-divider style; flat drawer style, or cube style with small cubelike spaces for inserting rolled documents.	Folders for negatives and other sensitive material; guides, tabs, and labels.

Note: Numerous variations of the basic filing equipment and supplies described above—and additional. special-purpose equipment and supplies—are available from manufacturing and retail outlets. Refer to current equipment and supply catalogs for details concerning new features and style and size variations. Design consultants are frequently available to solve problems and to design efficient systems for specific needs.

INDEXING AND
ALPHABETIZING RULES

INDIVIDUALS

1. Transpose so that last name becomes the first indexing unit (Jones, John).
2. Index and file unfamiliar foreign names (Chiang Ching-kuo) as they occur rather than transpose them, but cross-reference to the other unit.
3. Treat hyphenated words as one word (St. Clair-Towers).
4. When names are identical, use the address to determine order (first city, then state, street name, direction, number).
5. Include a prefix (de) as part of the surname (de Reus).
6. Consider abbreviations as if they were spelled out (St. = Saint).
7. Ignore academic degrees and professional designations (Ph.D.; CPS), but place them in parentheses at the end of the name.
8. Treat a title preceding one name alone or part of a name as the first unit (Prince Andrew). Otherwise, ignore a title before a full name, but place it in parentheses after the name—for example, Smith, Michael (Dr.).
9. Retain seniority titles (Jr., Sr., II, III).
10. Treat Mrs. as an indexing unit when a woman is known only by her husband's name (Mrs. Henry Kilgore). Ignore Mrs. otherwise, but place the title and husband's name in parentheses if it is important to have this information—for example, Adams, Margaret (Mrs. Ward Adams).
11. After indexing the names, place them in alphabetical order, letter by letter, word by word, and unit by unit.
12. Cross-reference whenever a name might be filed in more than one place.

EXAMPLES

Paul S. Hart, 19 Third Street, Rochester, NY
Prince Andrew
John Jones
Sister Mary Walters
Mrs. Ward (Margaret) Adams
John Jones III
S. R. de Reus
Michael Smith, M.D.
Paul S. Hart, 1070 West Charles Street, Rochester, NY
Miss Jennifer St. Clair-Towers
Mrs. Henry Kilgore
Chiang Ching-kuo

Unit 1	Unit 2	Unit 3	Unit 4	Unit 5	Unit 6
Adams	Margaret (Mrs. Ward Adams)				
Chiang	Ching-kuo				
de Reus	S.	R.			
Hart	Paul	S.	Rochester	NY	Third
Hart	Paul	S.	Rochester	NY	Charles
Jones	John				
Jones	John	III			
Kilgore	Henry	Mrs.			
Prince	Andrew				
St. Clair-Towers	Jennifer				
Smith	Michael (Dr.)				
Walters	Mary (Sr.)				

BUSINESSES

1. Generally, index business names in the order they are written, but transpose the name of the first-mentioned individual and file by that name; cross-reference to any other individual names in the title (Snow, P. K., Inc.). Retain the original order in well-known names (Mark Cross).

2. Retain titles in a firm name (Mr. Y Sportswear).

3 Retain firm endings (Co., Corp., Inc., Ltd., Mfg., Son, Bros.) and treat them as if they were spelled out.

4. Generally, ignore articles, conjunctions, and propositions (a, an, the, and, &, for, in, of), but retain them in foreign words. Treat a foreign article as part of the word it precedes (l'Anglais).

5 Treat hyphenated surnames as one word (R. L. Douglas-Brown Co.), but if the hyphen replaces a comma or the word and, treat it as two words (The Douglas-Brown Co., meaning The Douglas and Brown Company).

6. Treat words that may be written as one or two words (Southwest, South West) as one indexing unit.

7. Generally, treat compound geographical names that are not hyphenated as separate units (<u>New York</u>), but treat them as one unit when the first part is foreign <u>Los Angeles</u>).

8. Disregard <u>s</u> when a word ends with apostrophe <u>s</u> (<u>Donnovan's</u>), but retain it when the word itself ends in <u>s</u> (<u>Burns'</u>).

9. Treat letters representing separate words or letters as separate indexing units (<u>N B C</u>).

10. Ignore accents (<u>Société</u>) in foreign words.

11. Treat coined names and trade names as one unit (<u>While-U-Wait</u>).

12. Treat numbers as if they were spelled out (<u>1200 Club</u> = <u>Twelve Hundred Club</u>).

13. When names are identical, use the address to determine order (first city, then state, street name, direction, number).

14. After indexing the names, place them in alphabetical order, letter by letter, word by word, and unit by unit.

15. Cross-reference whenever a name might be filed in more than one place.

EXAMPLES

P. K. Snow, Inc.
Henry Doyle and Samuel Goldstein Associates, Inc.
The New York Dance Studio
Cleaning While-U-Wait
Mr. Y Sportswear
Burns' Bridal Shop
Best Hardward, 1500 El Paso Drive, Dallas, TX
The 1200 Club
Société des Auteurs Français
Jones, Shore & Watts Ltd.
Donnovan's Quick Printing
Best Hardware, 92 Courtney Lane, Atlanta, GA
Jackson-Weber-Hill Mfg. Co.
Donnovans' Fast Food Service
Los Angeles Opera House
NBC

Unit 1	Unit 2	Unit 3	Unit 4	Unit 5	Unit 6
Best	Hardware	Atlanta	Georgia	Court-ney	Lane
Best	Hardware	Dallas	Texas	El Paso	Drive
Burns'	Bridal	Shop			

Unit 1	Unit 2	Unit 3	Unit 4	Unit 5	Unit 6
Cleaning	While-U-Wait				
Donnovan's	Quick	Printing			
Donnovans'	Fast	Food	Service		
Doyle	Henry (and Samuel Goldstein)	Associates	Incorporated		
Jackson	Webber	Hill	Manufacturing	Company	
Jones	Shore (&)	Watts	Limited		
Los Angeles	Opera	House			
Mr.	Y	Sportswear			
(The) New	York	Dance	Studio		
N(ational)	B(roadcasting)	C(ompany)			
Snow	P	K	Incorporated		
Société	des	Auteurs	Français		
(The) Twelve hundred	Club				

INSTITUTIONS AND GOVERNMENTAL BODIES

1. Generally, index institutions such as colleges and churches in the order written (College of the Ozarks), but place the significant word first if the name begins with a common word (University of Ohio = Ohio, University of).
2. Place articles in a name in parentheses before or after the name—for example,

The Research Institute = (The) Research Institute; otherwise, ignore them in indexing and alphabetizing, except in foreign names (LaSalle University).

3. Index a name with different addresses by location (Little Rock, Young Women's Christian Association).

4. When two or more names are identical, use the address to determine order (first city, then state, street name, direction, number).

5. Transpose names with common words to place the significant words first (Hotel Windsor = Windsor, Hotel).

6. Treat the geographic location of a bank as the first unit (First National Bank of Boulder = Boulder, First National Bank).

7. Names of U.S. federal governmental departments, bureaus, commissions, and so on are always preceded by the three indexing units United States Government.

8. Place governmental classifications such as Department, Bureau, and City after the descriptive word (Department of Commerce = Commerce, Department of), or place the classification in parentheses and disregard it, for example Commerce (Dept. of).

9. Retain words such as Board and Department in nongovernmental organizations, but index them after the descriptive term (Board of Education, City of Memphis = Memphis, City of, Education, Board of), with the city of location first.

10. Index foreign governmental names first by name of country, next by general classification (Republic of), and then by subdivision (Defense, Ministry of).

11. After indexing the names, place them in alphabetical order, letter by letter, word by word, unit by unit.

12. Cross-reference whenever a name might be filed in more than one place.

EXAMPLES

The Research Institute
Federal Trade Commission
Washington High School
GSA
Newark Public Library
Department of Education, France
Finance Department of Milwaukee, WI
Sacramento Highway Department
City Sewer Department, Richmond, VA
College of the Ozarks

Young Women's Christian Association, 200 Walsh Avenue, Birmingham, AL

U.S. Department of Interior

Board of Education, City of Memphis, TN

State of Wyoming, Department of Parks and Recreation

First National Bank of Boulder

University of Ohio

Young Women's Christian Association, 14 Main Street, Little Rock, AR

Hotel Windsor

Unit 1	Unit 2	Unit 3	Unit 4	Unit 5	Unit 6
Birming- ham (AL)	Young	Women's	Christian	Associa- tion	Walsh
Boulder (CO)	First	National	Bank (of)		
College (of the)	Ozarks				
France	Republic (of)	Education (Dept. of)			
Little Rock (AR)	Young	Women's	Christian	Associa- tion	Main
Memphis (TN)	City (of)	Educa- tion	Board (of)		
Milwau- kee (WI)	City (of)	Finance (Dept. of)			
Newark	Public	Library			
Ohio	University (of)				
(The) Research	Institute				
Richmond (VA)	City (of)	Sewer (Dept. of)			

Unit 1	Unit 2	Unit 3	Unit 4	Unit 5	Unit 6
Sacra-mento (CA)	City (of)	Highway (Dept. of)			
United	States	Govern-ment	Federal	Trade	Commis-sion
United	States	Govern-ment	G(eneral)	S(er-vices)	A(d-ministra-tion)
United	States	Govern-ment	Interior (Dept. of)		
Washing-ton	High	School			
Windsor	Hotel				
Wyoming	State (of)	Parks and Recrea-tion (Dept. of)			

GUIDE TO RECORDS RETENTION

Legend for Authority to Dispose

AD—Administrative Decision
ASPR—Armed Services Procurement
    Regulation
CFR—Code of Federal Regulation
FLSA—Fair Labor Standards Act
ICC—Interstate Commerce Com-
    mission
INS—Insurance Company Regulation
ISM—Industrial Security Manual, At-
    tachment to DD Form 441

Legend for Retention Period

AC—Dispose After Completion of Job
    or Contract
AE—Dispose After Expiration
AF—After End of Fiscal Year
AM—After Moving
AS—After Settlement
AT—Dispose After Termination
ATR—After Trip
OBS—Dispose When Obsolete
P—Permanent
SUP—Dispose When Superseded

Type of Record	Retention Period (Years)	Authority
ACCOUNTING & FISCAL		
Accounts Payable Invoices	3	ASPR-STATE, FLSA
Accounts Payable Ledger	P	AD
Accounts Receivable Invoices & Ledgers	5	AD
Authorizations for Accounting	SUP	AD
Balance Sheets	P	AD
Bank Deposits	3	AD
Bank Statements	3	AD
Bonds	P	AD
Budgets	3	AD
Capital Asset Record	3*	AD
Cash Receipt Records	7	AD
Check Register	P	AD
Checks, Dividend	6	
Checks, Payroll	2	FLSA, STATE
Checks, Voucher	3	FLSA, STATE
Cost Accounting Records	5	AD
Earnings Register	3	FLSA, STATE
Entertainment, Gifts & Gratuities	3	AD
Estimates, Projections	7	AD
Expense Reports	3	AD
Financial Statements, Certified	P	AD
Financial Statements, Periodic	2	AD
General Ledger Records	P	CFR
Labor Cost Records	3	ASPR, CFR
Magnetic Tape and Tab Cards	1**	
Note Register	P	AD
Payroll Registers	3	FLSA, STATE
Petty Cash Records	3	AD
P & L Statements	P	AD
Salesman Commission Reports	3	AD
Travel Expense Reports	3	AD
Work Papers, Rough	2	AD
ADMINISTRATION RECORDS		
Audit Reports	10	AD
Audit Work Papers	3	AD
Classified Documents: Inventories, Reports, Receipts	10	AD

* After Disposed   ** Normally   † Govt. R&D Contracts

Type of Record	Retention Period (Years)	Authority
Correspondence, Executive	P	AD
Correspondence, General	5	AD
Directives from Officers	P	AD
Forms Used, File Copies	P	AD
Systems and Procedures Records	P	AD
Work Papers, Management Projects	P	AD
COMMUNICATIONS		
Bulletins Explaining Communications	P	AD
Messenger Records	1	AD
Phone Directories	SUP	AD
Phone Installation Records	1	AD
Postage Reports, Stamp Requisitions	1 AF	AD
Postal Records, Registered Mail & Insured Mail Logs & Meter Records	1 AF	AD, CFR
Telecommunications Copies	1	AD
CONTRACT ADMINISTRATION		
Contracts, Negotiated, Bailments, Changes, Specifications, Procedures, Correspondence	P	CFR
Customer Reports	P	AD
Materials Relating to Distribution Revisions, Forms, and Format of Reports	P	AD
Work Papers	OBS	AD
CORPORATE		
Annual Reports	P	AD
Authority to Issue Securities	P	AD
Bonds, Surety	3 AE	AD
Capital Stock Ledger	P	AD
Charters, Constitution, Bylaws	P	AD
Contracts	20 AT	AD
Corporate Election Records	P	AD
Incorporation Records	P	AD
Licenses—Federal, State, Local	AT	AD
Stock Transfer & Stockholder	P	AD
LEGAL		
Claims and Litigation Concerning Torts and Breach of Contracts	P	AD
Law Records—Federal, State, Local	SUP	AD

Type of Record	Retention Period (Years)	Authority
Patents and Related Material	P	AD
Trademark & Copyrights	P	AD
LIBRARY, COMPANY		
Accession Lists	P	AD
Copies of Requests for Materials	6 mos.	AD
Meeting Calendars	P	AD
Research Papers, Abstracts, Bibliographies	SUP, 6 mos. AC	AD
MANUFACTURING		
Bills of Material	2	AD, ASPR
Drafting Records	P	AD†
Drawings	2	AD, ASPR
Inspection Records	2	AD
Lab Test Reports	P	AD
Memos, Production	AC	AD
Product, Tooling, Design, Engineering Research, Experiment & Specs Records	20	STATUTE LIMITA- TIONS
Production Reports	3	AD
Quality Reports	1 AC	AD
Reliability Records	P	AD
Stock Issuing Records	3 AT	AD, ASPR
Tool Control	3 AT	AD, ASPR
Work Orders	3	AD
Work Status Reports	AC	AD
OFFFICE SUPPLIES & SERVICES		
Inventories	1 AF	AD
Office Equipment Records	6 AF	AD
Requests for Services	1 AF	AD
Requisitions for Supplies	1 AF	AD
PERSONNEL		
Accident Reports, Injury Claims, Settlements	30 AS	CFR, INS, STATE
Applications, Changes & Terminations	5	AD, ASPR, CFR
Attendance Records	7	AD
Employee Activity Files	2 or SUP	AD
Employee Contracts	6 AT	AD

Type of Record	Retention Period (Years)	Authority
Fidelity Bonds	3 AT	AD
Garnishments	5	AD
Health & Safety Bulletins	P	AD
Injury Frequency Charts	P	CFR
Insurance Records, Employees	11 AT	INS
Job Descriptions	2 or SUP	CFR
Rating Cards	2 or SUP	CFR
Time Cards	3	AD
Training Manuals	P	AD
Union Agreements	3	WALSH-HEALEY ACT
PLANT & PROPERTY RECORDS		
Depreciation Schedules	P	AD
Inventory Records	P	AD
Maintenance & Repair, Building	10	AD
Maintenance & Repair, Machinery	5	AD
Plant Account Cards, Equipment	P	CFR, AD
Property Deeds	P	AD
Purchase or Lease Records of Plant Facility	P	AD
Space Allocation Records	1 AT	AD
PRINTING & DUPLICATING		
Copies Produced, Tech. Pubs., Charts	1 or OBS	AD
Film Reports	5	AD
Negatives	5	AD
Photographs	1	AD
Production Records	1 AC	AD
PROCUREMENT, PURCHASING		
Acknowledgments	AC	AD
Bids, Awards	3 AT	CFR
Contracts	3 AT	AD
Exception Notices (GAO)	6	AD
Price Lists	OBS	AD
Purchase Orders, Requisitions	3 AT	CFR
Quotations	1	AD
PRODUCTS, SERVICES, MARKETING		
Correspondence	3	AD
Credit Ratings & Classifications	7	AD

Type of Record	Retention Period (Years)	Authority
Development Studies	P	AD
Presentations & Proposals	P	AD
Price Lists, Catalogs	OBS	AD
Prospect Lines	OBS	AD
Register of Sales Order	NO VALUE	AD
Surveys	P	AD
Work Papers, Pertaining to Projects	NO VALUE	AD

PUBLIC RELATIONS & ADVERTISING

Type of Record	Retention Period (Years)	Authority
Advertising Activity Reports	5	AD
Community Affairs Records	P	AD
Contracts for Advertising	3 AT	AD
Employee Activities & Presentations	P	AD
Exhibits, Releases, Handouts	2–4	AD
Internal Publications	P (1 copy)	AD
Layouts	1	AD
Manuscripts	1	AD
Photos	1	AD
Public Information Activity	7	AD
Research Presentations	P	AD
Tearsheets	2	AD

SECURITY

Type of Record	Retention Period (Years)	Authority
Classified Material Violations	P	AD
Courier Authorizations	1 mo. ATR	AD
Employee Clearance Lists	SUP	ISM
Employee Case Files	5	ISM
Fire Prevention Program	P	AD
Protection—Guards, Badge Lists, Protective Devices	5	AD
Subcontractor Clearances	2 AT	AD
Visitor Clearance	2	ISM

TAXATION

Type of Record	Retention Period (Years)	Authority
Annuity or Deferred Payment Plan	P	CFR
Depreciation Schedules	P	CFR
Dividend Register	P	CFR
Employee Withholding	4	CFR
Excise Exemption Certificates	4	CFR
Excise Reports (Manufacturing)	4	CFR
Excise Reports (Retail)	4	CFR
Inventory Reports	P	CFR

Type of Record	Retention Period (Years)	Authority
Tax Bills and Statements	P	AD
Tax Returns	P	AD
TRAFFIC & TRANSPORTATION		
Aircraft Operating & Maintenance	P	CFR
Bills of Lading, Waybills	2	ICC, FLSA
Employee Travel	1 AF	AD
Freight Bills	3	ICC
Freight Claims	2	ICC
Household Moves	3 AM	AD
Motor Operating & Maintenance	2	AD
Rates and Tariffs	SUP	AD
Receiving Documents	2–10	AD, CFR
Shipping & Related Documents	2–10	AD, CFR

Source: Electric Wastebasket Corporation, a division of Michael Business Machines Corp., 145 West 45th Street, New York, NY 10036.

Note: State retention statutes vary widely, and both federal and state statutes may be revised from time to time. Consult your attorney or accountant for current federal and state retention requirements that may affect your organization.

BUSINESS MACHINES AND SYSTEMS

Machine/System	Primary Function
Addressing equipment	Machines that prepare mailing addresses by mechanical or electronic means. Machines that stamp addresses onto the paper often use inked cards or metal plates. Computers store and print out addresses electronically.
Audiovisual equipment	Equipment such as projectors; often used in making sales presentations, in conducting training programs, and in delivering conference papers.
Automatic bookkeeping and accounting equipment	Machines using coded instructions that automatically tabulate, extend, post, and total figures on reports and statements and in ledgers. Computers use spreadsheets and other accounting software to record, calculate, and print data electronically.

Machine/System	Primary Function
Automatic shredder	A machine that shreds documents ready for disposal, so that they are no longer readable. Some security shredders will reduce microfilm and microfiche into unreadable microfine hairs.
Billing machine	A typewriter with a built-in automatic calculator that handles various functions such as posting to ledger accounts and accumulating posting totals; often computer integrated.
Binding equipment	Machines that perform binding operations such as drilling, gluing, stitching, trimming, and inserting and molding plastic tubes.
Calculator	A machine that handles arithmetic functions such as adding, subtracting, dividing, and multiplying. Calculators vary in size from small handheld models to large desk machines. Printing models record on paper. Electronic models illuminate figures on a small screen. Some have both screen and paper. Programmable models can handle advanced mathematical functions.
Check signer/tallyprinter	A security-controlled document processor that will quickly and accurately perform tasks such as count, date, number, imprint, sign, or endorse checks, stocks, bonds, certificates, transportation tickets, and other documents.
Closed-circuit television	A private video system with large-screen projection systems or television monitors in soundproof conference rooms within a company or within a network such as a company's headquarters and its branches. Used primarily for meetings, seminars, and training programs. Sites are sometimes joined by satellite transmission for mass audience viewing (e.g., to introduce a new product).
Collator	A machine that automatically assembles individual pages into sets of material. Models vary in size, speed, and other features, with some high-speed models containing up to 100 stations or bins.
Computer	An electronic device that receives input data, stores it, operates on it in response to a specific set of program instructions, displays it on a videolike screen, and

Machine/System	Primary Function
	prints it out on paper. Computers range in size from very large central terminals to very small travel units. Features vary widely from model to model. Desktop computer systems consist of a keyboard, one or more disk drives and/or a hard disk, a display screen, a printer, and the central processor. Computers are used in almost all phases of business activity and for specialized functions such as typesetting. Very large systems are sometimes used on a time-sharing basis.
Computer-aided designer	A design system that is linked to a computer, with a display screen and other features to assist in design drafting and three-dimensional modeling work.
Copier	A reproduction machine that makes single or multiple copies of material. Size, speed, type of paper used, reproduction quality, and other factors vary widely among available equipment. Some machines with advanced features are capable of producing art-quality copies, can copy on two sides of the paper, and can reduce the size of original documents.
Dictation equipment	Recording and playback machines of various sizes and styles, from pocket-size travel units to desk-top executive communication models. Portable models use discrete media such as cassettes, disks, and belts. Permanent, continuous-loop models use a dictator-to-transcriber circular tape.
Document feeder	An automatic or semiautomatic machine that feeds original documents into a copier.
Document reader	A machine that reads individual pages, converts them into digital characters, and transfers the characters to a word processor. Such automatic document-entry terminals are intended to relieve busy word-processor operators of the text-entry operation.
Duplicating equipment	Various machines used to duplicate copies, including the mimeograph (using a stencil, to 5,000 copies, good quality); the spirit duplicator (using a master, to 500 copies; medium quality); and the offset duplicator (using a master, to 10,000 copies, excellent quality). (See also *Copier*.)

Machine/System	Primary Function
Electronic filing system	Computer-assisted filing and retrieval equipment that locates microfilm (see *Microform equipment*) or paper documents in a matter of seconds and transports containers or displays documents on a screen or prints out a hard copy.
Electronic mail opener	A machine that automatically feeds and adjusts to open mail of different sizes and thicknesses.
Electronic PBX/CBX	Computer phone systems, the Private Branch Exchange (PBX) and Central Branch Exchange (CBX) can automatically perform a variety of functions from transferring calls to notifying a user when a busy line is free. Systems can be connected to computers, which allows the transmittal of communications to receiving phones anywhere in the system.
Electronic weighing systems	A machine with a weighing platform and keyboard console that selects and displays the correct rate of postage for the intended mode of shipment.
Facsimile equipment (FAX)	High-speed electronic transmitter-receiver equipment that will convert all sorts of documents including graphic displays into a form that can be sent over the regular telephone lines to a destination where the receiver equipment reproduces it in a duplicate hard-copy format.
Folding equipment	Machines that automatically fold items for insertion into envelopes, often at high speeds. Different models handle different paper sizes, for example 11 × 17 or 14 × 21 inches.
Inserting equipment	Machines that automatically insert items in envelopes, often at high speeds. Most models will open envelopes, insert a certain number of items, fold the envelope flaps, seal the envelopes, and stack them.
Mail-sorting system	A unit with numerous trays, racks, and sacks, sometimes rotary or otherwise movable, arranged in a logical work-flow order so that each piece of mail can be quickly dropped into the appropriate slot.
Microform equipment	Machines designed to reduce documents to a fraction of the original size and store the images on film strips (*microfilm*), film sheets (*microfiche*), or opaque cards

Machine/System	Primary Function

(microcard). For rapid retrieval, readers magnify the material on a screen for viewing. Printers make a hard copy of the document. Sometimes the two functions are combined in one unit.

Optical scanner — A device that reads typed images at high speed. It is designed to free word processors for text editing and allow office typewriters to be used as an input terminal. Three types of scanners are optical character readers (OCR), optical mark readers (OMR), and bar code readers, each of the three designed especially to recognize alphanumeric characters, placement of particular marks, or heavy lines and bars.

Postage accounting systems — An electronic device used in conjunction with an electronic postage meter to provide accurate accountability for postage expenditures by department or account, by batch, and by day, week, or month.

Postage meter — A machine that imprints a meter stamp on mailing material. One purchases a desired amount of postage and has the machine set for that amount at the post office or by telephone with a remote meter-setting feature. Metered mail need not be dated, canceled, or postmarked at the post office. Some automatic meter-mailing machines will feed, seal, transport, stack, and automatically imprint both U.S. Post Office and United Parcel Service tapes.

Tabulating machine — A machine that can sort and tabulate information recorded by another machine—for example, sorting punched cards into some desired order and tabulating the information punched on the card.

Telephone answering machine — A telephone message playback-recorder, often with a remote-control feature that allows one to call the device from another location to activate message playback.

Teleprinter/teletypewriter — A keyboard machine that is connected to the telephone lines over which one can send, receive, and print out data. Various models have features such as memory storage of multiple messages; used in telex transmission.

Machine/System	Primary Function
Time recorder	A mechanical or electromechanical control device used to monitor time spent by persons or machines. Time devices range from simple time stamps to sophisticated time-management systems. Units for time-recording applications are used to provide payroll and various production information.
Time system	Payroll processing machines that automatically process time cards for payroll accounting. An optical feature will link a machine through telephone lines to a central computer for large network applications.
Typesetting equipment	A variety of machines that produce typeset copy suitable for reproduction. Examples are *phototypesetting equipment,* which use film to produce a photographic result; *digital composition machines,* which store type on floppy disks; *linotype machines,* which cast individual metal lines, and *monotype machines,* which produce individual type characters rather than lines; and *computers* and advanced *typewriters,* which print out camera-ready copy.
Typewriter	*Electronic typewriters* are capable of performing routine functions (such as centering and underscoring) automatically. In addition to having a standard typewriter keyboard, the machines have special keys for the various automatic functions. A memory for phrase, line, or page storage with automatic playout and text-revision capability are features of many models. Some are upgradable to a higher level approaching word-processor capability. The *electric typewriter* is the forerunner of the electronic model without the many automatic functions.
Voice-mail system	An integrated system combining a telephone system with electronic computer transmission. Voice mail can transmit, receive, and store messages and can be accessed from almost any telephone worldwide.
Word processor	A dedicated computer designed primarily to process reports, correspondence, and other word-based information. Word processors handle text like a typewriter with additional features such as memory, automatic printing, and electronic intelligence. They perform

Machine/System	Primary Function

functions such as checking spelling in different languages and verifying your figures against the figures you're typing from. Material is generally stored on floppy disks or diskettes, cassette tapes, or hard disks.

Note: Because of wide variation in equipment features and capabilities, as well as rapid technological change, readers should consult manufacturers and retail outlets for current specifications on any desired machine or system.

CHECKLIST OF DICTATION AND TRANSCRIPTION MATERIALS

Taking Dictation

Spiral-bound notebook(s)	( )
Rubber bands	( )
Pens (e.g., ballpoint)	( )
Sharpened lead pencils	( )
Colored pencils	( )
Paperclips	( )
Rubber finger to turn pages	( )
Small calendar	( )
Address lists	( )
Special files	( )
Folder for miscellaneous reference material and correspondence	( )
Shorthand notebook(s)	( )
Transcription belt, disk, or cassette	( )
Files and reference material	( )
Address lists	( )
Stationery	( )
Envelopes and mailing labels	( )
Typing paper	( )
Carbon paper	( )
Erasers	( )
Correction tape or fluid	( )
Paperclips	( )

TYPEWRITER AND PRINTER RIBBONS

Type of Ribbon	Principal Uses
Carbon	Carbon ribbons are available in film, polyethylene, paper, and acetate, with the carbon film ribbon being one of the most popular ribbons. Used for all high-quality and general typing and printing to produce clean, crisp images. Carbon ribbons are generally discarded after using them one time.
Fabric	Fabric ribbons are available in cotton, silk, and nylon, with the nylon fabric ribbon producing the best image of the three. Used for general typing and printing, fabric ribbons produce a poorer quality image than some of the nonfabric ribbons such as the carbon film ribbon. Unlike carbon ribbons, fabric ribbons are generally reused, although the image fades with repeated uses.
Correctable	Correctable ribbons are used for quality correspondence. Errors are lifted from the page in conjunction with a correction tape.
Color	Colors are available with most types of ribbons—carbon, nylon, and so on. Two-color ribbons have the most frequently used color on top. They are often used in typing offset reproduction masters and in other work where additional color is advantageous.
Stencil	Stencil ribbons are made of clear plastic material. They are commonly used for typing stencils that do not have a cover sheet.
Photostat	Photostat ribbons contain a special ink for use in reproduction processes with ultraviolet light.
Offset	Offset ribbons are designed especially for typing masters in offset reproduction work.
Opaque	Opaque ribbons are used to type material intended for reproduction in the Diazo copying machine.

BASIC OFFICE PAPERS

Type of Paper	Chief Characteristics
Stationery	Paper with a heading printed or engraved on it; usually, twenty- or twenty-four-pound weight cotton content (25, 75, or 100 percent) on high-quality bond paper in a white or conservative color, with matching envelopes. Traditional business letterhead size is 8½ by 11 inches.
Bond paper	A plain paper used for multiple purposes (drafts, reports, and so on). It is graded by brightness and opacity. A No. 1 bond, the highest quality, is sometimes used for stationery. Lower grades are used for photocopying, drafting, and so forth. Standard letter size is 8½ by 11 inches. Tractor bond is regular bond paper with perforated edges designed to feed into a computer printer. Most copiers will accept any type of bond (or cotton-content) paper.
Carbon paper	Lightweight coated paper used in making carbon (duplicate) copies. A single-weight solvent carbon coated on a film base is durable and long lasting and will not tear or smear. Wax-coated paper ranges from a four-pound to a seven-pound weight. Use a standard weight for making up to five copies, a medium weight or light weight for up to ten, and a light weight or extra-light weight for more than ten. Carbon sets consist of a sheet of carbon paper attached at one end to lightweight bond, or onionskin, copy paper. Carbonless paper is treated to produce a carbonlike image on copies simply by striking the original sheet without inserting a wax or solvent-coated carbon paper between the copies; often used for invoices.
Copier paper	*See* Bond paper.
Computer paper	*See* Bond paper.
Facsimile paper	Unlike other cotton or bond paper used in typewriters, computers, and the like, FAX paper is as yet not interchangeable. The paper must be selected so that the coating of the paper matches the print head on the machine.

OFFICE REPRODUCTION MACHINES

Machine	Chief Characteristics
Photocopier	A common business machine found in offices of all sizes. It makes few or numerous copies. Models vary widely in speed; type and size of paper used; general image quality; availability of two-sided copying, size reduction, color copying, and art-quality reproduction; and other factors. Many office models average 1,000 to 2,000 copies an hour. Reproduction quality is usually good to excellent, and most photocopiers are easy to operate and require minimal operator training time.
Mimeograph machine	A hand or electronically operated reproduction machine. Mimeograph machines, or stencil duplicators, require typing of a stencil, which may produce black and white or full-color copies. Reproduction quality is good, and from a hundred to several thousand copies can be produced from a single stencil. Some models operate at 5,000 to 10,000 copies an hour. Operator training time may run from a few hours to a few days. The mimeograph is useful in producing bulletins, notices, informal newsletters, programs, and similar material of more than 100 copies a run.
Fluid, or spirit, duplicator	A hand or electrically operated reproduction machine, producing copies of medium quality (but the poorest quality of the four machines described here). Fluid duplicators require typing of a master, and they produce copy in various colors, purple usually being the sharpest. Up to 500 copies can be produced from a master, and machines will operate at speeds reaching 5,000 copies an hour. One to six hours of operator training time are usually needed. Fluid duplicators are suitable for bulletins and similar material where high quality is not essential.
Offset duplicator	A good-to-excellent-quality full-color reproduction machine for 10 to 10,000 copies. Offset duplicators require typing of a master or the preparation of an offset plate. They often average speeds of 8,000 to 10,000 copies an hour. Up to two days' of operator

Machine	Chief Characteristics
	training time may be required. Offset duplicators are useful in printing newsletters, bulletins, and other material requiring speed, quantity, and quality beyond that of the other machines listed here.

Note: Features and capabilities vary according to manufacturer and model. Consult manufacturers and retail outlets for current specifications.

CORRECTION METHODS FOR REPRODUCTION MATERIALS

Reproduction Material	Correction Method
Photocopy	Since most copies are made from other typed or printed material, errors should be corrected in the usual manner on the original document or on the copy being used as a master. In the case of typewritten copy, for example, use materials such as correction fluid, tape, and typewriter erasers.
Mimeograph stencil	Stencils must be handled carefully to avoid damaging the coated surfaces. Set aside the film sheet on top of the stencil and correct errors with a stencil correction fluid that matches the color of the stencil (e.g., blue), allowing it to dry before retyping on it. If the stencil has a cushion sheet, burnish the error with a paperclip before applying the correction fluid. You also can cut out the error and patch the spot with a fresh piece of stencil, using correction fluid to bond the patch to the main sheet. Then replace the cushion sheet, retype the material, and proceed as usual. If possible, correct errors while the stencil is still in the typewriter.
Fluid, or spirit, master	Handle masters carefully to avoid smudging them. Set aside the carbon on the reverse side of the master. Cut out the error and tape in a fresh piece of master and a fresh piece of carbon. Or cover the error on the carbon side with correction tape. Or scrape off or erase the error and coat it with correction fluid

Reproduction Material	Correction Method
	and tape a small piece of fresh carbon back of it. After retyping, throw away any carbon scraps before continuing. If possible, correct errors while the master is still in the typewriter.
Offset master	Handle paper masters carefully to avoid smudging them. Use an orange offset eraser for errors made by a fabric ribbon and a white offset eraser followed by an orange one for errors made by a carbon ribbon. If possible, correct errors while the master is still in the typewriter.

GUIDELINES FOR TYPING SPECIAL CHARACTERS

Character	Method of Typing	Example
Brackets	*Left bracket:* type underscore, backspace, and type diagonal; roll platen forward and type underscore again for top of bracket. *Right bracket:* type underscore and diagonal, backspace, roll platen forward, and type underscore again for top of bracket.	$\lceil \quad \rceil$
Caret	Type diagonal, backspace, roll platen forward, and type underscore. Or type underscore and diagonal.	7 or _/
Cedilla	Type lowercase *c*, backspace, roll platen slightly forward, and type comma.	ç
Division sign	Type a colon, backspace, and overtype a hyphen.	÷
Equation sign	Type a hyphen, backspace, turn platen slightly, and overtype another hyphen.	=

Character	Method of Typing	Example
Exclamation sign	Type an apostrophe, backspace, and type a period.	!
Paragraph mark	Type a capital *P*, backspace, and overtype a lowercase *l*.	¶
Plus sign	Type a hyphen, backspace, and overtype a diagonal.	+
Pound sterling sign	Type a capital *L*, backspace, and overtype either a hyphen or lowercase *f*. Or type a lowercase *f*, backspace, and overtype a lowercase *t*.	Ł or £ or £
Section sign	Type a lowercase *s*, backspace, roll the platen slightly forward, and overtype *s* again.	§

RULES FOR SPACING AFTER PUNCTUATION MARKS

Number of Spaces	Rule
No space	*Before or after:* dash, hyphen, and apostrophe, unless it begins or ends a word.
	Between: quotation marks and matter enclosed, parentheses or brackets and matter enclosed, any word and punctuation following it, initials that make up a single abbreviation (f.o.b.), and initials in a state abbreviation (NY).
One space	*Before and after:* × used for *by* (3 × 5 inch).
	After: comma, semicolon, period following an abbreviation, period in a person's name (J. A. Doe), and exclamation mark within a sentence.
Two spaces	*After:* colon, sentence, and period following a number or letter at the beginning of a line in a list of items.

RULES FOR CHECK ENDORSEMENT

Type of Endorsement	Purpose	Example
Blank endorsement	To make a check negotiable by anyone without further endorsement. Payee simply signs name on back of check. Since anyone can cash a check with a blank endorsement, the signer should deposit or cash it immediately.	*John Jones*
Special endorsement (also: specific or full endorsement)	Specifies the person or company to whom the payee wants to transfer the check. The words *Pay to . . .* may be typed, but the payee must also include his or her signature. In the example here, James Smith must also endorse the check before cashing it.	Pay to the order of James Smith
Restrictive endorsement	Limits the endorsee's use of funds, with words such as *Pay to the order of . . .* or *For deposit in the . . . to the credit of. . . .* Typewritten or rubber-stamped endorsements are acceptable when a business endorses a check to a bank. An individual should sign his or her name. If the name of the payee on the check is incorrect, include both the incorrect name and the correct name beneath it (e.g., Leroy Smith, Lee Roy Smith). Checks sent by mail should always contain a restrictive endorsement.	Pay to the order of First Bank and Trust of Philadelphia ABC COMPANY Pay to the order of FIRST BANK AND TRUST of Sacramento For Deposit Only *John Jones*
Endorsement without recourse	A qualifying phrase typed on the back of a check above the payee's signature that relieves him or her of any future liability in transferring payments.	Pay to the order of Henry Steele Without Recourse *John Jones*

STATIONERY AND ENVELOPE SIZES AND APPLICATIONS

Classification	Common Sizes	Typical Applications
Standard letterhead	8½ × 11 inches	Routine business correspondence
Monarch (or executive) letterhead	7¼ × 10½ inches	Personal executive correspondence
Memo stationery	Various sizes	In-house communication; informal, routine external communication with colleagues; and standard order/request-reply communications
Second sheets	8½ × 11 inches	File copies and carbon copies
No. 9 envelope	3⅞ × 8⅞ inches	Standard letterhead, memo, and miscellaneous mailings
No. 10 envelope	4⅛ × 9½ inches	Standard letterhead, memo, and miscellaneous mailings
Monarch (or executive) envelope	3⅞ × 7½ inches	Personal executive correspondence and memo mailings
No. 6¾ envelope	3⅝ × 6½ inches	Memo and miscellaneous mailings
No. 5 Baronial	4⅝ × 5⁵⁄₁₆ inches	Personal executive correspondence, memo, and miscellaneous mailings

GUIDELINES FOR TRAINING ASSISTANTS

Item	Method
Supplies, where they are kept and how they are stored	Show trainee where each item is kept. Provide a diagram (if available) of supply cabinet showing where each item is stored.
Stationery supplies and use of each	Show trainee each type of stationery. Explain how each is used.

Item	Method
	Give trainee a folder of stationery on which is typed instructions for its use, including computer, word processor, and typewriter format specifications, number of copies to make, and distribution of copies.
Forms	Give trainee sample of each form filled out.
	Explain the use of each form.
	Attach to each form a typed memo about the number of copies to make and the distribution.
Company practice in writing letters and memos	Have trainee study manual (if any) containing sample letters on company letterhead.
	Mark in manual parts that apply to company practice, including computer-word processor and typewriter preparation. Have trainee study them.
	If there is no manual, give trainee sample letters written on company letterhead. Include computer-word processor and typewriter format specifications.
Typing aids: feeding small cards, chain feeding, decimal tabulation, making special characters, typing narrow labels	Refer trainee to *Guidelines for Typing Special Characters* in this chapter and to the appropriate item in other books.
	Have trainee apply procedure explained there.
	Demonstrate if necessary.
Neat arrangement of typed work, especially the setup of tables	Show trainee samples.
	Explain setup process on typewriter and computer-word processor format procedures.
Inserting carbon paper and numerous copies in machine	Show trainee how a folded sheet of paper can help as starter.
	Explain and have trainee apply procedure.
	Demonstrate again if necessary.
Improvement of text preparation	Point out defects in trainee's work.
	Demonstrate operations of parts of typewriter or computer-word processor that help in text preparation.

Item	Method
	Review correction steps with typewriter and computer-word processor
	Compliment trainee on work well done.
Operation of dictaphone transcriber	Explain mechanical operation and demonstrate.
	Watch while trainee uses machine.
	Demonstrate again if necessary.
Operation of reproduction and photocopy equipment, when to use each, and difference in cost	Demonstrate operation of each machine.
	Explain each step as you perform it.
	Watch while trainee performs each step.
	Explain when and why machine is used.
	Tell trainee the number of copies a machine can make and the comparative cost.
	Give trainee booklets from manufacturers.
Care of equipment: typewriter, computer-word processor, dictaphone equipment, reproduction equipment, photocopier, facsimile, teleprinter, other equipment	Explain and demonstrate the care that should be given each piece of equipment.
	Set an example by properly caring for your own equipment.
	Give trainee booklets from manufacturers.
	Give trainee chart showing costs of machines to emphasize the necessity of proper care.
	Refer trainee to *Business Machines and Systems* in this chapter.
Filing	Point out to trainee the types of materials filed in each cabinet or group of cabinets, including computer diskettes and printouts and odd-sized material such as blueprints.
	Open each drawer and explain the arrangement of the files.
	Provide list of cabinets and contents.
	Demonstrate, step by step, proper method of filing, explaining each step.
	Refer trainee to *Common Filing Systems* in this chapter.

Item	Method
	Mark material for trainee to file. Watch trainee file some material, correcting any misconceptions.
	After trainee is thoroughly familiar with system, let him or her mark material.
	Point out to trainee any inaccurately marked material, explaining inaccuracy. (When assistant can mark correctly, it will not be necessary to check the material before it is filed.)
	Explain use of central filing department.
Telephone facilities and their use	Explain and demonstrate use of office telephone facilities such as voice-data terminals.
	Have trainee practice operation of any unusual facilities.
	Give trainee directory of officers, department heads, and key employees.
	Refer trainee to *Telecommunications Services* in Chapter 2.
	Explain how to handle incoming calls including out-of-the-ordinary calls.
	Have trainee place outgoing calls and take incoming calls.
Office facilities, such as telegraphic and messenger	Enumerate and explain to trainee when and how each facility is used.
	As need arises, have trainee use facilities. (Forms used with the facilities should have been given to trainee with other forms.)
Company products and nomenclature	Take trainee on tour of company plant or offices, pointing out different products.
	Refer trainee to company manual.
	Provide list or dictionary of technical terms.
	Point out to trainee any misuse or misspelling of technical terms in his or her work.
Improvement of grammar	Point out errors in work prepared by trainee.

Item	Method
	Point out the rules of grammar in Chapter 4 that are applicable to trainee's errors.
Improvement of spelling, syllabication, punctuation, capitalization	Refer trainee to rules in Chapter 4.
	Point out errors in work prepared by trainee.
	See that trainee uses dictionary and doesn't guess.
	Compliment trainee for work well done.
Handling incoming mail	Explain any practices peculiar to the procedure followed in your office.
	Refer trainee to directory of officers, department heads, other key employees, and branch offices.
	Give trainee routing lists for any mail or periodicals received and routed by your office.
Handling outgoing mail	Explain any practices peculiar to the procedure followed in your office.
	Explain the procedure for nontraditional mail such as electronic mail and telex.
Preparing reports	Give trainee sample report.
	Point out any specific points to follow, such as numbering of headings and subheadings and other typewriter or computer-word processor format requirements.
	Refer trainee to Chapter 6.
Correspondence without dictation	Refer trainee to Chapter 5.
	Point out sample letters that trainee is to write without dictation.
	Suggest improvements in trainee's letters
Specific duties of trainee's position	Prepare a job breakdown of each duty.
	Explain procedure in each duty.
	Point out trainee's errors in any step.
	Commend trainee on accomplishments.

Source: Adapted from *Private Secretary's Encyclopedic Dictionary*, 3rd ed., rev. by Mary A. De Vries. © 1984 by Prentice-Hall, Inc. Published by Prentice-Hall, Inc., Englewood Cliffs, NJ 07632.

CHAPTER 2

Postal
and
Telecommunications
Services

CLASSES OF DOMESTIC POSTAL SERVICES

Class of Mail	Type of Service

Express Mail®

Express service, the fastest postal delivery, offers reliable, expedited delivery of high-priority shipments within the United States and to certain foreign countries. Mailers who use Express Mail Next Day Service take shipments to any designated Express Mail Post Office by the time designated at the facility. The mailing is delivered by 3 P.M. the next day, or it can be picked up by the addressee at a designated destination post office as early as 10:00 A.M. the next business day. This service comes with a postage-refund provision, and shipments are insured against loss or damage at no additional cost. Additional services include Express Mail Same Day Airport Service, Custom Designed Service, and International Service.

First-class mail

Mail (under 12 ounces) that receives expeditious handling and transportation and may not be opened for postal inspection. Any mailable matter may be sent as first-class mail. Postcards, personal correspondence, matter wholly or partially in writing or typewriting, bills, and statements of account must be mailed as first-class mail. When first-class matter such as a letter is included with second-, or third-, or fourth-class matter, postage at the first-class rate is required for the letter. (This does not apply to secondary material such as an invoice in a package sent at the fourth-class rate.) Packages should be marked "Letter Enclosed." First-class mail is delivered overnight locally and to certain designated areas if properly addressed (including zip code) and deposited in time. The designated overnight delivery area is dependent on transportation accessibility and scheduling. Second-day delivery is scheduled for locally designated states nationwide to which transportation is available for consistent achievement of two-day delivery. Third-day delivery encompasses all remaining outlying areas nationwide.

First-class presort mail

The presort rate, which is less than the regular rate for letters and postcards, is charged on each piece

Class of Mail	Types of Service
	that is part of a group of 10 or more pieces sorted to the same five-digit zip code or a group of 50 or more pieces sorted to the same first three-digit zip code. To qualify, a mailing must consist of at least 500 pieces. Mail that cannot be separated to five or three digits is counted toward the minimum volume but does not qualify for the lower rate. Customers are required to pay an annual fee to take advantage of the presort rate.
First-class zone-rated (priority) mail	First-class mail over 12 ounces, with rates based on zoned distances. Generally, the maximum weight limit is 70 pounds, and the maximum size is 108 inches, length and girth combined. Other weight and size limitations apply in cases of APO and FPO mail to and from the 48 contiguous states. Priority mail may be registered or insured or sent COD or special delivery if the charges for these services are paid in addition to the regular priority mail rate.
Second-class mail (newspapers and other periodicals)	Newspapers and other periodicals issued at least four times a year. A second-class permit must be obtained from the Postal Service. To qualify for second-class rates, publishers must normally distribute primarily to paid subscribers. Second-class publications may not be designed primarily for advertising purposes. The regular second-class postage rate varies depending on the distance mailed, the advertising portion of the publication's content, and whether the publication is mailed to an address within the county of publication. Anyone can mail individual complete copies of a second-class publication at the "transient" rate: address an envelope, slit the ends, and wrap the entire newspaper or periodical in it; write "Second-Class Matter" above the address, "To" in front of the address, and "From" in front of the return address. To call attention to a special passage in the text, mark with symbols, *not words*, in colored pencil. Write "Marked Copy" on the wrapper.
Requester publications mail	Publishers using this category may mail at second-class rates, whether the publication is free or paid by subscribers. Like second-class mail, each issue

Class of Mail	Types of Service
	must contain at least 24 pages and must be issued at least four times a year. Additionally, no issue may contain more than 75 percent advertising; the publication may not be owned or controlled by any person(s) or any business(es) as a means to promote the owners, controllers, or the mail business; and there must be a list of persons who request the publication, with at least 50 percent of the copies going to such requesters. However, a request is not deemed legitimate if it is more than three years old or if a special inducement is used to secure the request, such as a premium.
Third-class mail (advertising mail and merchandise weighing less than 1 pound)	Circulars, booklets, catalogs, and other printed materials not required to be sent as first-class mail; also merchandise, farm products, and keys. Each piece is limited to less than 16 ounces. There are two subcategories: single-piece rate and bulk rate. Third-class mail is subject to postal inspection but may be sealed if clearly marked "Third Class" on the outside. It is advisable to designate the contents on the wrapper, such as "Merchandise" or "Printed Matter." Writing, except something in the nature of an autograph or inscription, is not permitted. "Do not open until Christmas," or a similar legend, may be written on the wrapper; other directions or requests may not. Corrections of typographical errors may be added. Bulk rate requires a bulk-mail permit, for which an annual fee is charged, and is applicable to mailings of pieces separately addressed to different addresses in quantities of not less than 200 pieces or 50 pounds. The pieces must be zip coded, presorted, and bundled or sacked.
Fourth-class mail (parcels)	Parcels weighing 1 pound or more are mailable as fourth-class mail. Generally, parcels weighing a maximum of 70 pounds and measuring up to 108 inches in girth and length combined can be mailed anywhere in the United States. Other weight and size limitations apply in the case of APO and FPO mail to and from the 48 contiguous states. For larger parcels, contact the post office for instructions. There are special rates for a number of specific items mailed by certain mailers. Do not seal a package unless you state on it

Class of Mail	Types of Service
	that it may be opened for postal inspection. Enclosed communications or a letter fastened to the outside of the parcel requires additional postage, but invoices and customer's orders that relate entirely to the mailing article may be enclosed, and seasonal greetings may be enclosed too. With enclosures such as a letter, write "First-Class Mail Enclosed." Special-handling postage entitles fourth-class mail to the same handling as first-class mail but not to special delivery. Nor does special handling insure the safe delivery of the mail.

Note: Since postal rules, regulations, and rates change from time to time, consult your local post office in specific instances for current information and request copies of free postal publications. Customer Service Representatives (CSRs) are available at many post offices and at mail-processing facilities to help answer questions and solve mailer problems.

SPECIAL POSTAL SERVICES

Service	Provisions
Business-reply mail	A service for senders who want to encourage responses by paying the postage for those responses. Application is made by filling out U.S. Postal Service Form 3614, for which there is no charge. Mailers guarantee that they will pay the postage for all replies that are returned along with a business-reply surcharge. If an advance deposit is made at the post office, the mailer may pay an accounting charge plus a nominal amount per piece returned. If no deposit is made, there is no accounting charge; however, the mailer must pay for each piece returned. Mailers who will receive large numbers of business-reply mail annually will find it economical to establish an advance deposit account. The required format elements for business-reply mail may be found in the free publication. "A Guide to Business Mail Preparation" (Publication 25).

Service	Provisions
Registered Mail	A high-security service available for all items mailed as first-class mail; the safest way to send valuable and irreplaceable articles. Registered mail is accounted for during each phase of mail processing and delivery. Registry fees include proof of mailing and proof of delivery, indemnity protection up to $25,000, and are based on the value of the article. A return receipt showing delivery information is available for an additional fee. All registered mail, except second- and third-class mail valued at not more than $100, must be sealed. Mail without intrinsic value may be registered for the minimum fee or certified (see Certified Mail). Registered mail closes earlier than ordinary mail at the post office. Priority mail may be registered, and registered mail may be sent COD.
Certified mail	Available for all mailable matter of no intrinsic value mailed as first-class mail; provides proof of mailing and delivery. A return receipt showing delivery information is available for an additional nominal fee. Restricted delivery service is also available for an additional fee. Certified mail does not offer indemnity protection and is not available for international mail.
Insurance	Provides indemnity protection against loss and damage up to $500 for merchandise. Indemnity levels are based on a graduated fee schedule. Return receipt and restricted delivery services are available for parcels insured above $25. Do not seal, but wrap the mail securely. All insured mail is sent with the understanding that forwarding or return postage is guaranteed. The priority mail system handles insured mail if it is sent at the priority mail rate of postage plus insurance fees. Return receipt may be requested for an extra fee.
Collect on delivery (COD)	A merchandise-payment system that permits customers to mail an article for which they have not been paid and have the price of the article as well as the postage collected from the addressee. COD service includes indemnity and is available for first-, third-, and fourth-class mail. Fees are graduated and are

Service	Provisions
	based on the amount to be collected or indemnity protection desired. The service is not available for international mail. The sender of a COD parcel must guarantee return and forwarding postage. COD mail may be sent special delivery or special handling if fees applying to these services are paid in addition to postage and COD charges.
Special delivery	Available for all classes of mail except Express Mail®, at offices served by city carriers and within a one-mile radius of any post office, station, or branch, except contract stations, branches, or community post offices. Special delivery mail is delivered during pre-scribed hours on a fixed schedule basis, with schedules coordinated with major mail receipts. To the extent it is practical, it receives preferential handling in pro-cessing; expedited delivery is provided after reaching the destination post office. It is also delivered on Sundays and holidays. (However, most businesses are closed on those days.) Fees vary depending on the class of service used and the weight of the article. Special delivery mail bearing the correct postage and fees can be deposited at all points that first-class mail can be deposited, but it should be deposited at postal facilities to insure the best service. Special delivery labels can be obtained free from the post office.
Special handling	Provides expeditious handling in dispatch and trans-portation for third- and fourth-class mail but does not provide special delivery. It is available for a fee based on weight and the class of mail.
Domestic money orders	A safe and convenient way to send money through the mail, money orders may be purchased at all post offices. They are available in amounts up to $500 nationwide. Should a money order be lost or stolen, it will be replaced. Money orders can be redeemed at many banks, stores, and businesses, as well as at all post offices.
Mailgram service	A service that enables you to send a message to virtu-ally any address in the continental United States and Canada for delivery on the next business day. Call Western Union's toll-free number and dictate your

Service	Provisions
	message to the operator. The message is transmitted electronically to a serving post office close to the recipient where it is delivered by a regular carrier the next business day. To insure next-day delivery, be sure to have your message in before 7:00 P.M. destination time. Single or multiple messages may also be sent on your own telecommunications terminals. Messages going to a large number of people may be placed directly into the system by computer.
Self-service postal centers	Customer-operated vending and mailing equipment located in post office lobbies, shopping centers, college campuses, and so on. Centers provide complete mailing information and services for letters and parcels as well as sales of stamps, envelopes, postal cards, stamp booklets, parcel insurance, and individual stamps. Most centers are open 24 hours a day, 7 days a week. All postal items in U.S. Postal Service machines are sold at face value.
Post office lockbox and caller service	Premium services provided for the convenience of the public at an additional charge. These two services, provided in addition to available carrier or general delivery, afford customers privacy and permit them to obtain their mail at their convenience. Lockboxes are accessible during the hours the lobby is open, and caller service is accessible during the hours that window service is available. Both services make use of the traditional post office box number as the address.
Philatelic mail order service	The Philatelic Sales Division provides mail order service for current postage stamps, postal stationery, and philatelic products, such as commemorative mint sets and *Stamps and Stories*. A free catalog of all items available can be obtained by writing to the Philatelic Sales Division, Washington, D.C. 20265.
First-day cover service	To obtain first-day of issue cancellations, send self-addressed envelopes to the postmaster of the official first-day city. Customers may purchase their own new stamps from their local post offices, affix them in the upper right-hand corner of the envelopes, and submit them for cancellation service. Or customers may request the post office to affix the stamps (limit

Service	Provisions
	of 50 covers); such requests must include a check or money order to cover the value of the postage affixed. Covers bearing customer-affixed stamps will be given preferential service. Cancelled covers will not be returned in protective envelopes even when furnished by the customer. All requests must be post-marked no later than 15 days after the date of issuance for stamps and no later than the date of issuance for stationery items. A schedule of upcoming issuances can be obtained by writing to the Philatelic Sales Division, Washington, D.C. 20265

Note: Since postal rules, regulations, and rates change from time to time, consult your local post office for current information and request copies of free postal publications.

INTERNATIONAL POSTAL SERVICE

Class/Service	Type of Service
Postal union mail	*LC mail* (letters and cards) consists of letters, letter packages, aerogrammes, postcards, and postal cards. *AO mail* (other articles) includes printed matter, matter for the blind, and small packets.
1. Letters and letter packages	Written or recorded communications resembling actual and personal correspondence must be sent as letter mail. Unless prohibited by the country of destination, dutiable merchandise may be transmitted in packages prepaid at the letter rate. The rate for letters and letter packages varies according to the country of destination and for surface or air transport. Typewritten material must be sent as "letters," not printed matter. Write *Letter* (*lettre*) on the address side of letters or letter packages that might be mistaken for other articles. Airmail should be clearly marked *Par Avion*. Merchandise subject to customs duty may be forwarded in letters or letter packages to many countries, prepaid at the letter rate if the importation of the article is permitted by the country of destination.

Class/Service	Type of Serivce
	Consult the post office regarding forms to be filled out, labels to be affixed, and various restrictions and requirements per country.
2. Aerogrammes	Sheets that can be folded in the form of an envelope and sealed. They can be sent to all foreign countries at a uniform rate. Messages are written on the inside with no enclosures allowed. Aerogrammes with printed postage and airmail markings are sold at all post offices. Those manufactured by private concerns, if approved by the U.S. Postal Service, may also be used.
3. Postcards	Only single cards are acceptable in international mail, not reply-paid cards or folded (double) cards. The maximum size is 6 × 4¼ inches, and the minimum size is 5½ × 3½ inches. Rates vary by country, with surface or air rates applying.
4. Printed matter	Paper on which letters, words, characters, figures or images, or any combination thereof, not having the character of actual or personal correspondence, have been reproduced in several identical copies by any process other than handwriting or typewriting. Manuscripts of literary works or of newspapers and scores or sheets of music in manuscript are also admitted as "Printed Matter." *Regular printed matter* is all printed matter other than books, sheet music, and publisher's second-class and controlled-circulation publications. The rate for printed matter varies according to the country of destination, with surface and air rates applying. Printed matter may be sealed if postage is paid by permit imprint, postage-meter stamps, precancelled stamps, second-class or controlled-circulation indicias. Write *Printed Matter* on the wrapper and specify type of printed matter, such as *Books* or *Sheet Music*, since special rates apply to these categories.
5. Matter for the blind	Consult the post office regarding matter admissible in international mail as matter for the blind. Weight limit is 15 pounds. It should not be sealed. Rates vary according to country of destination and for air transport. The surface rate is free. Write *Matter for*

Class/Service	Type of Service
	the Blind in the upper right corner and add *Par Avion* for air service.
6. Small packets	Small packets designed to permit the mailing of small items or merchandise and samples to countries that will accept them. Philatelic items may be mailed under this classification only to Canada. The postage rates are lower than for letter packages or parcel post and vary according to country of destination, with surface and air rates applying. Mark the address side of the packet *Small Packet* or the equivalent in a language known in the country of destination. Small packets, whether or not they are subject to customs inspection, must bear the green customs label, Form 2976. You may enclose a simple invoice and a slip showing the names and addresses of the sender and addressee of the packet but not a letter, note, or document having the character of actual personal correspondence; coins, bank notes, paper money, postage stamps (cancelled or uncancelled), or any values payable to the bearer; platinum, gold, or silver (manufactured or unmanufactured); precious stones, jewelry, or other precious articles. Consult the post office for restrictions and requirements per country.
Parcel post	Parcel post may be sent to almost every country in the world, either by direct or indirect service. The parcels are sent from the United States by surface vessel or by airplane to a port in the country of destination or to a port in an intermediate country to be sent from there to the country of destination. In the latter case, the parcels are subject to transit charges in the intermediate country. Customs and other restrictions and regulations vary by country. Pack in canvas or similar material, double-faced corrugated cardboard boxes, solid fiber boxes or cases, thick cardboard boxes, or strong wooden boxes of material at least half an inch thick. It is permissible to use heavy wrapping paper or waterproof paper as the outside covering of a carton or box, not as the only covering. Boxes with lids screwed or nailed on and bags sewed at the openings may be used, provided they conform to the special provisions of the country of destination.

Class/Service	Type of Service
	Consult the post office for other restrictions and requirements.
Special services	Insurance and air service are available to some countries. Special handling entitles parcels to priority handling between the mailing point and the U.S. point of dispatch; fees vary. COD and certified mail are not available. Special delivery is available to most countries for articles other than parcel post. Registration is available to all countries except Kampuchea for articles other than parcel post. Return receipts may be purchased at time of mailing. Restricted delivery is available to many countries for registered articles only. Other services are express mail for high-speed delivery to and from designated countries, reply coupons to prepay mail from other countries, and money orders for safe transmission of money to certain countries. For more information consult the post office.

Note: Since numerous restrictions and regulations apply to international mail, consult the post office for current information and ask for free publications pertaining to international postal rates and regulations.

GUIDELINES FOR SENDING MAILABLE ITEMS

Item	How to Send
Bills and Statements of Account	First-class
Birth Announcements	First-class
Bonds: Negotiable	Registered fist-class
Nonnegotiable	First-class or certified first-class
Books	Fourth-class

    (Special rates apply to books. The book may be autographed. Mark the package "Special Fourth-Class Rate: Books.")

Catalogs	Third-, fourth-class

    (Special rates apply to printed catalogs individually addressed, consisting of 24 pages or more and not weighing over 10 pounds. Each piece must be clearly marked "Catalog.")

Item	How to Send
Checks, Filled Out	First-class
Canceled	First-class
Certified	Registered first-class
Endorsed in blank	Registered first-class
Circulars	Third-class
Currency	Registered first-class
Documents: No intrinsic value	Certified mail
With intrinsic value	
Signed originals	Registered first-class
Copies	First-class
Drawings	Third-class
Form Letters	Third-class

(Check with the post office for the category of third-class mail best suited to your needs.)

Greeting Cards	First-class
Jewelry	Registered first-class

(Limit of liability is $25,000. Consult postmaster on limits if other insurance is carried.)

Letters

Carbon copies	First-class
Duplicate copies	First-class
For delivery to addressee	
only	Registered or certified first-class
Form (see Form letters)	
Handwritten or typed	First-class
Magazines	Second-class
Manuscript, without	
proof sheets	Fourth-class, insured

(Mark the package "Special Fourth-Class.")

Accompanied by proof sheets	Third- or fourth-class, depending on weight

(Corrections on proof sheets may include insertion of new matter, as well as marginal notes to the printer. The manuscript of one article may not be enclosed with the proof of another unless the matter is mailed at the first-class rate.)

Merchandise (see Packages)	
Money Orders	First-class
Newspapers	Second-class
Packages	
Up to 16 ounces	Third-class
16 ounces and over	Parcel post

(Packages may be sealed if they bear an inscription authorizing inspection

Item	How to Send

by the postmaster. Packages containing articles valued at not more than $500 may be insured, but if they contain articles valued at more than $500, they should be sealed and registered. First-class postage will then apply, and the liability limit is $25,000.

      Containing personal messages (see Fourth-class mail, page 50)

Periodicals	Second-class
Photographs	Third-class

(Wrap with a cardboard protection and mark the envelope "Photograph— Do Not Bend." Photographs may be autographed.)

Postal cards	First-class
Postcards	First-class

(To be mailed at postcard rates, cards cannot be smaller than 3½ × 5 inches or larger than 4½ × 6 inches. If the card is enclosed in an envelope, it cannot be mailed at the postcard rate. Cards carrying a statement of a past-due account cannot be mailed at the card rate because they must be enclosed in an envelope.)

Plants, Seeds, Cuttings, Scions Bulbs, Roots	Third-class or parcel post depending on weight
Printed Matter	
Less than 16 ounces	Third-class
16 ounces or over	Fourth-class
Stock Certificates	
Negotiable	Registered first-class
Nonnegotiable	First-class or certified
Tapes and cassettes	
Nonpersonal	Special fourth-class, marked "Sound Recording"
Personal	First-class
Typewritten Material (see Manuscript)	First-class

Source: Adapted from *Private Secretary's Encyclopedic Dictionary*, 3rd ed., rev. by Mary A. De Vries. © 1984 by Prentice-Hall, Inc. Published by Prentice-Hall, Inc., Englewood Cliffs, NJ 07632.

POSTAL AND TRADITIONAL STATE ABBREVIATIONS

State	Traditional Abbreviation	Postal Abbreviation
Alabama	Ala.	AL
Alaska	Alaska	AK
American Samoa*	Amer. Samoa	AS
Arizona	Ariz.	AZ
Arkansas	Ark.	AR
California	Calif.	CA
Canal Zone*	C.Z.	CZ
Colorado	Colo.	CO
Connecticut	Conn.	CT
Delaware	Del.	DE
District of Columbia	D.C.	DC
Florida	Fla.	FL
Georgia	Ga.	GA
Guam*	Guam	GU
Hawaii	Hawaii	HI
Idaho	Idaho	ID
Illinois	Ill.	IL
Indiana	Ind.	IN
Iowa	Iowa	IA
Kansas	Kans.	KS
Kentucky	Ky.	KY
Louisiana	La.	LA
Maine	Maine	ME
Maryland	Md.	MD
Massachusetts	Mass.	MA
Michigan	Mich.	MI
Minnesota	Minn.	MN
Mississippi	Miss.	MS
Missouri	Mo.	MO
Montana	Mont.	MT
Nebraska	Nebr.	NE
Nevada	Nev.	NV
New Hampshire	N.H.	NH
New Jersey	N.J.	NJ
New Mexico	N.Mex.	NM
New York	N.Y.	NY
North Carolina	N.C.	NC

State	Traditional Abbreviation	Postal Abbreviation
North Dakota	N.Dak.	ND
Ohio	Ohio	OH
Oklahoma	Okla.	OK
Oregon	Oreg.	OR
Pennsylvania	Pa.	PA
Puerto Rico*	P.R.	PR
Rhode Island	R.I.	RI
South Carolina	S.C.	SC
South Dakota	S.Dak.	SD
Tennessee	Tenn.	TN
Texas	Tex.	TX
Utah	Utah	UT
Vermont	Vt.	VT
Virginia	Va.	VA
Virgin Islands*	V.I.	VI
Washington	Wash.	WA
West Virginia	W.Va.	WV
Wisconsin	Wis.	WI
Wyoming	Wyo.	WY

* U.S. territories and possessions (by treaty, the Panama Canal will revert to Panama by 1999). Guam and Puerto Rico are self-governing U.S. territories. American Samoa and three of the Virgin Islands (St. Croix, St. Thomas, St. John) are nonself-governing U.S. territories.

ENVELOPE ADDRESSING REQUIREMENTS
FOR AUTOMATED SORTING

Address Data	Position on Envelope
Address block	Single-spaced in block form (flush left margin), at least 1 inch from left and ⅝ inch from bottom of envelope; no print to the right or below address block. Window envelope inserts should show ¼-inch margin all around the address in the window.

Address Data	Position on Envelope
	XRM 4401-2-63 ABC COMPANY ATTN JOHN DOE 500 W THIRD ST RM 4112 DALLAS TX 75222
Account number, date, and other nonaddress data	First line above addressee's name.
Addressee	First line of actual address data.
Information and attention lines	First line after addressee's name
Street address and box number	Line immediately above city, state, zip code. If address has both a line for the street and a line for the post office box number, place the one that mail is to be delivered to on the next to the last line of the address, immediately above the city, state, zip code. Place the other one directly above the line selected for actual delivery of mail. A unit number such as *Room 4112* should be on the same line as the street if there is room; otherwise, place it on the line immediately above the street.
City, state, zip code	Last line of the address block; one space between city and state and two spaces between state and zip code. Use nine-digit zip codes where they are available.

UNITED STATES POSTAL SERVICE STANDARDS
(Zip-Coded Mail Only)

	Overnight	Overnight Requirements	2nd Day	3rd Day	4th Day	5th Day	6th Day	7th Day	8th Day	9th Day	10th Day
First-Class Mail	Locally designated cities and SCF's	Up to and including 5:00 P.M. collections	Locally designated states	Remaining outlying areas	—	—	—	—	—	—	—
First-Class Zone-Rated (Priority Mail)	Designated cities	Stated at mailing post office	Nationwide	—	—	—	—	—	—	—	—
Surface Preferential	Up to 150 miles	5:00 P.M. mailings	300 miles / zone 3	600 miles / zone 4	1,000 miles / zone 5	1,400 miles / zone 6	1,800 miles / zone 7	Over 1,800 miles / zone 8	—	—	—
Ordinary Second- and Third-Class Mail	As developed locally	—	Intra-SCF (for 5:00 P.M. carrier presorted mailings	Designated SCF's and nonpresorted intra-SCF	Up to 150 miles / zone 2	300 miles / zone 3	600 miles / zone 4	1,000 miles / zone 5	1,400 miles / zone 6	1,800 miles / zone 7	Over 1,800 miles / zone 8
Parcel Post	See separate standards issued for each bulk-mail center.										
Plant Loaded	Delivery schedules worked out between USPS and mailer.										

Note: Second- to 10th-day delivery targets cover all of a day's mailings, excepted as noted.

PRIVATE DELIVERY SERVICES

Service	Chief Characteristics
Basic services	Local, national, and international private delivery services transport letters and packages by both air and ground transportation. Whereas some companies are devoted exclusively to message and package delivery, other organizations such as bus lines and airlines provide letter and package delivery as a supplementary service.
	A large private delivery service might offer ground and air delivery, telex and facsimile service, electronic mail, and messenger service. Additionally, it would likely place Western Union and other messages for you. Sometimes delivery services do not have their own delivery vehicles but act as an intermediary and simply send your material through another service. Since the services, rates, and regulations vary so widely, it is helpful to develop a file of private services and update it regularly. Check the yellow pages for names and addresses and call the organizations operating in your area for current data.
	Most companies offer a variety of delivery times and schedules. Large organizations may provide anything from overnight, door-to-door service to second-day delivery or third-day delivery to charter service. Contact each company for its own available services and schedules.
Pickup and delivery	Many of the private delivery companies provide pickup and delivery service. Most also maintain local offices or, in certain cities, offices where you may deliver your letters or packages in person. Some of the private delivery services provide free kits containing mailing envelopes and boxes. Usually, you can open an account with the company and charge your mailings (*see* Company account).
Fast delivery	Fast delivery services are more expensive than conventional U.S. Postal Service delivery. To avoid unnecessary expense, consider the urgency of the message

Service	Chief Characteristics
	and the advantages in fast delivery. Overnight service might be useless in some cases. Although a letter mailed through the Postal Service might take several days in transit, an overnight letter might be wasted if it is mailed on Friday and would simply have to wait at the destination anyway until the business office opened again on Monday. To make cost-conscious decisions, compare rates, regulations (size and weight limits, amount of insurance coverage provided, and so on), and delivery time of the private delivery companies servicing your area as well as the options available through the U.S. Postal Service.
Company account	Most large private delivery services will open a company account for you. Thereafter, when you have a letter or package to send, you only have to telephone the service, give your account number, and request pickup. The service will charge the cost to your account and bill you later.

Note: Consult the nearest delivery service office for current rates, regulations, and domestic and international network served. In addition to the U.S. Postal Service Express Mail service and large private delivery companies such as Federal Express and United Parcel Service, numerous other courier and airline companies provide package- and letter-delivery services domestically and internationally. The current edition of *The National Directory of Addresses and Telephone Numbers* lists numerous courier and airline companies that provide letter-, document-, and package-delivery services.

MAIL ROOM SUPPLIES AND EQUIPMENT CHECKLIST

Stamps ( )
Miscellaneous supplies: string, tape, package-marking pens, postal-handling stickers, sponges, paperclips, scissors, rubber fingers, rubber bands, etc. ( )
Manual and automatic letter/package openers ( )
Manual and automatic time/date stamps ( )
Address/shipping labels and packing slips ( )
Mailing envelopes/cartons ( )
Record-keeping forms/books ( )
National Zip Code and Post Office Directory ( )

Miscellaneous mailing/shipping instruction guides and rate lists   ( )
Equipment-operation instruction guides   ( )
Storage containers/files   ( )
Mailbags/trays   ( )
Mail-sorting trays/bins/cells   ( )
Rolling carts   ( )
Work tables (some with rails)   ( )
Postage metering/sealing machine   ( )
Postal scale (electronic model for weighing, computing postage)   ( )
Electronic postage accounting machine   ( )
Collating/folding/counting/inserting equipment   ( )
Addressing equipment   ( )
Photocopy equipment   ( )
Microfilm/microfiche and related equipment   ( )
Other (required for your particular operation): ____   ( )

MONEYSAVING MAILING PRACTICES

Requirements	Recommended Practice
Class of mail and mail service	Do not use a more expensive class of mail or mail service than is necessary; for example, avoid the use of special delivery when regular first-class mail will be delivered as fast.
Mailing time	Always schedule your mail and deposits early for fastest service when deadlines are important (e.g., "time is money").
Postage	Apply only the correct amount of postage and use a postage meter rather than stamps for numerous pieces.
Envelopes	Make more use of timesaving business-reply and window envelopes; use combination envelopes for mailing first-class letters and lower-class material in the same package rather than send it all first class.
Packaging	Package and label parcels properly, selecting the lightest possible weight cartons and envelopes that are nevertheless sufficiently sturdy for the hazards of shipment.

Requirements	Recommended Practice
Enclosures	Avoid unnecessary enclosures, including paperclips and other clasps.
Stationery	Avoid unnecessarily heavy letterheads, envelopes, and other stationery.
Mail groupings	Put letters and material to the same person or to the same office (e.g., a branch office) in one envelope.
Insurance	Insure material that needs coverage and protection but do not overinsure or insure needlessly.
Addressing	Follow postage guidelines for optical character reading and use five- (or nine-) digit zip codes.
Mail sorting	Sort and bundle mail strictly according to postal requirements; deliver sorted and bundled mail to save processing time at the post office.
Bulk mailings	Use third-class bulk rate for mass mailings.
Mailroom	Maintain a mailroom equipped appropriately for the type of mailing you do and organize it for efficient movement of personnel and rapid succession of each step in the mailing process.
Equipment	Use modern, efficient mailing equipment (e.g., sorting tables, scales, meters, openers) suitable for the type of mailing needs you have, allowing for anticipated expansion of operations; periodically check equipment such as scales for accuracy.
Microfilm/microfiche	Consider reducing certain material to one of the film-storage media and ship film instead of the heavier original document whenever possible.
Alternative services	Compare costs and service between postal and courier methods (e.g., UPS, Federal Express Corporation).
Mailing information	Maintain up-to-date postal/shipping rules and regulations and current forms (e.g., customs forms) to avoid costly mistakes.

CLASSES OF TELEGRAPH SERVICE

Class	Type of Service
Domestic telegram	*Fast telegram*: The quickest service, usually hand delivered within a few hours. Charges are based on a minimum of 15 words, with an additional charge for each word thereafter. Address and signature do not count as words. Messages may be sent in code. Call Western Union.
	Night letter: A less expensive message than the fast telegram, which may be filed at any time until 2:00 A.M. Delivery is usually made the next business day. Charges are based on a minimum of 100 words, with an additional charge for each group of 5 words thereafter. Address and signature do not count as words. Messages may be sent in code. Call Western Union.
	Mailgram: Mailgrams are sent by a variety of means such as toll-free telephone call, telex, computer, and tape. Messages are routed by certified carriers to the post office nearest the addressee, where they are printed out and delivered with the next regular mail. Mailgrams of 100 words can be sent at a lower cost than a 15-word telegram.
	Money orders: Money orders may be sent directly through Western Union (e.g., orders phoned in may be charged to Visa or Mastercard credit cards).
Cablegram service	*Full-rate message(FR)*: Fast service for regular or coded messages. Charges vary according to destination, with a minimum charge per message. Call Western Union for cablegrams and radiograms, or file directly using your own telex equipment, or call an international carrier such as ITT World Communications, RCA Global Communications, or MCI International.
	Letter telegram (LT): Overnight service to certain countries often used for longer messages that can wait until the next day. Regular language only, except a registered code address may be used. Charges are less than for full-rate messages, with a minimum charge per message. Call Western Union or one of the international carriers.

FAST-MESSAGING SERVICES

Service	Type of Communication
Electronic mail	Electronic mail (or E-mail) is a form of computer message transmission. A sender who subscribes to an E-mail network types a message on a computer or word processor terminal and sends it over the telephone to a receiving computer terminal. (Some terminals may be directly wired together in a local area network [LAN].) Users can set up computer mailboxes where the messages they receive are stored until they are ready to retrieve them from the computer's memory. Messages prepared on one's own computer for mailing on an E-mail network can be edited the same as any other computer document. (A *voice-data system* combines or integrates the use of telephone [voice] and electronic data systems.)
Telex	Telex I and Telex II use a keyboard-to-keyboard method of sending messages. Teleprinters are hooked to the telephone lines where messages are converted for transmission to the receiving machine. Users subscribe to a network and can locate other subscribers through a *Telex Directory*. Teleprinter messages are usually poor quality in appearance; however, users can convert computers or word processors into a telex center for a better quality product. Equipment varies according to the manufacturer, and options vary according to the network to which one subscribes.
Teletex	Teletex service is faster than telex transmission, although telex and Teletex users can send to one another. The messages are much higher quality than standard telex and resemble a regular business letter. Contact Western Union for rates and subscriber fees.
Facsimile service	Rapid transmission of all sorts of data, including documents with graphics, by use of facsimile (FAX) transmission equipment (often called transceivers since the machines both send and receive) and the regular telephone lines. Senders without equipment can transmit by mailing or delivering their documents to a facsimile bureau. Documents can also be sent to a destination bureau using one's own equipment and

Service	Type of Communication
	then delivered to receivers who do not have their own equipment.
Radio photo service	Transmission of photographs, drawings, designs, contracts, and so on by radio. This service is available through organizations such as RCA Global Communications.
Leased-channel service	A private communications line between any two national or international points that can be leased from a common carrier such as AT&T. It allows greater speed and economy for high-volume users. Channels are leased for various speeds. (A *tie line* directly links two offices, for example, two branch offices.)
Computer-access service	Communication between computers and data systems. A variety of devices can be linked and a variety of databases are available through an access service.
Marine service	Radio, telex, or cablegram communication to and from persons on ships at sea. Messages may be filed with an international carrier or with Western Union, which will transfer them to the carrier you specify on the message.
Satellite service	Worldwide transmission of messages by beaming to and from a space satellite. Subscribers can send voice, facsimile, and other forms of communication by satellite.

Note: For current rate information, request a rate chart from the international carriers you wish to use. Telex numbers are listed in the *Telex Directory*. Contact the international carriers for information on the selection and registration of a code for use in addressing cablegrams and for information about the specific services offered by each carrier.

GLOBAL TIME CHART

To determine the time in listed countries, add the number of hours shown under your time zone (or subtract, if preceded by a minus sign) to your local time. Time differences are based on standard time, which is observed in the U.S. (in most states) from the last Sunday in October until the last Sunday in April. This may vary in other countries.

Time Difference to—	U.S. Time Zones			
	EST	CST	MST	PST
American Samoa	−6	−5	−4	−3
Andorra	6	7	8	9
Argentina	2	3	4	5
Australia (Sydney)*	16	17	18	19
Austria	6	7	8	9
Bahrain	8	9	10	11
Belgium	6	7	8	9
Belize	−1	0	1	2
Bolivia	1	2	3	4
Brazil (Rio de Janeiro)*	2	3	4	5
Chile	2	3	4	5
Colombia	0	1	2	3
Costa Rica	−1	0	1	2
Cyprus	7	8	9	10
Denmark	6	7	8	9
Ecuador	0	1	2	3
El Salvador	−1	0	1	2
Fiji	17	18	19	20
Finland	7	8	9	10
France	6	7	8	9
French Antilles	1	2	3	4
French Polynesia	−5	−4	−3	−2
German Dem. Rep.	6	7	8	9
Germany, Fed. Rep. of	6	7	8	9
Greece	7	8	9	10
Guam	15	16	17	18

Time Difference to—	U.S. Time Zones			
	EST	CST	MST	PST
Guatemala	−1	0	1	2
Guyana	2	3	4	5
Haiti	0	1	2	3
Honduras	−1	0	1	2
Hong Kong	13	14	15	16
Iceland	5	6	7	8
Indonesia (Jakarta)*	12	13	14	15
Iran	8½	9½	10½	11½
Iraq	8	9	10	11
Ireland	5	6	7	8
Israel	7	8	9	10
Italy	6	7	8	9
Ivory Coast	5	6	7	8
Japan	14	15	16	17
Kenya	8	9	10	11
Korea, Rep. of	14	15	16	17
Kuwait	8	9	10	11
Liberia	5	6	7	8
Libya	7	8	9	10
Liechtenstein	6	7	8	9
Luxembourg	6	7	8	9
Malaysia (Kuala Lumpur)*	12½	13½	14½	15½
Mexico (Mexico City)*	−1	0	1	2
Monaco	6	7	8	9
Netherlands	6	7	8	9
Netherlands Antilles	1	2	3	4
New Caledonia	16	17	18	19
New Zealand	18	19	20	21

Time Difference to—	U.S. Time Zones			
	EST	CST	MST	PST
Nicaragua	−1	0	1	2
Nigeria	6	7	8	9
Norway	6	7	8	9
Panama	0	1	2	3
Papua New Guinea	15	16	17	18
Paraguay	2	3	4	5
Peru	0	1	2	3
Philippines	13	14	15	16
Portugal	5	6	7	8
Qatar	8	9	10	11
Romania	7	8	9	10
San Marino	6	7	8	9
Saudi Arabia	8	9	10	11
Senegal	5	6	7	8
Singapore	12½	13½	14½	15½
South Africa	7	8	9	10
Spain	6	7	8	9
Sri Lanka	10½	11½	12½	13½
Suriname	1½	2½	3½	4½
Sweden	6	7	8	9
Switzerland	6	7	8	9
Taiwan	13	14	15	16
Thailand	12	13	14	15
Tunisia	6	7	8	9
Turkey	7	8	9	10
United Arab Emirates	9	10	11	12
United Kingdom	5	6	7	8
Uruguay	2	3	4	5

Time Difference to—	U.S. Time Zones			
	EST	CST	MST	PST
U.S.S.R. (Moscow)*	8	9	10	11
Vatican City	6	7	8	9
Venezuela	1	2	3	4
Yugoslavia	6	7	8	9

* Has more than one time zone.
Source: Personal Directory for International Dialing, Bell System, May 1982.

PRINCIPAL TELECOMMUNICATIONS SERVICES

Type of Service	Chief Characteristics
Direct-distance dialing (DDD)	Long-distance communication by telephone, provided by AT&T, MCI, or one of the other common carriers, with charges based upon distance, call duration, time of day, and other factors as established by each independent carrier. With traditional long-distance dialing, station-to-station calls require no operator intervention; person-to-person calls are usually made by dialing 0 and the number—an operator will come on the line and request information before the call is completed. To dial direct to many countries, dial the international access code, plus the country code, plus the city code, plus the local number.
Other common carriers (OCC)	An alternative to traditional long-distance telephone service. OCC service is provided by independent carriers that use their own terrestrial and satellite circuits along with the regular telephone company lines. OCCs provide their own telephone directories and numbers. No special equipment is needed for persons who already have pushbutton phones. Customers may purchase new equipment from any available retail outlet
Private leased channel (PLC)	A service whereby a user is provided with an exclusive link between two points—for example, a company

Type of Service	Chief Characteristics
	and its branch office. PLCs can transmit voice, data, facsimile, and so on with charges calculated as a flat monthly rate. Companies that offer leased lines use a combination of terrestrial lines and satellites. Several types of lines are available. *Tie lines,* for example, enable users to dial any number in a distant city as though it were a local call.
WATS (Wide Area Telephone Service)	A type of discount subscriber service for long-distance calls, it may be inbound or outbound. A WATS line is installed for subscribers who then receive a number with an 800 prefix. Charges are borne by the subscriber. Customers who dial the 800 number do not pay for the call, and hence subscribers often use a WATS line to encourage customer response to their product or service.
Pushbutton systems	With a pushbutton, or key, system, telephones in one office are interconnected to telephones in another office and, with the other telephones, also connected to outside lines. There may be one telephone in a small office that one person answers or, in a slightly larger firm, a number of pushbutton telephones with buzzers interconnected so that the person answering can signal others to take incoming calls. All pushbutton systems have hold buttons, and many other features such as programming for automatic and speed dialing and a routing feature for transferring calls automatically from a remote location to another telephone. In a larger system, where all incoming calls are received by a receptionist or other operator, there may be a message feature with a light on the telephone that signals people that the operator has a message for them. A dial safeguard is a small device that prevents unauthorized persons from making outside calls. Call sequencers indicate the next call in line and may process unanswered calls after a certain number of rings.
Digital systems	Digital systems are replacing the older equipment in some companies. The digital process transmits signals in varying discrete steps based on bits (binary digits); the analog signal varies in a continuous manner. A

Type of Service	Chief Characteristics
	common feature of digital systems is the digital display monitor (like that on a digital watch) that shows various data such as the cost of the call. Since digital systems are software driven, they can be upgraded without replacing the equipment. Some offices have integrated various equipment and functions, and in those cases the digital system is easily linked to other computer activity such as electronic mail.
Telephone exchanges	A telephone system designed to interconnect users. Switching systems range in complexity from the once-familiar switchboards such as PBX (Private Branch Exchange) and the succeeding CBX (Computerized Branch Exchange) to newer third-generation systems that integrate voice, data, and office automation (e.g., word processing) work stations. Advanced systems use sophisticated microprocessor technology for immediate telephone usage feedback. Modern switching systems can interconnect not only people but machines—for example, person-person, person-machine, and machine-machine.
Answering services	Automatic (i.e., machine) and independent services designed to receive and give messages. *Independent services* tie into one's telephone line and employ trained operators who monitor and answer phones in the subscriber's absence. *Answering machines* give and record messages on tape. A remote-control feature allows users to telephone the machine from another location and activate the message playback.
Voice mail	A message service whereby subscribers dial a voice-mail access telephone number to receive messages. Users can also route messages or reply to them. Voice-mail systems are designed primarily for brief communications. The equipment can be leased or purchased to serve as either a stand-alone unit or a PBX component.
Remote-call forwarding	People who travel can have calls follow them by dialing a simple code plus the number where they can later be reached. Businesses may use forwarding as a means of maintaining a listed number in one

Type of Service	Chief Characteristics
	city with customer calls forwarded from there to the home office in another city.
Messenger calls	An operator at the destination is authorized to send a messenger for someone who does not have a telephone. The caller pays for the cost of the messenger in addition to the person-to-person telephone charge.
Paging	Because of the sound they emit, paging devices are called beepers. When you have an incoming call, they're activated to let you know that you should find a telephone and call your home or office. They operate only within a limited area, however.
Mobile calls	Local and long-distance calls can be placed to automobiles, trucks, aircraft, boats, and ships. The newer cellular radio transmission is an improved version of the traditional wireless equipment. It will accommodate more subscribers and has fewer delays in making calls. Dial 0 and ask for the mobile, marine, or highseas operator. Mobile numbers are listed in the regular telephone directory.
Teleconferencing/ videoconferencing	*Teleconferences* are meetings held by the simultaneous telephone connection of various participants. Telephone calls involving more than two persons are charged at the person-to-person rate for each participant. Ask the long-distance operator for the conference operator who will set up the desired conference. *Videoconferences* link two or more locations by closed-circuit television. Although the system is very expensive, large companies may set up a permanent private network. An alternative is a temporary network joined by satellite transmission. Another alternative is to hold a picturephone meeting (see *Speakerphone/picturephone*).
Speakerphone/picturephone	*Speakerphones* have a built-in microphone and loudspeaker that enable one to talk and listen without picking up a receiver, leaving one's hands free to do other work. *Picturephones* also enable one to see the other person. Although the cost has limited its use, the picturephone is used by some large corpora-

Type of Service	Chief Characteristics
	tions for meetings with participants in various locations (see *Teleconferencing/videoconferencing*).
Cordless telephone	A compact telephone without cord. The cordless phone can be carried from one place to another for use within its operational range (indoors and outdoors). Some models have features such as redialing the last number called at the push of a button.
Automatic dialers	Special units that store numbers and at the press of a button automatically dial them. Depending on the unit, the numbers may be stored on tape, plastic card, or some other medium.
Calling card	A telephone credit card. Users are given a card similar to a charge card with a number to use for charging calls to an office or home telephone number. Follow the instructions you receive with your card. Some phones in public places such as airports are labeled expressly for charge calls.

Note: Available telephone services vary, depending on location. For the latest information on services, equipment, and other communication matters, consult your local telephone company, AT&T, MCI, or one of the other common carriers.

INTERNATIONAL DIALING CODES

Dial 011 or 01 + Country Code + City Code + Local Number
Numbers beside countries are *country codes*.
Numbers beside cities are *city codes*.
For codes of cities not listed dial 0 (operator).
World Rate Regions are noted in Codes A–K.

AMERICAN		**BRAZIL**(E)	55	**FIJI**+(C)	579
SAMOA+(C)	584	Belem	91		
		Belo Horizonte	31	**FINLAND**(B)	358
ANDORRA(B)	33	Braqzilia	61	Helsinki	0
All points	078	Porto Alegra	512	Tampere	31
		Recite	81	Turku-Abo	21
ARGENTINA(E)	54	Rio de Janeiro	21		
Buenos Aires	1	Salvador	71	**FRANCE**(B)	33
Cordoba	51	Sao Paulo	11	Bordeaux	56
La Plata	21			Brest	98
Rosario	41	**CHILE**(E)	56	Grenoble	76
		Concepcion	42	Le Havre	35
AUSTRALIA(C)	51	Santiago	2	Lille	20
Adelaide	8	Valparaiso	31	Lyon	7
Brisbane	7			Marseille	91
Canberra	52	**COLOMBIA**(E)	57	Montpellier	67
Melbourne	3	Barranquilla	5	Nice	93
Perth	9	Bogota	*	Paris	1
Sydney	2	Bucaramanga	71	Reims	26
		Cali	3	Rennes	99
AUSTRIA(B)	43	Cartagena	59	Rouen	35
Graz	316	Medellin	4	St. Etienne	77
Linz	732			Strasbourg	88
Vienna	222	**COSTA RICA**+(G)	506	Toulon	94
				Toulouse	61
BAHRAIN+(F)	973	**CYPRUS**(B)	357		
		Limassoi	51	**FRENCH**	
BELGIUM(B)	32	Nicosia	21	**ANTILLES**+(D)	596
Antwerp	31	Paphos	61		
Brussels	2			**FRENCH**	
Ghent	91	**DENMARK**(B)	45	**POLYNESIA**+(C)	689
Liege	41	Aarhus	6		
Malines	15	Copenhagen	1 or 2	**GERMAN**	
		Odense	9	**DEMOCRATIC**	
BELIZE(G)	501			**REPUBLIC**(B)	37
Belize City	*	**ECUADOR**(E)	593	Berlin	2
Belmopan	09	Ambato	2	Dresden	51
Corozal Town	04	Cuenca	4	Leipzig	41
		Guayaquil	4		
BOLIVIA(E)	591	Quito	2		
Cochabamba	42				
La Paz	2	**EL SALVADOR**+(G)	503		
Santa Cruz	33				

GERMANY, FED.REP.OF[B]	**49**	**HONG KONG**[C]	**852**	**ITALY**[B]	**39**
Berlin	30	Castle Peak	0	Bari	80
Bonn	228	Hong Kong	5	Bologna	51
Bremen	421	Kowloon	3	Catania	95
Cologne	221	Kwai Chung	0	Florence	55
Dortmund	231	Lantau	5	Genoa	10
Duisburg	203	Ma Wan	5	Messina	90
Dusseldorf	221	Peng Chau	5	Milan	2
Essen	201	Sha Tin	0	Naples	81
Frankfurt	611	Tai Po	0	Palermo	91
Gelsenkirchen	209	Tsun Wan	0	Rome	6
Hamburg	40			Taranto	99
Hannover	511	**ICELAND**[B]	**354**	Trieste	40
Munich	89	Akureyri	6	Turin	11
Nuremberg	911	Hafnarfjordhur	1	Venice	41
Stuttgart	711	Reykjavik	1	Verona	45
Wuppertal	202				
		INDONESIA[C]	**52**	**IVORY COAST***[H]	**225**
GREECE[B]	**30**	Jakarta	21	**JAPAN**[C]	**81**
Athens	1	Medan	61	Amagasaki	6
Drama	521	Semarang	24	Fukuoka	92
Ioannina	651			Hiroshima	822
Iraklion	81	**IRAN**[F]	**58**	Kawasaki	44
Kalamai	721	Abadan	631	Kitakyushu	93
Kavala	51	Esfanhan	31	Kobe	78
Larissa	41	Mashad	51	Kyoto	75
Patrai	61	Tabriz	41	Nagoya	52
Piraeus	1	Teheran	21	Osaka	6
Serrai	321			Sakai (Osaka)	722
Thessaloniki	31			Sapporo	11
Volos	421	**IRAN**[F]	**964**	Tokyo	3
		Baghdad	1	Yokohama	45
GUAM*[C]	**671**	Basra	40		
		Hilla	30	**SPAIN**[B]	**34**
GUATEMALA[G]	**502**	Mosul	60	Barcelona	3
Amatitlan	•			Bilbao	4
Antigua	•	**IRELAND**[A]	**353**	Granada	58
Guatemala City	2	Cork	21	Las Palmas	
Quetzaitenango	•	Dublin	1	(Canary Is.)	28
Villa Nueva	•	Galway	91	Madrid	1
		Limerick	61	Palma de	
GUYANA[E]	**592**	Waterford	51	Mallorca	71
Bartica	05			Pamplona	48
Georgetown	02	**ISRAEL**[F]	**972**	Seville	54
		Bene Brak	3	Valencia	6
HAITI[D]	**509**	Bet Shean	65	Zaragoza	76
Cap Hatien	3	Haifa	4		
Gonaive	2	Jerusalem	2	**SRI LANKA**[J]	**94**
Port Au Prince	1	Petah Tikva	3	Colombo	1
		Ramat Gan	3	Kandy	8
HONDURAS*[G]	**504**	Tel Aviv	3	Moratuwa	72

SURINAME*(E)	597	UNITED ARAB EMIRATES(F)	971	Sheffield, Eng. Stoke-on-Trent.	742	
SWEDEN(B)	45	Abu Dhabi	2	Eng.	782	
Goteborg	31	Ajman	6	Wolverhampton,		
Malmo	40	Al Ain	3	Eng.	902	
Stockholm	8	Aweir	49			
Uppsala	18	Dubai	4	URUGUAY(E)	598	
Vasteras	21	Fujairah	91	Canelones	332	
		Jebel Dhana	5	Mercedes	532	
SWITZERLAND(B)	41	Khawanij	49	Montevideo	2	
Basel	61	Ras-Al-Kahaimah	7			
Berne	31	Sharjah	6	VATICAN CITY(B)	39	
Biel/Bienne	32	Umm-Al-Qaiwain	6	All points	6	
Geneva	22					
Lausanne	21	UNITED		VENEZUELA(E)	58	
Lucerne	41	KINGDOM(A)	44	Barcelona	81	
Winterthur	52	Belfast N.Ire	232	Barquisimeto	51	
Zurich	1	Birmingham,		Caracas	2	
		Eng.	21	Ciudad Bolivar	85	
TAIWAN(C)	685	Bradford, Eng.	274	Cumana	93	
Kaohsiung	7	Bristol, Eng.	272	Maracaibo	61	
Tainan	62	Cardiff, Wales	222	Maracay	43	
Taipei	2	Coventry, Eng.	203	Maturin	91	
		Edinburgh,		San Cristobal	76	
THAILAND(C)	66	Scot.	31	Valencia	41	
Bangkok	2	Glasgow, Scot.	41			
		Hillington, Eng.	485	YUGOSLAVIA(B)	38	
TUNISAI(H)	216	Huddersfield,		Belgrade	11	
Menzel		Eng.	484	Saraievo	71	
Bourguiba	2	Leeds, Eng.	532	Skoplje	91	
Tunis	1	Leicester, Eng.	533	Zagreb	41	
		Liverpool, Eng.	51			
TURKEY(B)	90	London, Eng.	1			
Adana	711	Manchester,				
Ankara	41	Eng.	61			
Istanbul	11	New Castle-on				
Izmir	51	Tyne, Eng.	632			
		Nottingham,				
UNION OF SOVIET		Eng.	602			
SOC.REP.(B)	7	Plymouth, Eng.	752			
Moscow	095					

*City codes not required.
WORLD RATE REGIONS

A.	United Kingdom/Ireland	F.	Near East
B.	Europe	G.	Central America
C.	Pacific	H.	Africa
D.	Caribbean/Atlantic	J.	Indian Ocean
E.	South American		

Source: Personal Directory for International Dialing,
Bell System, May 1982.

CHAPTER 3

Meetings and Travel

CHECKLIST FOR MEETING PREPARATION

( )   Meeting date/time/place selected: _____ (specify) _____

( )   Date/time/place confirmed with officers and participants
( )   Meeting notice sent: _____ (date) _____
( )   Agenda topics requested from officers/participants
( )   Agenda prepared/mailed: _____ (date) _____
( )   Meeting folder prepared for employer (reports, etc.)
( )   Supplies organized for employer to take to meeting (see *Checklist of Supplies for Business Trips*)
( )   Meeting room reservations made
( )   Hotel room reservations made for employer (and others, if required)
( )   Travel (car-train-air) reservations made for employer (and others, if required)
( )   Meal arrangements made: breakfast ( ), lunch ( ), dinner ( ), coffee breaks ( )
( )   Rental/delivery arrangements made for equipment: _____ (list) _____

( )   Equipment operator arrangements made (if required)
( )   Meeting room supplies—pencils, pads, blotters, ash trays, pitcher with water glasses, etc.—organized/delivered
( )   Meeting room inspected—for coat closets, temperature, lighting, seating, etc.—in advance ( ), before meeting ( )
( )   Refreshment delivery/service arrangements made (other than meal arrangements) and service area inspected (e.g., hallway, adjoining room, etc.)
( )   Message (telephone, telegraph, etc.) arrangements made for secretary, employer, and participants
( )   Minute book, resolution forms, rules of order, and related material organized ( ), carried to meeting ( )
( )   Other _____

PRELIMINARY CHECKLIST OF CONFERENCE/WORKSHOP PLANNING

( ) Define purpose of conference/workshop (e.g., educational).
( ) Define needs and interests of participants.
( ) Brainstorm with organizers (e.g., to anticipate problems).
( ) State specific objective(s) of organizers.
( ) State specific objectives of conference-workshop sessions.
( ) Secure support from key persons and organizations.
( ) Establish committees and chairpersons for key functions (e.g., program, facilities, publicity, registration, exhibits, finance).
( ) Identify key personnel and outside contacts (e.g., meeting coordinator, chairpersons, hotel sales representative, printer).
( ) Prepare a work schedule—with specific start-finish deadlines—for each committee (e.g., facilities arrangements) and miscellaneous activities (preparing recreational opportunities for spouses who accompany participants).
( ) Prepare a calendar for committee and other progress reports to go to the coordinator.
( ) Evaluate each step of the conference-workshop from concept to adjournment.

Note: Those who assist conference organizers should maintain a detailed calendar of start-finish deadlines for themselves and their employers, using checklists such as the above to follow progress and alert their employers to any deviations from schedule.

MEETING AGENDA FORMAT

AGENDA

Meeting Title

Time–Date–Place

1. Call to order
2. Roll call or verification of members present
3. Determination of quorum
4. Reading and correction of minutes of previous meeting
5. Approval of minutes

6. Reading of correspondence
7. Reports of officers
8. Reports of standing committees
9. Reports of special committees
10. Unfinished business
11. New business
12. Appointments of committees
13. Nominations and elections
14. Announcements
15. Adjournment

Note: For further guidelines on the amount of detail to include and any variation in topic order, study previous agendas in your organization and follow your employer's instructions as well as any legal requirements.

MEETING NOTICE AND PROXY FORMAT

NOTICE OF MEETING

You are hereby notified that the Annual Meeting of the stockholders of (company) will be held in (location), on (date), at (time). If you do not expect to attend, please sign this proxy card and mail it promptly. No postage is required.

PROXY

I hereby constitute (name), (name), and (name), who are officers or directors of the Company, or a majority of such of them as actually are present, to act for me in my stead and as my proxy at the Annual Meeting of the stockholders of (company), to be held in (location), on (date), at (time), and at any adjournment or adjournments thereof, with full power and authority to act for me in my behalf, with all powers that I, the undersigned, would possess if I were personally present.

Effective Date: _____

Signed: _____
                        Stockholder

City   State   ZipCode

PLEASE MAKE SURE THAT YOU HAVE COMPLETED THIS FORM WITH YOUR SIGNATURE AND ADDRESS BEFORE MAILING. NO POSTAGE REQUIRED.

FORM FOR RECORDING MEETING RESOLUTIONS

MEETING NAME

Time–Date–Place

RESOLUTION 1: _____

_____

_____

Proposed by: _____ For: _____

Seconded by: _____ Against: _____

RESOLUTION 2: _____

_____

_____

Proposed by: _____ For: _____

Seconded by: _____ Against: _____

RESOLUTION 3: _____

_____

_____

Proposed by: _____ For: _____

Seconded by: _____ Against: _____

RESOLUTION 4: _____

_____

_____

Proposed by: _____ For: _____

Seconded by: _____ Against: _____

RESOLUTION 5: _____

_____

_____

Proposed by: _____ For: _____

Seconded by: _____ Against: _____

RESOLUTION 6: _____

_____

_____

Proposed by: _____   For: _____
Seconded by: _____   Against: _____

FORMAT FOR MEETING MINUTES

STOCKHOLDERS' MEETING

TIME AND PLACE

A (special) meeting of the stockholders of _____
Corporation was held at the office of the Corporation at _____

(street), _____ (city), _____ (state), on the ____ day
of _____, 19__, at ____ o'clock __ M.

PRESIDING OFFICER; SECRETARY

_____ , president of the Corporation, presided at the meeting,
and _____ , secretary of the Corporation, acted as secretary of
the meeting, as provided by the Bylaws.

ROLL CALL

The secretary called the roll of stockholders, and all of the stockholders
were present either in person or by proxy. (State if less than all of the stockholders
were present.)

The following notice of the meeting was read by the secretary and ordered
entered into the minutes of this meeting: (insert notice)

PROOF OF NOTICE OF MEETING

The secretary presented an affidavit, showing that the notice of meeting
aforesaid had been duly mailed to each stockholder at his last known address,
more than __ weeks (or days) preceding this meeting.

PROOF OF PUBLICATION OF NOTICE OF MEETING

The secretary also presented an affidavit of publication of the aforesaid notice of meeting in the _____, a newspaper published and having a circulation in the county where the principal business office of the Corporation is located, on the ____ day of _____, 19__, and on the ____, ____, and ____ days of _____, 19__, as required by law and by the Bylaws of this Corporation. (If publication is not required, omit.)

INSPECTORS OF ELECTION

The president stated that the Board of Directors had heretofore chosen two inspectors, _____ and _____, and that it was desirable that their appointment be confirmed at the meeting.

Upon motion duly made and seconded, the appointment of _____ and _____ as inspectors was unanimously confirmed, and they and each of them took and subscribed to the prescribed oath.

The inspectors thereupon took charge of the proxies, and upon examination thereof and of the stock books, reported that there were present in person or by proxy stockholders of record owning _____ (__) shares of stock, being the entire outstanding capital stock of the Corporation.

VOTE ON RESOLUTIONS

On motion duly made and seconded, and after due deliberation, the following resolution was voted upon: (insert)

The inspectors of election canvassed the votes and reported that the aforesaid resolution had been adopted by the affirmative vote of all the stockholders of the Corporation. (State if defeated instead.)

ADJOURNMENT

No other business coming before the meeting, the meeting was thereupon adjourned.

_____
President

_____
Secretary

Source: From *Private Secretary's Encyclopedic Dictionary*, 3rd ed., rev. by Mary A. De Vries. © 1984 by Prentice-Hall, Inc. Published by Prentice-Hall, Inc., Englewood Cliffs, NJ 07632.

Note: Use as many subheadings and sections as are necessary and indicated by the business conducted at the meeting. Since the bylaws of organizations differ and states have different legal requirements, examine copies of previous minutes of your organization to determine the proper format and content. Generally, however, observe these typing guidelines: Capitalize and center the meeting title and indent paragraphs 10 spaces. But indent any lists of attendees or absentees 15 spaces. Double-space the text but single-space resolutions and indent them 15 spaces. Triple-space between sections. Capitalize *Board of Directors* and *Corporation* (when used in reference to your employer). Subheads (which may be set in the margins) should be all capitals. Leave a margin of 1½ or 2 inches for captions and indexing. Type *WHEREAS* and *RESOLVED* in all capitals and the word *That* with an initial capital. Write out sums of money and follow with the numerals in parentheses.

CHECKLIST OF SUPPLIES FOR BUSINESS TRIPS

Stationery and envelopes   ( )
Carbon paper   ( )
Note pads and legal pads (steno pad for secretary)   ( )
File folders and labels   ( )
Mailing envelopes, boxes, and labels   ( )
Postage stamps and mailing stickers   ( )
Address list   ( )
Business cards   ( )
Expense forms and other forms   ( )
Checkbook: office and personal   ( )
Cash, traveler's checks, letters of credit, credit cards, etc.   ( )
Calendar and appointment schedule   ( )
Timetables and itinerary   ( )
Reference material and documents   ( )
Dictating equipment, pocket calculator, and portable computer   ( )
Miscellaneous supplies: diskettes, dictation belts, pens, pencils, blotters,
erasers, paperclips, rubber bands, cellophane tape, ruler, bottle opener,
bandaids, rubber stamp, stamp pad, scissors, etc.   ( )

RAILROAD ACCOMMODATIONS CHART

Accommodations	Provisions
Coach seating	Individual reclining seats equipped with drop-down trays and overhead lighting. Some coach seats have leg and foot rests.
Slumbercoaches	Individual seats that convert to beds. Single has a fold-away bed, and double has an upper and lower bed. Private washing and toilet facilities.
Roomettes	Private accommodation for individual traveler. Larger than the slumbercoach, it has a seat for day travel with a fold-down bed for sleeping. Private washing and toilet facilities.
Bedrooms	More spacious than a roomette and suitable for two persons. Two separate berths for sleeping, with seating for day travel. Private washing and toilet facilities.
Economy bedroom (super-liner)	Seating by day for two and sleeping berths at night. Toilet facilities in each sleeping car.
Family bedroom (super-liner)	Accommodating two adults and two children, with seating for day travel and adult and children's beds for sleeping. Toilet facilities in each sleeping car.
Deluxe bedroom (super-liner)	A large sofa with two individual reclining sections and a reclining swivel chair, with ample bedding for sleeping. Toilet facilities in each sleeping car.
Special bedroom (super-liner)	Designed for travelers with travel-related handicaps and their companion. Room spans the width of one superliner. Sleeping space and use of toilet facilities designed for travelers with special needs.

Source: National Railroad Passenger Corporation, 400 North Capitol Street, N.W., Washington, DC 20001.

MAJOR U.S. AIRPORTS

Top U.S. Cities	Major Airport(s)
Albuquerque, N.Mex	Albuquerque International Airport
Atlanta, Ga.	William B. Hartsfield Atlanta International Airport
Austin, Tex.	Robert Mueller Municipal Airport
Baltimore, Md.	Baltimore-Washington International Airport
Birmingham, Ala.	Birmingham Municipal Airport
Boston, Mass.	Logan International Airport
Buffalo, N.Y.	Greater Buffalo International Airport
Charlotte, N.C.	Douglas Municipal Airport
Chicago, Ill.	O'Hare International Airport
Cincinnati, Ohio	Greater Cincinnati International Airport
Cleveland, Ohio	Cleveland Hopkins International Airport
Columbus, Ohio	Port Columbus International Airport
Dallas, Tex.	Dallas–Ft. Worth Airport
Denver, Colo.	Denver International Airport
Detroit, Mich.	Detroit Metropolitan Airport
El Paso, Tex.	El Paso International Airport
Ft. Worth, Tex.	Dallas–Ft. Worth Airport
Honolulu, Hawaii	Honolulu International Airport
Houston, Tex.	Houston Intercontinental Airport; W. P. Hobby Airport
Indianapolis, Ind.	Indianapolis International Airport
Jacksonville, Fla.	Jacksonville International Airport
Kansas City, Mo.	Kansas City International Airport
Las Vegas, Nev.	McCarran International Airport
Long Beach, Calif.	Long Beach Airport (Daugherty Field)

Top U.S. Cities	Major Airport(s)
Los Angeles, Calif.	Los Angeles International Airport
Louisville, Ky.	Standiford Field
Memphis, Tenn.	Memphis International Airport
Miami, Fla.	Miami International Airport
Milwaukee, Wis.	General Mitchell Field
Minneapolis–St. Paul, Minn.	Minneapolis–St. Paul International Airport
Nashville, Tenn.	Metropolitan Nashville Airport
Newark, N.J.	Newark International Airport
New Orleans, La.	New Orleans International Airport
New York, N.Y	John F. Kennedy International Airport; La Guardia Airport
Norfolk, Va.	Norfolk International Airport
Oakland, Calif.	Oakland International Airport
Oklahoma City, Okla.	Will Rogers World Airport
Omaha, Nebr.	Eppley Air Field
Philadelphia, Pa.	Philadelphia International Airport
Phoenix, Ariz.	Sky Harbor International Airport
Pittsburgh, Pa.	Greater Pittsburgh International Airport
Portland, Oreg.	Portland International Airport
St. Louis, Mo.	St. Louis International Airport
San Antonio, Tex.	San Antonio International Airport
San Diego, Calif.	San Diego International Airport
San Francisco, Calif.	San Francisco International Airport
San Jose, Calif.	San Jose Municipal Airport
Seattle, Wash.	Seattle-Tacoma International Airport
Tampa, Fla.	Tampa International Airport
Toledo, Ohio	Toledo Express Airport
Tucson, Ariz.	Tucson International Airport

Top U.S. Cities	Major Airport(s)
Tulsa, Okla.	Tulsa International Airport
Washington, D.C	Dulles International Airport; Washington National Airport

Sources: Rand McNally Road Atlas, 1982; *The National Directory of Addresses and Telephone Numbers*, 1983; *Information Please Almanac*, 1983.

PASSPORT AGENCIES

Location	Telephone Inquiries	
Room E123, John F. Kennedy Building Government Center Boston, MA 02203	Recording: Public:	617-223-3831 617-223-2946
Suite 380, Kluczynski Federal Building 230 South Dearborn Street Chicago, IL 60604	Recording: Public:	312-353-5426 312-353-7155
Room C-106, New Federal Building 300 Ala Moana Boulevard P.O. Box 50185 Honolulu, HI 96850	Recording: Public:	808-546-2131 808-546-2130
One Allen Center 500 Dallas Street Houston, TX 77002	Recording: Public:	713-226-5575 713-226-4581
Federal Building, 13th Floor 11000 Wilshire Boulevard Los Angeles, CA 90024	Recording: Public:	213-824-7070 213-824-7075
Room 804, Federal Office Building 51 Southwest First Avenue Miami, FL 33130	Recording: Public:	305-350-5395 305-350-4681
Room 400, International Trade Mart Two Canal Street New Orleans, LA 70130	Recording: Public:	504-589-6728 504-589-6161

Location	Telephone Inquiries	
Room 270, Rockefeller Center 630 Fifth Avenue New York, NY 10111	Recording: Public:	212-541-7700 212-541-7710
Room 4426, Federal Building 600 Arch Street Philadelphia, PA 19106	Recording: Public:	215-597-7482 215-597-7480
Room 1405, Federal Building 450 Golden Gate Avenue San Francisco, CA 94102	Recording: Public:	415-556-4516 415-556-2630
Room 906, Federal Building 915 Second Avenue Seattle, WA 98174	Recording: Public:	206-442-7941 206-442-7945
One Landmark Square Street Level Stamford, CT 06901	Recording: Public:	203-325-4401 203-325-3538
1425 K Street, N.W. Washington, DC 20524	Recording: Public:	202-783-8200 202-783-8170

Source: U.S. Department of State, *Your Trip Abroad* (Washington, D.C.: U.S. Government Printing Office, 1982).

Note: A 24-hour recording includes general passport information, passport agency location, and hours of operation. For other questions, call the public inquiries number.

FORM

TRAVEL EXPENSE REPORT

Name _____

Title _____

Period Covered _____

Department _____

Date	Transportation			Living Expenses		Entertainment	Phone, Tele-gram, Postage	Misc.	Daily Total
	Auto	Plane	Train	Hotel	Meals				
Total									

Item	Current Month	Previous Month	Year to Date
Mileage			
Expenses			
Budget			

Source: From *The Prentice-Hall Complete Secretarial Letter Book* by Mary A. De Vries. © 1984 by Prentice-Hall, Inc. Published by Prentice-Hall, Inc., Englewood Cliffs, NJ 07632.

CHAPTER 4

Grammar
and
Composition

COMMON ENGLISH ABBREVIATIONS

@	at (referring to price)
A-1	first-class
aa	author's alterations (printing)
aar, AAR	against all risks
ac	alternating current
a/c	account
A/C	account current
a/cs pay.	accounts payable
a/cs rec.	accounts receivable
a/d	after date
a.d.	before the day
ad fin.	to or at the end (*ad finem*)
ad inf.	without limit (*ad infinitum*)
ad int.	in the meantime (*ad interim*)
ad lib., ad libit.	at one's pleasure; freely to the quantity or amount desired (*ad libitum*)
ad loc.	to or at the place (*ad locum*)
ad val.	according to value (*ad valorem*). See *a/v*.
adv. chgs.	advance charges
agb	a good brand
aka	also known as
an.	arrival notice (shipping)
anon.	anonymous
a/o	account of
a to oc	attached to other correspondence
ap	additional premium
a/p	authority to pay
a/r	all risks; against all risks (marine insurance)
as.	at sight
a/s	after sight
Ast	Atlantic standard time
A/T	American terms (grain trade)
att.	attached
attn., atten.	attention
au.	author; astronomical unit
Au	gold
AV	authorized version
a/v	according to value (*ad valorem*). See *ad val*.
a/w	actual weight

aw	all water (transportation)
AWG	American wire gauge
b	born; brother
b/a	billed at
b7d, b10d, b15d	buyer 7 days to take up, etc. (stock market)
bal.	balance
bb	bail bond; break bulk
bbl	barrel(s)
B.C.	before Christ
b/c	bill for collection
b/d	barrels per day; brought down (accounting)
bd	bank draft
bdl.	bundle
BE	bill of exchange
B/E	bill of entry
b/f	brought forward (bookkeeping)
bf	boldface; brief (legal)
b/g	bonded goods
B/H	bill of health
bkpt.	bankrupt
bkt.	bracket
B/L	bill of lading
bl	bale(s)
b of m	bill of materials
bo	buyer's option; back order; branch office
b/o	brought over (accounting)
b/p	blueprint
bp	bills payable; bill of parcels
bpd	bank post bill; barrels per day
B/R	bills receivable; builders' risks
Bros.	Brothers
b/s	bill of sale; bill of store (commerce)
bsk.	basket(s)
Bs/L	bills of lading
B/St	bill of sight
bv	book value
bw	please turn page (*bitte werden*)
bx.	box
©, copr.	copyright
c	carat; chapter(s); about (*circa*)

C/	case(s)
ca	capital account; credit account; current account; chartered accountant; commercial agent; close annealed; about (*circa*)
CAF	cost, assurance, and freight
cal.	small calories; calendar; caliber
can.	cancelled; cancellation
cap.	capital; capacity
caps	capital letters
cart.	cartage
cb	cash book
cbd	cash before delivery
c/d	carried down (bookkeeping)
cd	cord; cash discount; certificate of deposit
C/D	commercial dock; consular declaration
c&d	collection and delivery
cert., ctf.	certificate; certification; certified
cf	compare
c/f	carried forward (bookkeeping)
c&f	cost and freight
cfi	cost, freight, and insurance
cfo	cost for orders
cge. pd.	carriage paid
ch.	chain; chapter; channel (TV); chemical; chart; candle hours
chap., chaps.	chapter; chapters
chg.	charge; change
c&i	cost and insurance
cif	cost, insurance, and freight
cir.	circuit; circular; circulation; circumference
cks.	cask(s); check(s)
cl	carload lots; center line
c/l	craft loss; cash letter
clt	collateral trust (bonds)
CLT	code language telegram
cm pf	cumulative preferred (stocks)
cn	credit note; consignment note; circular note
co.	company; county
c/o	carried over (bookkeeping); in care of; cash order
COD	cash, or collect, on delivery
col.	column
coll. tr., clt	collateral trust (bonds)
consgt.	consignment
coop	cooperative

corp.	corporation; corporal; to the body (*corpori*)
cos	cash on shipment
cp	carriage paid
CPA	certified public accountant
CPLS	certified professional legal secretary
CPS	certified professional secretary
cr	class rate; current rate; company's risk
cr.	credit; creditor
CST	central standard time
ct	central time
ctge	cartage
ctn.	carton
ctr.	center; counter
cum.	with; cumulative
cum. pref.	cumulative preferred (stocks)
cur.	current
cv	chief value
cvt	convertible (securities)
cv db	convertible debentures (securities)
cv pf	convertible preferred (securities)
cw	commercial weight
cwo	cash with order
D/A	deposit account; documents against acceptance; discharge afloat
db	debenture
dba	doing business as (company name)
dbk.	drawback
db rts.	debenture rights (securities)
dc	deviation clause; direct current
dd	delivered at docks; demand draft
dd	days after bill (bill of exchange)
deb.	debenture
dec.	decision; decimal
def.	deferred (securities)
deg.	degree(s)
dep. ctfs.	deposit certificates
df	dead freight
DFA	division freight agent
dia., diam.	diameter
diag.	diagram; diagonal
dis.	discount
div.	dividend; division

dkt.	docket
dl	demand loan
DL	day letter (telegraph)
dld	delivered
dlo	dispatch loading only
DLO	dead letter office
dls/shr	dollars per share
D/N	debit note
do.	ditto (the same); delivery order
dp	direct port
D/P	documents against (or for) payment
D/R	deposit receipt
dr.	debit; debtor; drawer
d/s	days after sight
DSC	distinguished service cross
DSM	distinguished service medal
D.V.	God willing (*Deo volente*)
D/W	dock warrant
dw	dead weight
dwc	dead weight capacity
dwt	pennyweight(s); deadweight tons
dwtf	daily and weekly till forbidden
dy	delivery
ea.	each
eaon	except as otherwise noted
ed.	editor; edition(s); education
Ed. Note	editorial note
EDP	electronic data processing
edt	eastern daylight time
EE	errors excepted
e.g.	for example (*exempli gratia*)
emp	end-of-month payment
enc.	enclosure
end.	endorse; endorsement
eng.	engine; engineer; engineering; engraved
eo	by authority of his office (*ex officio*)
eod	every other day (advertising)
e&oe	errors and omissions excepted
eohp	except as otherwise herein provided
eom	end of month (payments)
Esq.	esquire
est.	estate; estimated

EST	eastern standard time
eta	estimated time of arrival
et al.	and others (*et alii*)
etc.	and the others; and so forth (*et cetera*)
et seq.	and the following (*et sequens*)
et ux.	and wife (*et uxor*)
et vir.	and husband
ex	out of or from; without or not including
Ex/B/L	exchange bill of lading
ex cp	ex coupon
ex div.	without dividend
ex int.	not including interest
ex n	ex new (excluding right to new shares—stocks)
exp.	express; expenses; export
f	following (after a numeral); feminine
faa	free of all average (shipping)
fac.	facsimile; fast as can
FAM	Free and Accepted Masons
faq	fair average quality; free at quay
faqs	fair average quality of season
FAX	facsimile
FD	free discharge; free delivery; free dispatch
fd.	fund
f&d	freight and demurrage (shipping)
Fed. Reg.	Federal Register
ff	following (after a numeral); folios
ffa	free from alongside; free foreign agency
fia	full interest admitted
fig.(s)	figure(s)
fio	free in and out
fit.	free of income tax; free in truck
fiw	free in wagon
fln	following landing numbers (shipping)
fn.	footnote
fo	firm offer; free overside; for orders; full out terms (grain trade)
fob	free on board
foc	free on car; free of charge
fod	free of damage
fol.	folio; following
foq	free on quay
for.	free on rail

fos	free on steamer
fot	free on truck
FP	floating (or open) policy; fully paid premium
F/R	freight release
frof	fire risk on freight
frt.	freight
ft	full terms
fv	on the back of the page (*folio verso*)
fwd	fresh-water damage; forward
fx	foreign exchange
FYI	for your information (interoffice use)
G/A	general average (marine insurance)
gfa	good fair average
GFA	general freight agent
GI	government issue; general issue
GNP	gross national product
GPA	general passenger agent
gr.	grain
gro.	gross
gtc	good till cancelled or countermanded (brokerage)
gtm	good this month
gtw	good this week (becomes void on Saturday)
hc	held covered (insurance)
hdqs.	headquarters. See *HQ*
hdwe.	hardware
hfm	hold for money
hon.	honorable
HQ	headquarters. See *hdqs*.
hr.	hour(s)
HR	House bill (federal); House of Representatives
hw	high water
HWOST	high-water ordinary spring tide
hyp.	hypothesis
IB	invoice book; in bond
ibid.	in the same place (*ibidem*)
ibo	invoice book outward
ic&c	invoice cost and charges
id	the same (*idem*)
i.e.	that is (*id est*)
Inc.	Incorporated
inf.	infinity

in loc.	in the proper place
in re	in regard to
ins.	insurance
int.	interest
inv.	invoice
IQ	intelligence quotient
ital.	italics
iv	invoice value; increased value
JA	joint account
jg	junior grade
jnt. stk.	joint stock
k	carat; knot
kd	knocked down
l	line
LA	Lloyd's agent
L/A	letter of authority; landing account
lat.	latitude
lc	lowercase; letter of credit
LC	deferreds (cable messages)
L/C	letter of credit
LCL	less than carload lot
lcm	least common multiple
ldg.	loading; landing
ldg. & dely.	landing and delivery
lds.	loads
L. Ed.	Lawyers Edition
lf	lightface; ledger folio
lge.	large
lip.	life insurance policy
lkg. & bkg.	leakage and breakage
LL	lend-lease
Ll. & Cos.	Lloyd's and Companies
lmsc	let me see correspondence
loc. cit.	in the place cited (*loco citato*)
log.	logarithm
long.	longitude
lr	lire
ls	place of the seal (*locus sigilli*)
LT	letter message (cables)
ltd.	limited (British)

lt-v	light vessel (shipping)
lv.	leave
LW	low water
LWM	low-water mark
m	married; masculine
M	thousand; monsieur (*pl* MM); noon (*meridie*)
m/a	my account
mar.	marine; maritime; married
max.	maximum
max. cap	maximum capacity
mc	marked capacity (freight cars); marginal credit
MC	master of ceremonies; member of Congress
m/d	months after date
M/D	memorandum of deposit
mdse.	merchandise
med.	medium; medicine; medical
Messrs	Misters (Messieurs)
mfg.	manufacturing
mfr.	manufacturer
MH	main hatch; Medal of Honor
mi.	mile(s)
min.	minute(s); minimum
min. B/L	minimum bill of lading
mip	marine insurance policy
misc.	miscellaneous
Mlle.	Mademoiselle
mm	necessary changes being made (*mutatis mutandis*)
MM	Messieurs
Mme.	Madam
Mmes.	Mesdames
mo.	month(s)
mo	money order
MP	member of Parliament; military police
ms./mss.	manuscript(s)
m/s	months after sight
Msgr.	Monsignor; Monseigneur
mst.	measurement
MST	mountain standard time
mt	empty
mt.ct.cp.	mortgage certificate coupon (securities)
mtg.	mortgage
mv	market value

n	net; note; number
n/a	no account (banking)
N/a	no advice (banking)
NA	not available
natl.	national
naut.	nautical
N.B.	note well (*nota bene*)
nc	new charter; new crop
NCO	noncommissioned officer
ncup	no commission until paid
ncv	no commercial value
nd	no date
ne	not exceeding; no effects (banking)
NE	New England; Northeast
nes	not elsewhere specified
N/F	no funds (banking)
NG	no good
nhp	nominal horsepower
NL	night letter (telegraph)
NLT	night letter cable
NM	night message
N/m	no mark
no.	number
n/o	in the name of (finance); no orders (banking)
noe	not otherwise enumerated
nohp	not otherwise herein provided
nol. pros.	to be unwilling to prosecute (*nolle prosequi*)
nom.	nominative; nominal
nom. std.	nominal standard
non obst.	notwithstanding (*non obstante*)
non pros.	does not prosecute (*non prosequitur*)
non seq.	does not follow (*non sequitur*)
nop	not otherwise provided for
nos	not otherwise specified
NP	notary public
np	net proceeds; nonparticipating (stocks); no place; no publisher
npt	normal pressure and temperature
nr	no risk; net register
nrad	no risk after discharge
ns	new series
NS	national society
nsf	not sufficient funds (banking)

nspf	not specially provided for
N/t	new terms
ntp	no title page
nt. wt.	net weight
Nv	nonvoting (stocks)
ob	died (*obit*)
OB/L	order bill of lading
obs.	obsolete
oc	open charter; overcharge; over the counter; office copy
od	on demand
o/d	overdraft (banking)
oe	omissions excepted
OE	Old English
o/o	order of
oo	on order
op	out of print
op. cit.	in the work cited (*opere citato*)
opn.	opinion
or.	owner's risk (transportation)
o&r	ocean and rail (transportation)
os	old series
o/s	out of stock
OS	on sample; one side
os&d	over, short, and damaged (transportation)
ot	on truck; overtime
O/t	old terms (grain trade)
ow	one way (fare)
oz.	ounce(s)
p.	page
pa	by the year (*per annum*); private account; particular average; power of attorney
PA	purchasing agent
PABX	private automatic branch exchange (telephone)
pam.	pamphlet
part.	participating (securities)
pat.	patent
PBX	private branch exchange (telephone)
pc	percent; post card; petty cash
P/C	prices current
pct.	percent; precinct
PD	port dues

pd	per diem
pd.	passed; paid
pfd.	preferred
p&i	protection and indemnity
pkg.	package
pl	partial loss
p&l	profit and loss
P.M.	afternoon (*post meridiem*)
PM	postmaster; provost marshal
pm	premium money
pn	promissory note
p/n	please note
PO	post office
por	payable on receipt
pp	parcel post
pp.	pages
ppd.	prepaid; postpaid
ppi	parcel post insured; policy proof of interest
ppt	prompt loading
pr.	pair
pref.	preface; preferred
prin.	principal; principle
pro tem.	for the time being (*pro tempore*)
prox.	proximate; of the next month (*proximo*)
ps	postscript; public sale
PST	Pacific standard time
Pt	Pacific time
pw	packed weight
PX	please exchange; post exchange; private exchange (telephone)
Q	question; query
qda	quantity discount agreement
qed	which was to be proved or demonstrated (*quod erat demonstradum*)
qq	questions; queries
qr.	quarter
qv	which see (*quod vide*)
r	reigned; recto
R/A	refer to acceptor; return to author
R/C	reconsigned; recovered
rcd.	received

RD	refer to drawer
rd	running days
re	in regard to
recd., rec'd	received
ref.	referee; reference; referred
reg.	registered; regulation(s)
rep.	report
res.	residue; research; reserve; residence; resigned; resolution
rev. A/c	revenue account
rf., rfg.	refunding (bonds); radio frequency
RI	reinsurance
r&l	rail and lake (transportation)
rl&r	rail, lake, and rail (transportation)
rm.	ream (paper); room(s)
r&o	rail and ocean (transportation)
rog	receipt of goods
rom.	roman (type)
rop	run of paper
rotn. no.	rotation number
rp	return premium; reply paid (cable)
RR	railroad
RSVP	please reply (*répondez, s'il vous plaît*)
Rt.	right(s) (stock)
r&t	rail and truck
RVSVP	please reply at once (*répondez vite, s'il vous plaît*)
r&w	rail and water (transportation)
rw	railway
s	son; substantive
/s/	signed
s7d, s10d, s15d	seller 7 days to deliver, etc. (stock market)
sa	subject to approval; safe arrival; without year (*sine anno*); under the year (*sub anno*)
sanr	subject to approval no risk (no risk until insurance is confirmed)
s/b	statement of billing (transportation)
sc	small capital letters; same case (legal); namely, to wit (*scilicet*); salvage charges
s&c	shipper and carrier
sd	without a day being named (*sine die*); sight draft
sdbl	sight draft, bill of lading attached

SE	stock exchange; Southeast
sec., secy., sec'y	secretary
sec.(s)	section(s)
seq.	the following; in sequence
ser.	series
SF	sinking fund
S&FA	shipping and forwarding agent
sgd.	signed
sh.	share
shpt.	shipment
sh. tn.	short ton
sic	so; thus (to confirm a word that might be questioned)
sit.	stopping in transit (transportation)
sk.	sack(s)
sl	salvage loss; without place (*sine loco*)
sn	shipping note
so.	seller's option; shipping order; ship's option
soc.	society
sol.	solicitor(s); solution
SOL	shipowner's liability
SOP	standard operating procedure
sp	supra protest; stop payment
spd	steamer pays dues
ss	namely (*scilicet*)
SS	steamship
s to s	station to station
SST	supersonic transport
st	let it stand (*stet*)
St.	saint
sta.	station
stat.	statute(s)
std.	standard
stg.	sterling; storage
stk.	stock
str.	steamer
sup.	above (*supra*)
supp.	supplement
supt.	superintendent
sv	sailing vessel; same year; under the word (*sub verbo*)
svp	if you please (*s'il vous plaît*)
sw	shipper's weights
syn.	synonymous

taw	twice a week (advertising)
tb	time base
tc	until countermanded
td	time deposit
TE	trade expenses
tel.	telegram; telegraph; telephone
tf	till forbidden (advertising)
tl	time loan
tlo	total loss only (marine insurance)
tm	true mean; landmark
T/o	transfer order
t/r	trust receipt; tons registered (shipping)
tr.	transpose
trans.	transitive; translated; transportation; transaction
treas.	treasurer
ts	typescript
TT	telegraphic transfer
twp.	township
tws	time wire service (telegraph)
U	university
UA	underwriting account (marine insurance)
uc	uppercase
ud	as directed
ugt	urgent (cable)
ui	as below (*ut infra*)
ult.	of the last month (*ultimo*)
univ.	university
up.	under proof
us.	as above (*ut supra*)
ut	universal time
up sup.	as above (*ut supra*)
u/w	underwriter
v	versus; value
vc	valuation clause
vi	see below (*vide infra*)
vid.	see (*vide*)
viz.	namely (*videlicet*)
vol.	volume
vop	value as in original policy
vs	verse; versus
vt.	voting (stock)
vv	vice versa

wa	with average (insurance); will advise
wd.	warranted; word
wf	wrong font (typesetting)
wg	weight guaranteed; wire gauge
whsle.	wholesale
wi	when issued (stock exchange)
wk.	week
woc	without compensation
wp	without prejudice; weather permitting; wire payment
wpp	waterproof paper packing
wr	with rights (securities); warehouse receipt
w&r	water and rail (transportation)
wt.	weight
ww	with warrants (securities); warehouse warrant
xcp	without coupon (bonds)
xd	without dividend (stocks)
xi	without next interest (bonds)
xn	ex new
xp	express paid
x per	without privileges
x rts.	without rights (stocks)
xw	without warrants (securities)
yb.	yearbook
yr.	year
z.	zone; zero
zhr.	zero hour

ABBREVIATIONS OF ORGANIZATIONS

ABA	American Bankers Association; American Bar Association; American Booksellers Association
AEC	Atomic Energy Commission
AFL-CIO	American Federation of Labor and Congress of Industrial Organizations
AIB	American Institute of Banking
AID	Agency for International Development
AMA	American Medical Association
AP	Associated Press

ARC	American (National) Red Cross
ARS	Agricultural Research Service
ASA	American Standards Association; American Statistical Association
ASTA	American Society of Travel Agents
BLS	Bureau of Labor Statistics
BTA	Board of Tax Appeals
CA	Civil Air Patrol
CCC	Commodity Credit Corporation
CEA	Commodity Exchange Administration
CEC	Commodity Exchange Commission
CED	Committee for Economic Development
CIA	Central Intelligence Agency
CID	Criminal Investigation Department
CORE	Congress of Racial Equality
CPSC	Consumer Product Safety Commission
CSC	Civil Service Commission
EEC	European Economic Community
EEOC	Equal Employment Opportunity Commission
EPA	Environmental Protection Agency
FAA	Federal Aviation Agency
FBI	Federal Bureau of Investigation
FCA	Farm Credit Administration
FCC	Federal Communications Commission
FDA	Food and Drug Administration
FDIC	Federal Deposit Insurance Corporation
FHA	Federal Housing Administration
FMC	Federal Maritime Commission
FPC	Federal Power Commission
FRB	Federal Reserve Board; Federal Reserve Bank
FRS	Federal Reserve System
FSA	Federal Security Agency
FTC	Federal Trade Commission
GAO	General Accounting Office
GHQ	General Headquarters (Army)
GPO	Government Printing Office
GSA	General Service Administration

HHFA	Housing and Home Finance Agency
HUD	Housing and Urban Development (Department of)
ICC	Interstate Commerce Commission
IFC	International Finance Corporation
IFTU	International Federation of Trade Unions
ILO	International Labor Organization
ILP	Independent Labour Party (British)
IMF	International Monetary Fund
INP	International News Photos
INS	International News Service
IRO	International Refugee Organization
IRS	Internal Revenue Service
ITO	International Trade Organization
IWW	Industrial Workers of the World
KC	Knights of Columbus
KKK	Ku Klux Klan
NAACP	National Association for the Advancement of Colored People
NALS	National Association of Legal Secretaries
NAM	National Association of Manufacturers
NAS	National Academy of Sciences
NASA	National Aeronautics and Space Administration
NATO	North Atlantic Treaty Organization
NBS	National Broadcasting Service
NEA	National Educational Association; National Editorial Association
NIH	National Institutes of Health
NLRB	National Labor Relations Board
NMB	National Mediation Board
NOW	National Organization for Women
NPS	National Park Service
NRC	Nuclear Regulatory Commission
NSC	National Security Council
NSF	National Science Foundation
OAS	Organization of American States
OECD	Organization for Economic Cooperation and Development
PHA	Public Housing Administration
PHS	Public Health Service

PSI	Professional Secretaries International
REA	Rural Electrification Administration
ROTC	Reserve Officers' Training Corp
RRB	Railroad Retirement Board
SBA	Small Business Administration
SEATO	Southeast Asia Treaty Organization
SEC	Securities and Exchange Commission
SSA	Social Security Administration
SSS	Selective Service System
TC	Tax Court of the United States
TVA	Tennessee Valley Authority
UN	United Nations
UNESCO	United Nations Educational, Social, and Cultural Organization
USIA	United States Information Agency
UNICEF	United Nations Children's Fund
UNRRA	United National Relief and Rehabilitation Administration
UPI	United Press International
UPS	United Parcel Service
USDA	United States Department of Agriculture
USIA	United States Information Agency
VA	Veterans Administration
VFW	Veterans of Foreign Wars
VISTA	Volunteers in Service to America
WHO	World Health Organization

ABBREVIATIONS OF FOREIGN COUNTRIES AND REGIONS

Country/Region	Abbreviation
Africa	Afr.
Albania	Alb.
Argentina	Argen.
Australia	Austl.
Austria	Aus.

Country/Region	Abbreviation
Belgium	Belg.
Bolivia	Bol.
Brazil	Braz.
Burma	Burma
Canada	Can.
Chile	Chile
China	China
Colombia	Colom.
Czechoslovakia	Czech.
Denmark	Den.
Dominican Republic	Dom. Rep.
East Germany	E. Ger.
Ecuador	Ecuador
Egypt	Egypt
El Salvador	El Sal.
Europe	Eur.
England	Eng.
Finland	Fin.
France	Fr.
Ghana	Ghana
Great Britain	Gr. Brit.
Greece	Greece
Guatemala	Guat.
Haiti	Haiti
Honduras	Hond.
Hong Kong	H.K.
Hungary	Hung.
Iceland	Ice.
India	India
Ireland	Ir.
Israel	Isr.
Italy	Italy
Japan	Japan
Korea	Korea
Luxembourg	Lux.
Mexico	Mex.
Netherlands	Neth.
New Zealand	N.Z.
Nicaragua	Nicar.
Nigeria	Nig.
Norway	Nor.
Pakistan	Pak.

Country/Region	Abbreviation
Panama	Pan.
Paraguay	Para.
Philippines	Phil.
Poland	Pol.
Portugal	Port.
Rhodesia	Rhodesia
Romania	Rom.
Scotland	Scot.
South Africa	S. Afr.
Spain	Spain
Sweden	Swed.
Switzerland	Switz.
Turkey	Turk.
Uganda	Uganda
U.S.S.R.	U.S.S.R.
United Kingdom	U.K.
Uruguay	Uru.
Venezuela	Venez.
Wales	Wales
West Germany	W.Ger.
Yugoslavia	Yugo.
Zambia	Zambia
Zimbabwe	Zimb.

TECHNICAL ABBREVIATIONS

a; amp.	ampere
Å	angstrom
af	audiofrequency
a-h	ampere-hour
a/m	ampere per meter
AM	amplitude modulation
at.	atmosphere
at. no.	atomic number
at. vol.	atomic volume
at. wt.	atomic weight
av.; avdp.	avoirdupois

bbl	barrel
bbl/d	barrel per day
bhp	brake horsepower
bm	board measure
bp	boiling point
Btu; BTU	British thermal unit
bu.	bushel
C	Celsius; Centigrade; centi (prefix: one-hundredth)
c	cycle (radio)
cd. ft.	cord foot
cg	centigram
c-h	candle-hour
cl	centiliter
cm	centimeter
c/m	cycles per minute
cm^2	square centimeter
cm^3	cubic centimeter
cp	candlepower
d	deci (prefix: one-tenth)
da	deka (prefix: 10)
dag	dekagram
dal	dekaliter
dam	dekameter
dam^2	square dekameter
dam^3	cubic dekameter
dB	decibel
dBu	decibel unit
dg	decigram
dl	deciliter
dm	decimeter
dm^2	square decimeter
dm^3	cubic decimeter
dr.	dram
dwt	deadweight ton; pennyweight
dyn	dyne
EHF	extremely high frequency
EMF	electromotive force
erg	erg
esu	electrostatic unit
eV	electronvolt

F	Fahrenheit; farad
fbm	board foot; board foot measure
FM	frequency modulation
ft.	foot
ft.^{2}	square foot
ft.^{3}	cubic foot
ft.H_2O	conventional foot of water
G	gauss; giga (prefix: 1 billion)
g	gram; gravity
gal.	gallon
GeV	gigaelectronvolt
GHz	gigahertz
h	hecto (prefix: 100)
H	henry
ha	hectare
hf	high frequency
hg	hectogram
hl	hectoliter
hm	hectometer
hm^2	square hectometer
hm^3	cubic hectometer
hp	horsepower
Hz	hertz
ihp	indicated horsepower
in.	inch
in.^{2}	square inch
in.^{3}	cubic inch
J	joule
k	kilo (prefix: one thousand)
kc	kilocycle
keV	kiloelectronvolt
kG	kilogauss
kg	kilogram
kgf	kilogram-force
kHz	kilohertz
kl	kiloliter
km	kilometer
km^2	square kilometer

km^3	cubic kilometer
kn	knot (speed)
kt	kiloton; carat
kV	kilovolt
kVa	kilovoltampere
kW	kilowatt
kWh	kilowatthour
l	liter
lf	low frequency
lin. ft.	linear foot
l/m	lines per minute
l/s	lines per second
M	mega (prefix: one million); thousand
m	meter; milli (prefix: one-thousandth)
m^2	square meter
m^3	cubic meter
ma	milliampere
mbar	millibar
Mc	megacycle
mc	millicycle
MeV	megaelectronvolts
mF	millifarad
mG	milligauss
mg	milligram
mH	millihenry
MHz	megahertz
mHz	millihertz
mi.	mile (statute)
$mi.^2$	square mile
min.	minute (time)
ml	milliliter
mm	millimeter
mm^2	square millimeter
mm^3	cubic millimeter
mph	miles per hour
ms	millisecond
Mt	megaton
mV	millivolt
MW	megawatt
mW	milliwatt
μ	micro (prefix: one-millionth)

μF	microfarad
μg	microgram
μH	microhenry
μin	microinch
μm	micrometer
μs	microsecond
μV	microvolt
μW	microwatt

n	nano (prefix: one-billionth)
na	nanoampere
nm	nanometer
nmi.	nautical mile
ns	nanosecond
oz.	ounce (avoirdupois)

p	pico (prefix: one-trillionth)
pct.	percent
pk.	peck
p/m	parts per million
ps	picosecond
pt.	pint
pW	picowatt

ql	quintal
qt.	quart

R	rankine; roentgen
rms	root mean square
rpm; r/m	revolutions per minute
rps; r/s	revolutions per second

s	second (time)
shp	shaft horsepower

T	tera (prefix: one trillion); tesla
tMW	thermal megawatt

u	atomic mass unit
uhf	ultrahigh frequency

V	volt
Va	volt ampere

vhf	very high frequency
V/m	volt per meter
W	watt
Wh	watthour
yd.	yard
yd.^{2}	square yard
yd.^{3}	cubic yard

Note: Authorities differ in matters of capitalization and punctuation of abbreviations. When appropriate, follow the practices in your profession or the preferred style in your office.

COMPUTER ACRONYMS AND ABBREVIATIONS

ABM	automated batch mixing
abort	abandon activity
ABP	actual block processor
abs	absolute
AC	automatic/analog computer
ACF	advanced communication function
ACL	Audit Command Language
ACM	area composition machine
ADAPS	automatic displayed plotting system
ADC	analog-to-digital converter
ADIS	automatic data interchange system
ADP	automatic/advanced data processing
ADR	address; adder; analog-to-digital recorder
AFR	automatic field/format recognition
ALCOM	algebraic computer/compiler
ALGOL	Algorithmic Language
ALP	automated language processing
ALU	arithmetic and logic unit
ANACOM	analog computer
AOC	automatic output control
AP	attached processor
APL	A Programming Language
APT	Automatic Programmed Tools (language)
AQL	acceptable quality level

ARQ	automatic report request; automatic request for correction
ARU	audio response unit
ASC	automatic sequence control
ASCII	American Standard Code for Information Interchange
ASDI	automated selective dissemination of information
ASM	auxiliary storage management
ASP	attached support processor
ASR	answer, send, and receive
ATLAS	Automatic Tabulating, Listing, and Sorting System
AUTODIN	automated digital network
B	bit; magnetic flux density
BA	binary add
BAM	basic access method
BASIC	Beginner's All-Purpose Symbolic Instruction Code
BC	binary code
BCD	binary-coded decimal
BDU	basic device/display unit
BIM	beginning of information marker
bit	binary digit
BIU	basic information unit
BN	binary number system
BOS	basic operating system
BOT	beginning of tape
bpi	bits per inch
bps	bits per second
BPS	basic programming support
BS	backspace character
BTU	basic transmission unit
C	computer; compute; control
CA	channel adapter
CAD	computer-aided design
CAD/CAM	computer-aided design/computer-aided manufacturing
CAI	computer-aided instruction
CAI/OP	computer analog input/output
CAL	computer-aided learning
CAM	computer-aided manufacturing
CAN	cancel character
CAR	computer-assisted retrieval
CAT	computer-assisted training/teaching
CDC	call directing code
CHAR	character

CIM	computer-input microfilm
CIOCS	communications input/output control system
CIU	computer interface unit
CLAT	communication line adapter
CLK	clock
CLT	communication line terminal
CMC	code for magnetic characters
CMND	command
CMS	conversation monitor system
CNC	computer numerical control
COBOL	Common Business-Oriented Language
COL	Computer-Oriented Language
COM	computer-output microfilm
CP	central processor
cph	characters per hour
cpm	characters per minute; cards per minute; critical path method
CP/M	controlled program monitor; control program/microcomputers
CPS	conversational programming system; central processing system
CPU	central processing unit
cr	carriage return
CR	call request; control relay
CRAM	card random access method
CROM	control read-only memory
CRT	cathode ray tube
CSL	Computer-Sensitive Language
CST	channel status table
CTR	computer tape reader
CTU	central terminal unit
CU	control unit
CWP	communicating word processor
DAA	direct-access arrangement
DAC	data acquisition and control; digital/analog converter
DASD	direct-access storage device
DBAM	database access method
DBMS	database management system
DD	digital data
DDL	Data-Description Language
DDS	digital-display scope
DE	display element
DIP	dual in-line package

DLC	data-link control
DMA	direct memory access
DNC	direct numerical control
DOS	disk operating system
DOV	data over voice
DP	data processing
DRL	Data-Retrieval Language
DRO	destructive read-out
DTR	data terminal ready
DUV	data under voice
EDP	electronic data processing
EOF	end of file
EOJ	end of job
EOR	end of record/run
ESI	externally specified index
ETB	end of transmission block
F	feedback
FACT	Fully Automatic Compiling Technique
FDOS	floppy-disk operating system
FF	flip-flop
FIRST	fast interactive retrieval system
FORTRAN	Formula Translation (language)
GDT	graphic display terminal
GP	general program
GPC	general-purpose computer
HSM	high-speed memory
HSP	high-speed printer
HSR	high-speed reader
IC	integrated circuit; input circuit
ID	identification
I/O	input/output
IOB	input-output buffer
IOC	input-output controller
ipm	impulses per minute
IR	infrared
ISR	information storage and retrieval
k	about a thousand (in storage capacity)
KB	keyboard

kb	kilobytes
KSR	keyboard send and receive
LCD	liquid crystal display
LIFO	last in, first out
LILO	last in, last out
LP	linear programming
lpm	lines per minute
lsc	least significant character
lsd	least significant digit
M	mega
mag	magnetic
Mb	megabyte
MC	master control
MCP	master control program
MIS	management information system
MPS	microprocessor system
msc	most significant character
msd	most significant digit
MSU	modem-sharing unit
MT	machine translation
MUX	multiplexer
n	nano-
NAM	network access machine
NAU	network addressable unit
NC	numerical control
NCP	network control program
NL	new-line character
NO-OP	no-operation instruction
ns	nanosecond
OCR	optical character recognition
ODB	output to display buffer
OEM	original equipment manufacturer
OLRT	on-line real time
OP	operations
opm	operations per minute
OR	operations research
OSI	open-system interconnection
p	pico-
PA	paper advance

PC	program counter
PCI	process control interface
PCM	punch-card machine
PCS	punch-card system
PDN	public data network
PERT	program evaluation and review technique
PIO chip	programmable input/output chip
PIU	path information unit
PRT	production-run tape
RAM	random-access memory
RAX	remote access
READ	real-time electronic access and display
REM	recognition memory
ROM	read-only memory
RT	real time
RTU	remote terminal unit
R/W	read/write
RWM	read-write memory
RZ	return to zero
SAM	sequential-access method; serial-access memory
S/F	store and forward
SLT	solid-logic technology
SOP	standard operating procedure
STX	start of text
TLU	table look-up
TOS	tape operating system
UCS	user control storage
USASCII	USA Standard Code for Information Interchange
VDI	visual display input
VDT	video display terminal
WC	write and compute
WFL	work-flow language
WIP	work in progress
WO	write out
WS	working storage/space
XMT	transmit

Note: See also *Technical Abbreviations* in this chapter.

ABBREVIATION GUIDELINES

Rule	Examples
General abbreviations should not be used in nontechnical writing, except in footnotes, tables, charts, invoices, and so on.	Write *administration* (not *admin.*); *inch* (not *in.*); *Sunday* (not *Sun.*)
In specialized areas, follow the style in your profession or the practices of your office.	A law office commonly uses *In re* to introduce the subject line in correspondence, but a business office would use the word *Subject*, spelled out.
Be consistent in your use of abbreviations.	25 *kilometers* west and 15 *kilometers* north (not 25 *km* west and 15 *kilometers* north)
Certain abbreviated words are rarely spelled out.	Personal and professional titles (*Mr.*, *Dr.*); scholarly degrees (*Ph.D.*, *Sc.D.*); time-date abbreviations (A.M., P.M.; A.D., B.C.)
Always abbreviate *Jr.*, *Sr.*, and *Esq.* after a personal name.	Mr. Henry Forrest, *Jr.*; Lucille Jenkins, *Esq.*
In informal writing, when religious, military, and honorary titles are preceded by *the* and when they precede a surname alone, spell them in full; otherwise you may abbreviate the title.	The *Reverend* John Jones; *Captain* Steiner; *Maj.* Lynda Fenton; *Hon.* Henry McKellen
A few prominent persons are sometimes referred to by their initials in informal writing. Use no space and no periods.	*FDR*; *JFK*. But: Harry Truman (not *HT*)
Abbreviate *company* when it is part of an organization's official name and when it appears in footnotes and bibliographies; otherwise, spell it in full.	Missouri Press *Co.* (actual name); the *company*
In general writing, spell out the name of an organization the first time you mention it, followed by the initials in parentheses, unless the name is espe-	Atomic Energy Commission (*AEC*); Cooperative for American Remittances to Europe (*CARE*). But: NAACP, YMCA, FBI, AFL-CIO

Rule	Examples

cially well known. Use capital letters, no periods, and no space between letters.

Well-known acronyms and popular abbreviations may be used without spelling them out the first time mentioned (in informal writing), although some authorities insist that they should always be spelled out in general text material. Some popular abbreviations should be avoided even in informal writing.

GNP; *SALT*. But: railroad (not *RR*); tuberculosis (not *TB*); post office (not *PO*)

Do not abbreviate days and months, except in tables and other supporting material, in invoices, and so on.

Generally, spell out the names of countries, except for the USSR. Some informal writing permits initials when used as an adjective.

the *United States*; *U.S.* currency

Spell out states in general business writing, but use traditional state abbreviations in footnotes, bibliographies, and so on and two-letter postal abbreviations in correspondence mailing addresses.

Sentence: I visited *New Jersey* yesterday.

Footnote: Englewood Cliffs, *N.J.*: Prentice-Hall, Inc.

Letter mailing address: Prentice-Hall, Inc./Englewood Cliffs, *NJ* 07632

Spell out prefixes of geographic names in general writing.

Saint (Not *St.*) Louis

Compass points may be abbreviated following a street name, using no space.

1634 Hillary Street, S.W.; 101 West Avenue, N.E.

Some abbreviations are short forms for Latin terms.

ls for locus sigilli (place of the seal)

Abbreviate rather than use a contraction when feasible.

Govt. (not *gov't*); *cont.* (not *con't*)

The trend is toward the use of lowercase (small) letters, although certain

CST (central standard time); *b/c* (bill for collection); *rpm* (revolutions per

Rule	Examples
terms remain more familiar in capital letters. Since authorities differ, you should follow the practices in your profession and in your office.	minute); *av* (audiovisual); *TV* (television); *IQ* (intelligence quotient); *C* (Celsius); *PST* (Pacific standard time). See the various lists of abbreviations in this chapter.
The trend is to omit periods in abbreviations unless an abbreviation spells an actual word and is not written in solid capitals. Exception: Some abbreviations such as academic degrees still retain periods, with no space between them.	*NAACP*, *YMCA* (organizations); *ac* (alternating current); *asap* (as soon as possible); *TV* (television); *mm* (millimeter). But: *in.* (for inch, not the word *in*); A.M. (for ante meridiem, not the word *am*); *op. cit.* (not *op. cit.*); *LL.D.* (not *LL.D.*)
Some short forms of words have been accepted as complete words, not abbreviations, and hence have no periods.	*memo* (not *memo.*); *ad* (not *ad.*); *math* (not *math.*)
Using periods with abbreviations of first and middle names but not nicknames.	*Thos.*; *Jas.* But: *Tom*; *Jim*
Do not use a period when a person is referred to by a letter of the alphabet.	Mr. *A* (not Mr. *A.*); Ms. *X* (not Ms. *X.*)
When a word is written as a contraction (in informal writing), omit the period after it.	*nat'l* (not *nat'l.*); *isn't* (not *isn't.*)
Do not use periods after symbols representing chemical elements.	H_2O (not $H_2O.$); CH_3 (not $CH_3.$)

FAMILIAR FOREIGN WORDS

abaca	ad hoc	apropos
aide memoire	ad infinitum	auto(s)-da-fe
a la carte	alma mater	barranca
a la king	angstrom	blase
a la mode	aperitif	bona fide
a priori	applique	boutonniere

brassiere
cabana
cafe
cafeteria
caique
canape
carte blanche
cause celebre
chateau
cliche
cloisonne
comedienne
communique
confrere
consomme
cortege
coulee
coup de grace
coup d'etat
coupe
creme
crepe
crepe de chine
debacle
debris
debut
debutante
decollete
dejeuner
denouement
depot
dos-a-dos
eclair
eclat
ecru
effendi
elan
elite
entree

etude
ex officio
facade
faience
fazenda
fete
finance
frappe
garcon
glace
grille
gruyere
habeas corpus
habitue
ingenue
jardiniere
laissez faire
litterateur
materiel
matinee
mea culpa
melange
melee
menage
mesalliance
metier
moire
naive
naivete
nee
non sequitur
opera bouffe
opera comique
papier mache
pasha
per annum
per se
piece de resistance
pleiade

porte cochere
porte lumiere
portiere
pousse cafe
premiere
prima facie
pro rata
pro tem
protege
puree
quid pro quo
rale
recherche
regime
remuda
rendezvous
repertoire
resume
risque
role
rotisserie
roue
saute
seance
senor
smorgasbord
soiree
souffle
status quo
suede
table d'hote
tete-a-tete
tragedienne
trattoria
vice versa
vicuna
vis-à-vis
weltschmerz

Note: Familiar foreign words and Anglicized words do not require diacritical marks and need not be italicized. However, since different professions adopt different styles, follow the practices in your office.

GREEK ALPHABET

Alphabet and pronunciation

A	α	*Aa*	alpha	*a* in *father*
B	β	*Bb*	beta	*v*
Γ	γ	*Gg*	gamma	*y* in *yes* before αι, ε, ει, η, ι, οι, υ, υι; *ng* in *singer* before γ, κ, ξ, χ; somewhat like *g* in *go* everywhere else
Δ	δ	*Dd*	delta	*th* in *this*, except in νδρ, pronounced *ndr*
E	ε	*Ee*	epsilon	*e* in *met*
Z	ζ	*Zz*	zeta	*z*
H	η	*Hn*	eta	*ee* in *eel*; *y* in *yet*; when after a consonant and before a vowel
Θ	θ		theta	*th* in *thin*
I	ι		iota	*ee* in *eel*; *y* in *yet* when initial or after a consonant, before a vowel
K	κ	*Ku*	kappa	*k*
Λ	λ	*Ll*	lambda	*l*
M	μ	*Mm*	mu	*m*
N	ν	*Nn*	nu	*n*
Ξ	ξ	*Zz*	xi	*x* (=*ks*)
O	ο	*Oo*	omicron	*o* in *for*
Π	π	*Po*	pi	*p*
P	ρ	*Pp*	rho	*r*, somewhat like the Scotch trilled *r*
Σ	σs*	*Lgs*	sigma	*z* before β, γ, δ, λ, μ, ν, ρ; *s* everywhere else
T	τ	*Tt(t)*	tau	*t*
Y	υ	*Vv*	upsilon	*ee* in *eel*; *y* in *yet*, after a consonant and before a vowel
Φ	φ	*Pp*	phi	*f*
X	χ	*Xx*	chi	like a strong *h* (like German *ch*)
Ψ	ψ	*Yy*	psi	*ps*
Ω	ω	*Ww*	omega	*o* or *or*

* The character σ is used in initial and medial positions in a word. The character *s* is used in the final position.

Source: *U.S. Government Printing Office Style Manual*, rev. ed. (Washington, DC: U.S. Government Printing Office, 1984).

PARTS OF SPEECH AND GRAMMATICAL TERMS

PARTS OF SPEECH

Term	Function	Example
Adjective	Modifies a noun or pronoun.	a *cold* day
Adverb	Modifies a verb, adjective, or another adverb	He walked *quickly*.
Conjunction	Connects other words.	he *and* she
Interjection	Expresses a strong or sudden feeling.	*Wow*!
Noun	Name of a person, place, thing, action, idea, or quality.	*New York University* [proper noun]; a *university* [common noun]
Preposition	Shows the relation between its object and another word.	*of*
Pronoun	Used in place of a noun.	*it*
Verb	Denotes action or state of being.	*is*

GRAMMATICAL TERMS

Term	Function	Example
Active voice	Indicates that the subject of a sentence is providing the action. (See also *Passive voice*.)	I *saw* the movie.
Antecedent	Noun or pronoun to which another pronoun refers.	*Evelyn* [noun] finished her [pronoun] work.
Appositive	Identifies or explains another word(s).	Donald Smith, *secretary*, proposed the new rule.

Term	Function	Example
Article	Adjectives *a* and *an* (indefinite articles) and *the* (definite article).	*the* typewriter
Auxilliary verb	Helps another verb form or verb phrase.	The students *are studying*.
Case	Property of a noun or pronoun showing its relation to other words. *Nominative case* means the noun or pronoun is used as the subject of a sentence; *objective case*, the object of a verb or preposition; *possessive case*, to show ownership.	*They* are late [nominative]. The company sent it to Adam and *me* [objective]. *My* work is finished [possessive].
Collective noun	Name of a group or collection of objects.	*team*
Comparative degree	Used when comparing two persons or things. (See also *Superlative degree*.)	Our product is *stronger* than theirs.
Complement	Completes the meaning of a verb.	The manager wrote the *letter*.
Compound predicate	Two or more connected verbs or verb phrases.	She *wrote* and *mailed* the article.
Compound sentence	Has two or more independent clauses.	(1) The machine broke down, but (2) the service department repaired it.
Compound subject	Two or more words joined by *and, or, nor*.	The *manager* and her *secretary* arrived by plane today.
Coordinate conjunction	Connects words, phrases, and clauses of equal importance.	I dictated *and* he typed.

Term	Function	Example
Dangling modifier	Does not refer to another word or does not modify any other word. (See also *Misplaced modifier*.)	*Upon hearing* from Weston Industries, the plans were made [dangling]. *Upon hearing* from Weston Industries, we made the plans [refers to *we*].
Dependent (subordinate) clause	Group of words in a sentence with a subject and predicate that alone does not express a complete thought.	The person *who spoke first* is an expert in neurology.
Direct object	Noun or noun equivalent that receives a verb's action. Answers the question *what* or *whom* after the verb.	He initiated [what?] the *project*.
Expletive	Introductory word such as *it* and *there* that fills the position of the subject when the actual subject comes after the verb.	*There* are two awards being offered. [Better: Two awards are being offered.]
Future perfect tense	Denotes action to be completed at a definite future time.	I *will have finished* the report by the time you arrive.
Future tense	Denotes future time.	I *will attend* the conference next month.
Gerund	Verb form ending in -*ing* used as a noun. May be a subject, direct object, object of a preposition, subjective complement, or an appositive.	*Running* is a popular activity.

Term	Function	Example
Imperative mood	Expresses a command or request. Always present tense, second person.	*Close* that file.
Indicative mood	Used to say something or ask something.	The receptionist greeted the visitor [statement].
Indirect object	Noun or noun equivalent usually indicating to whom or for whom something is done. Occurs before the direct object.	The manager sent the *insurance company* [indirect object] a letter [direct object].
Infinitive	Verb form used as a noun, objective, or adverb, usually preceded by *to*.	She wanted to *meet* the director.
Intransitive verb	One that has no object. (See also *Transitive verb*.)	The time *passed* quickly.
Linking verb	Links a subject with another word that explains or describes it.	The author *is* a scientist.
Misplaced modifier	One positioned in a sentence so it appears to modify the wrong word. (See also *Dangling modifier*.)	They *only* visited the museum [misplaced]. They visited *only* the museum [properly placed].
Modifier	Word(s) that restricts or qualifies the meaning of another word.	a *cool* day.
Mood	Expresses the attitude of the speaker or writer (statement; question; wish; expression of possibility or doubt; command).	See *Imperative mood*, *Indicative mood*, and *Subjunctive mood*.

Term	Function	Example
Nominative case	Indicates the case of a subject or a predicate noun.	Our *supervisor* [subject] is a former *secretary* [predicate nominative].
Nonrestrictive clause	Subordinate clause that is nonessential to the meaning of the sentence, usually set off with commas.	The car, *which was just serviced*, is hard to start.
Objective case	Indicates the case of a dirct object, an indirect object, or the object of a preposition.	We saw him in the *play* [object of *in*].
Participle	Verb form used as an adjective or predicate adjective.	The *increasing* costs are a matter of record.
Passive voice	Indicates that the subject of a sentence is receiving the action (is being acted upon). See also *Active Voice*, above.	The movie *was seen by me*.
Past perfect tense	Denotes action completed at some definite time in the past.	I *had started* to type when the telephone rang.
Past tense	Denotes past time	I *started* to type.
Person	Indicates who is speaking: *first person* (the one speaking); *second person* (the one being spoken to); *third person* (the person or thing spoken about).	*I* opened the door [first]. *You* open the door, please [second]. *They* will open the door [third].
Possessive case	Shows possession.	the *man's* hat; *my* coat.

Term	Function	Example
Predicate	Part of a sentence containing the verb and other words that make a statement about the subject.	My neighbor Louise *is an artist*.
Predicate adjective	Follows linking verb, modifies the subject.	The report is *informative*.
Present tense	Denotes action occurring now.	I *hear* the music.
Present perfect tense	Denotes action completed at the time of speaking or writing (that also may be continuing into present).	He *has received* the supplies.
Relative adjective	Relative pronoun (e.g., *whose*) used as an adjective.	She is the doctor *whose* license was revoked.
Relative adverb	Adverb (e.g., *where*, *when*, *why*) referring to an antecedent in the main clause and modifying a word in subordinate clause.	I scheduled my typing for a time *when* I had few interruptions.
Relative pronoun	Pronoun (e.g., *who/ whom*, *which/that*) that takes the place of a noun and joins a dependent clause to a main clause.	He is the person *who* has the most to gain.
Restrictive clause	Clause essential to the sentence's meaning.	The room *that has the TV monitor* will be ready for tomorrow's sales meeting.
Subject	Word or group of words in a sentence about which a statement is made.	*The job* is diffiult.

Term	Function	Example
Subjunctive mood	Used to express beliefs, doubts, wishes, uncertainty, and contrary-to-fact conditions.	If I *were* younger, I would return to college.
Subordinate conjunction	Words such as *since*, *so that*, and *although* used to link subordinate and main clauses.	I stated late *because* I wanted to finish the bookkeeping.
Superlative degree	Used to compare more than two persons or things. See also *Comparative degree*.	Our company is the *largest* in the industry.
Tense	Change in a verb's form to distinguish time.	See *Present tense*, *Present perfect tense*, *Future tense*, *Future perfect tense*, *Past tense*, and *Past perfect tense*.
Transitive verb	Expresses action or state of being and has a direct object. See also *Intransitive verb*.	I *studied* [what?] the procedures manual.
Verbal	Verbal form used as another part of speech.	See *Gerund*, *Infinitive*, and *Participle*.
Voice	Indicates whether a subject is doing the acting or is receiving the action (being acted upon).	See *Active voice* and *Passive voice*.

PROPER USE OF COMPOUND NOUNS

Type	Definition	Examples
Open compound	Nouns consisting of two or more closely associ-	*Quasi* words (*quasi corporation*); nouns

Type	Definition	Examples
	ated words that form a single concept but are written as separate words.	expressing a type of relationship (*parent company*); temporary compounds (*decision maker*); job titles denoting a single office (*secretary general*)
Hyphenated compounds	Nouns consisting of two or more closely associated words that are joined by hyphens	Temporary compounds with *vice-* (*vice-president*); *in-laws* (*mother-in-law*); *great-* relations (*great-grandfather*); *self-* compounds (*self-examination*); fractions (*two-thirds*, *twenty-two hundredths*); *-elect* compounds (*governor-elect*); *ex-* compounds (*ex-senator*); compounds of equal weight (*teacher-educator*); descriptive personal nouns (*Johnny-on-the-spot*)
Closed compounds	Nouns consisting of two or more words or elements that are written as one word	Permanent compounds (*textbook*; *greenhouse*; *bookkeeping*); *grand-* relations (*grandmother*); *-ache* compounds (*headache*)

Note: Many compound nouns do not follow the styles described here. Check a modern dictionary or a current stylebook when in doubt. See also *General Rules for Writing Compounds* in this chapter.

PROPER USE OF COMPOUND ADJECTIVES

Types	Definitions	Examples
Open compounds	Adjectives consisting of two or more parts that together modify a noun or pronoun but are written separately	Adjective-noun combinations that are well established or that do not appear before the noun they modify (*social security* office; her position is *full time*); *-ly* adverb-participle combinations (*numerically controlled* machine); adverb-adjective combinations (*very interesting* man); participle-adverb combinations that do not appear before the noun (the containers are *filled up*); number-noun combinations that do not appear before the noun they modify (a charge of 25 *dollars*); proper names (*United States* citizen); adverb-participle combinations where the participle is part of the verb (the rain *was* much *needed*); independent adjectives preceding the noun (*steady* and *delicate* hand)
Hyphenated compounds	Adjectives consisting of two or more parts that together modify a noun or pronoun and are linked by hyphens	Adjective-noun combinations appearing before a noun (*high-level* office); number-noun combinations appear-

Types	Definitions	Examples
		ing before a noun (*20-degree* angle); separate proper names before a noun (*Mexico-United States* alliance); some noun-adjective combinations appearing before and after the noun (*tax-exempt, duty-free*); some noun-participle combinations appearing before and after the noun (*tailor-made, time-consuming*); adjective-participle combinations appearing before the noun (*high-ranking* official); participle-adverb combinations appearing before the noun (*filled-up* containers); adjective-phrase compounds appearing before the noun (*up-to-date* listing); *self-, half-, quasi-, cross-,* and *all-* compounds before and after the noun (*all-inclusive*)
Closed compounds	Adjectives consisting of two or more parts that together modify a noun or pronoun and are written as one word.	Compounds with *-like*, except for those consisting of proper names or ending in *ll* (*birdlike* features. But: *hill-like* construction); compounds with *-wide* (*statewide* elections); compounds with *-fold* (*fourfold* increase); ad-

Types	Definitions	Examples
		jectives including most prefixes (*counterproductive* policy), *multinational* force)

Note: Since some adjectives are exceptions to the general style described here, consult a modern stylebook or dictionary when in doubt. See also *General Rules for Writing Compounds* in this chapter.

GENERAL RULES FOR WRITING COMPOUNDS

Rule	Example
Hyphenate most compound adjectives before a noun.	*ten-story* building
Hyphenate certain expressions and coined phrases.	*devil-may-care*
Hyphenate words of equal importance.	*soldier-statesman*
Hyphenate *in-law* and *great-* relations.	*mother-in-law, great-grandfather*
Hyphenate *vice-*, *self-*, *-elect*, and *ex-* compounds.	*self-appointed*
Hyphenate most compound numbers.	*fifty-two, 4-1* ratio, *six hundred and ninety-seven, four thirty-sevenths*
Hyphenate compounds when the first word (non-literal) has an apostrophe or if it is a single letter.	*crow's-nest, T-square*
Write most compound predicate adjectives open.	He was *well informed.*
Write well-established compounds open.	*real estate* broker
Write most temporary compound nouns open.	*decision making*
Write *-ly* adverb combinations open.	*highly respected* company

Rule	Example
Write nouns with *quasi* open.	the *quasi corporation*
Write words of relationship with a noun open.	*mother figure*
Write most single-office job titles open, except for some that are hyphenated before a proper name.	*attorney general, Commander-in-Chief* Lewis
Write a compound formed from a proper name open.	*North American* continent
Write most permanent compounds with *-house*, *-book*, *-ache*, and *-like* closed.	*headache*
Write most prefixes and suffixes closed.	*pre*determined, manage*ment*

Note: Exceptions to the general rules stated here exist in many of the categories. When in doubt, consult a modern stylebook or dictionary. See also *Proper Use of Compound Nouns*, *Proper Use of Compound Adjectives*, *Rules of Word Division*, and *Spelling Rules* in this chapter.

TRITE EXPRESSIONS

Trite Expression	Example	Preferred Expression	Example
acknowledge receipt of	This will *acknowledge receipt of* your order.	received	We *received* your order.
advise	I want to *advise* you about our new policy.	say, tell	I want to *tell* you about our new policy.
after giving due consideration to	*After giving due consideration to* each application, we have made a decision.	after considering	*After considering* each application, we have made a decision.

Trite Expression	Example	Preferred Expression	Example
allow me to express our appreciation for	*Allow me to express our appreciation for* your suggestion.	thank you for, we appreciate	*Thank you for* your suggestion.
along these lines	I plan to speak *along these lines.*	*Be specific.*	I plan to discuss *economies in manufacturing.*
and oblige	Kindly send the following items *and oblige.*	*Delete.*	Please send the following items immediately.
as per	The books have been set up *as per* your instructions.	according to	The books have been set up *according to* your instructions.
as soon as possible	I'd like your answer *as soon as possible.*	*Be specific.*	I'd like your answer *by Monday, December 5, 19__.*
at all times	We are happy to hear from you *at all times.*	always	We are *always* happy to hear from you.
at an early date, at your convenience	Please return the enclosed questionnaire *at your convenience.*	*Be specific.*	Please return the enclosed questionnaire *by Thursday, November 11, 19__.*
at this time	We would like to begin work *at this time.*	now	We would like to begin work *now.*
at hand	We have your proposal *at hand.*	*Delete.*	We have your proposal.
attached please find, enclosed please find	*Enclosed please find* our latest catalog.	attached, enclosed	*Enclosed* is our latest catalog.
at the present writing	The economy is improving *at the present writing.*	now	The economy is improving *now.*

Trite Expression	Example	Preferred Expression	Example
awaiting your favor	*Awaiting your favor*, I remain,	I hope to hear from you soon.	*I hope to hear from you soon.*
beg, beg to inform you that	I *beg to inform you that* the company has opened a branch office.	*Delete.*	The company has opened a branch office.
contents carefully noted	Yours of the 8th received and *contents carefully noted.*	*Delete.*	The recommendations in your May 8 letter will be discussed at our next meeting.
duly	Your inquiry has been *duly* forwarded to our sales department.	*Delete.*	We have sent your inquiry to our sales department.
enclosed please find	See *attached please find.*	———	———
esteemed	We received your *esteemed* favor of the 4th.	*Delete.*	Thank you for your letter of October 4.
favor	Thank you for your *favor* of June 7.	*Be specific.*	Thank you for your *order* of June 7.
for your careful consideration	I am enclosing a proposal on refinancing *for your careful consideration.*	*Delete.*	I am enclosing a proposal on refinancing.
for your information	A brochure is enclosed *for your information.*	*Delete.*	A brochure is enclosed.
hand you	We herewith *hand you* our remittance of $67.99.	enclosed is	*Enclosed is* our check for $67.99.
have before me	I *have before me* your application.	in answer to, in reply to, thank you for	*Thank you for* your application.

Trite Expression	Example	Preferred Expression	Example
hereto	I am attaching *hereto* the price list you requested.	*Delete.*	Here is the price list you requested.
herewith	Enclosed *herewith* is your copy of the contract.	*Delete.*	Enclosed is your copy of the contract.
in re	This is a study *in re* alcoholism at work.	regarding, concerning	This is a study *concerning* alcoholism at work.
in receipt of	We are *in receipt of* the revised specifications.	we received, thank you for	*Thank you for* the revised specifications.
in the amount of	Enclosed is our check *in the amount of* $117.52.	for	Enclosed is our check *for* $117.52.
in the event that	I will drive *in the event that* a bus is not provided.	if, in case	I will drive *if* a bus is not provided.
line	The company will introduce its new *line* next month.	merchandise, line of goods	The company will introduce its new *line of goods* next month.
our Miss McCord	*Our Miss McCord* will know how to reach me.	Ms. McCord	*Ms. McCord* will know how to reach me.
per day, month, etc.	The lease is $98 *per month*.	a day, month, etc.	The lease is $98 *a month*.
permit me to say that	*Permit me to say that I* thoroughly enjoyed the tour.	*Delete.*	I thoroughly enjoyed the tour.
please be advised that	*Please be advised that* the meeting will begin at 10:30 A.M.	*Delete.*	The meeting will begin at 10:30 A.M.

Trite Expression	Example	Preferred Expression	Example
recent date	We received your check of *recent date*.	*Be specific.*	We received your *August 11, 19__,* payment.
replying to yours of	*Replying to yours of* the 5th, I have the resource list you requested.	thank you for	*Thank you for* your letter of May 5; the resource list you requested is enclosed. *Or*: Here is the resource list you requested.
same	The parts you ordered are being assembled now. We will ship *same* on July 21, 19__.	it, they, them	The parts you ordered are being assembled now. We will ship *them* on July 21, 19__.
state	I'll *state* my strategy at the Monday sales meeting.	say, tell	I'll *tell* you my strategy at the Monday sales meeting.
take pleasure	We *take pleasure* in announcing the opening of our new East Coast plant.	are pleased, are happy, are glad	We *are happy* to announce the opening of our new East Coast plant.
thanking you in advance	*Thanking you in advance* for any information you may have.	I would appreciate	*I would appreciate* any information you may have.
thank you kindly	*Thank you kindly* for the invitation to speak at your annual conference.	thank you	*Thank you* for the invitation to speak at your annual conference.
the undersigned	*The undersigned* will appreciate any suggestions you may have.	I	*I* will appreciate any suggestions you may have.

Trite Expression	Example	Preferred Expression	Example
the writer, this author, etc.	*This writer* used the same method.	I	*I* used the same method.
this letter is for the purpose of	*This letter is for the purpose of* introducing our new computer keyboard, which has revolutionized composition.	*Delete.*	Our new computer keyboard has revolutionized composition.
this will acknowledge receipt of	*This will acknowledge receipt* of your proposal.	thank you for	*Thank you for* your proposal.
too numerous to mention	The benefits are *too numerous to mention.*	numerous, many	The benefits are *numerous.*
under separate cover	The report was mailed *under separate cover.*	*Be specific.*	The report was sent *by registered first-class mail.*
up to this writing	Registrations have been numerous *up to this writing.*	until now	Registrations have been numerous *until now.*
valued	Thank you for your *valued* order.	*Delete.*	Thank you for your order.
we regret to inform you that	*We regret to inform you that* this item is out of stock.	we are sorry that	*We are sorry that* this item is out of stock.
I wish to say that, wish to state that, would say that	*I would say that* the concept is basically sound.	*Delete.*	The concept is basically sound.
you claim, say, state, etc.	*You claim* that you wrote to us on October 14.	*Delete.*	We are sorry that your letter of October 14 never reached us.

Trite Expression	Example	Preferred Expression	Example
yours of	Thank you for *yours of* recent date.	*Be specific.*	Thank you for *your order* of February 7, 19__.

COMPARISON OF EFFECTIVE AND INEFFECTIVE WORDS AND PHRASES

Ineffective Words/Phrases	Effective Substitute
accordingly	so
accounted for by	due to, caused by
add the point that	add that
advice and inform	advise (*or* inform)
aggregate	total
a great deal of	much
along the line of	like
a majority of	most
analyzation	analysis
an example of this is the fact that	for example
another aspect of the situation to be considered	as for
a number of	about
appraise and determine	determine (*or* appraise)
approximately	about
are of the opinion that	think that
as per	(*delete*)
as regards	about
as related to	for, about
assist, assistance	help
as to	about
at a later date	later
at a time	when
attempt	try
at the present writing	now
based on the fact that	because
bulk of	most

Ineffective Words/Phrases	Effective Substitute
chemotherapeutic agent	drug
close proximity	proximity, near
collect together	collect
commence	begin
communicate	write, talk, etc.
concerning, concerning the nature of	about
consequently	so
construct	build
deeds and actions	deeds (*or* actions)
demonstrate	show, prove
depressed socioeconomic area	slum
donate	give
due to the fact that	because
during the time that	while
employ	use
endeavor	try
except in a small number of cases	usually
exhibit a tendency to	tend to
facilitate	ease
few (many) in number	few (many)
final conclusion	conclusion, end
first and foremost	first
firstly (secondly, etc.)	first (second, etc.)
for the purpose of	for, to
for the reason that	because
from the point of view	for
future prospect	prospect
help and assist	help
hopes and aspirations	hopes
if at all possible	if possible
implement	do, start
inasmuch as	because
in case, in case of	if
in close proximity	near
in favor of	for, to
initial	first
in light of the fact that	because
in order to	to
(have an) input into	contribute to
inquire	ask
in rare cases	rarely
in (with) reference to, in regard to	about

Ineffective Words/Phrases	Effective Substitute
in relation with	with
in terms of	in, for
in the case of	(*avoid*)
in the case that	if, when
in the course of	during
in the event that	if
in the first place	first
in the majority of instances	usually
in the matter of	about
in the nature of	like
in the neighborhood of	about
in the normal course of our procedure	normally
in the not-too-distant	soon
in the opinion of this writer	in my opinion, I believe
in the vicinity of	near
in view of the fact that	therefore
involve the necessity of	require
is defined as	is
is dependent upon	depends on
it is clear that	therefore, clearly
it is observed that	(*delete*)
it is often the case that	often
it is our conclusion in light of investigation	we conclude that
it should be noted that the . . .	the . . .
it stands to reason	(*delete*)
it was noted that if	if
it would not be unreasonable to assume	I assume
leaving out of consideration	disregarding
locate	find
linkage	link
make an examination of	examine
marketing representative	salesperson
mental attitude	attitude
modification	change
month of January	January
mutual compromise	compromise
necessitate	require, need
not of a high order of accuracy	inaccurate
notwithstanding the fact that	although
numerous	many
objective	aim, goal
obtain	get

Ineffective Words/Phrases	Effective Substitute
of considerable magnitude	big, large, great
of very minor importance	unimportant
on account of the conditions described	because of the conditions
on account of the fact that	because
on a few occasions	occasionally
on the grounds that	because
out of	of
outside (inside) of	outside (inside)
partially	partly
perform	do
perform an analysis of	analyze
personal friend	friend
positive growth	growth
presently	now
prior to, in advance of	before
proceed	go
proceed to investigate	investigate
prompt and speedy	prompt, quick, speedy
purchase	buy
refer to as	call
refuse and decline	refuse (*or* decline)
relative to this	about this
remainder	rest
renovate like new	renovate
resultant effect	effect
right and proper	right (*or* proper)
short minute	minute, moment
solid facts	facts
subsequent to	after
successful triumph	triumph
sufficient	enough
synthesize	unite
taking this factor into consideration, it is apparent that	therefore, therefore it seems
terminate, termination	end
that is, i.e.,	(*avoid*)
the data show that . . . can	. . . can
the existence of	(*avoid*)
the foregoing	the, this, that, these, those
the fullest possible	most, completely, fully
the only difference being that	except
the question as to whether	whether

Ineffective Words/Phrases	Effective Substitute
the year of 19__	19__
there are not very many	few
tire and fatigue	tire
to be sure	of course
to summarize the above	in sum, in summary
transmit	send
under way	begun, started
usage	use
utilize	use
veritable	true
visualize	foresee
within the realm of possibility	possible, possibly
with reference to	about
with the exception of	except
with the result that	so that
with this in mind, it is clear that	therefore, clearly

DICTIONARY OF CORRECT WORD USE

a while/while

> *A while*, a noun phrase, refers to a period or interval. (Let's wait for *a while* and see if the rain stops.)

> *Awhile*, an adverb, means "for a short time." (We should work *awhile* before leaving.) Do not use *for* with *awhile* since *for* is implied.

adapt/adept/adopt

> *Adapt* means "to change something for one's own purpose; to adjust." (I *adapted* the meter to our console.)

> *Adept* means "proficient, skilled." (She is *adept* in foreign languages.)

> *Adopt* means "to accept something without changing it." (They *adopted* the resolutions.)

affect/effect

> *Affect*, a verb, means "to influence." (How will this policy *affect* our schedule?)

Effect, as a noun, means "a result." (What *effect* did the speech have on the audience?) As a verb, it means "to bring about." (The new policy will *effect* better customer relations.)

aid/assist/help

Aid means "to provide relief or assistance" and suggests incapacity or helplessness on the part of the recipient. (The government provided *aid* to flood victims.)

Assist means "to support or aid" and suggests a secondary role. (Her staff will *assist* in the presentation.)

Help means "to assist; to promote; to relieve; to benefit" and suggests steps toward some end. (He *helped* them move the machine.)

all right/alright

All right means "safe; acceptable; yes." (The schematic looks *all right* to me.)

Alright is a misspelling of *all right*.

although/though

Although means "regardless; even though." It is preferred over *though* at the beginning of a sentence. (*Although* the plan failed, we learned a lot from the experience.)

Though means the same thing but is used more to link words and phrases in the middle of a sentence. (It is true, *though*, that the index is too high.)

among/between

Among refers to the relationship of more than two things. (The exchange of opinions *among* the participants was hostile.)

Between refers to the relationship of two things or more than two things if each one is individually related to the others. (The exchange of opinions *between* Smith and Wright was hostile).

anxious/eager

Anxious refers to uneasiness or worry. (I am *anxious* to know about the outcome of the surgery.)

Eager suggests earnest desire or anticipation. (I am *eager* to start my new job.)

apt/liable/likely

Apt means "fit" (*apt* in journalism) or "inclined to do something" (*apt* to come early).

Liable means "obligated by law; responsible." (The company is *liable* if an accident occurs on the property.)

Likely means "probable." (An economic slowdown is *likely*.)

as/since

As is a less effective conjunction than *since*, but it has other uses in the English language: preposition, adverb, and pronoun.

Since (or *because*, *when*) is more effective and is preferred. (*Since* this issue is late, we will have to reschedule the next issue.)

as . . . as/so . . . as

As . . . as is preferred for positive expressions. (The next conference will be *as* successful *as* the last one.)

So . . . as is often preferred, but not essential, for negative expressions. (The revised proposal is not *so* good *as* the original version.)

as if/as though/like

As if is less formal than *as though*. (She hesitated to begin the project *as if* she were afraid it would fail.)

as if/as though/like

As though is used in the same sense, and like *as if*, it is followed by a verb in the subjunctive mood. (He angrily rejected the proposal *as though* it were a personal affront.)

Like is widely used and misused in informal conversation (*like* I said), but authorities still recommend that it be used as a preposition and with a noun or pronoun that is *not* followed by a verb. (The president acts *like* a dictator.)

assure/ensure/insure

Assure means "to guarantee." It is used only in reference to persons. (I can *assure* you that we intend to complete the job on schedule.)

Ensure, a less common variation of *insure*, means "to make certain." (This long-range policy will *ensure* our continuing success.)

Insure, the preferred spelling of ensure, also means "to make certain; to guard against risk or loss." (The mail room will *insure* the package.)

balance/remainder

> *Balance* refers to "a degree of equality" (we want to *balance* the budget)
> or to "bookkeeping" (please double-check the *balance* in our account).
>
> *Remainder* should be used in all other instances to mean "what is left
> over." (Five hundred of the 1,000 brochures were mailed this morning,
> and the *remainder* are almost ready for mailing now.)

barely/hardly/scarcely

> *Barely* means "meagerly; narrowly." (He could *barely* fit into the small
> foreign car.)
>
> *Hardly* means "with difficulty." (She could *hardly* control the car in
> the driving rain.)
>
> *Scarcely* means "by a narrow margin" and suggests something hard to
> believe. (He could *scarcely* believe his application was rejected.)
>
> Do not use a negative with any of these terms since each already has a
> negative quality (*not* not barely, not hardly, or not scarcely.)

because/due to

> *Because* should be used with nonlinking verbs. (They were exhausted
> *because* of overwork.)
>
> *Due to* means "caused by" and is followed by a linking verb. (Their
> exhaustion was *due to* overwork). *Due to* is often used by careless business
> writers as a wordy substitute for *since* or *because*.

capital/capitol

> *Capital* means "a stock or value of goods." (The company needed more
> *capital* to expand.) It also means "the city that is the seat of government."
> (Concord is the *capital* of New Hampshire.)
>
> *Capitol* refers to a state building. It is always capitalized in reference to
> the seat of the United States Congress. (The *Capitol* in Washington,
> D.C., is a magnificent structure.)

close/near

> *Close* means "very near" (*close* race) or "intimate"' (*close* friend).
>
> *Near* means "closedly related" (*near* neighbors) or "narrow margin"
> (a *near* victory).

compare/contrast

> *Compare* means "to examine for difference or similarity, mostly similar-
> ity." *Compare* is followed by *with* when specifics are examined. (She

compared her record with his.) But in a general reference, *compare* is followed by *to*. (*Compared to* yesterday, today is tranquil.)

Contrast means "to show only differences." The noun form of *contrast* is followed by *to*. (The new typewriters have correcting features in *contrast* to the old models.) But the verb *contrast* is usually followed by *with*. (His present position *contrasts* markedly *with* his old one.)

complement/compliment

Complement means "to complete." (The new study *complements* the previous report.)

Compliment means "to flatter or praise." (His employer *complimented* him on his achievement.)

compose/comprise

Compose means "to make up by combining." (Seven rooms *compose* the suite. *Or* The suite is *composed* of seven rooms.) A general rule is that the parts (seven rooms) *compose* the whole (the suite).

Comprise means "to include." (The company *comprises* two hundred employees.) A general rule is that the whole (the company) *comprises* the parts (the employees).

continual/continuous

Continual means "always going on; repeated over and over," and often implies a steady or rapid succession. (The company is *continually* seeking part-time help.)

Continuous means "connected; unbroken; going on without interruption." (The computer is in *continuous* operation, day and night.)

convince/persuade

Convince means "to lead someone to understand, agree, or believe." (She *convinced* her employer that funding was inadequate.)

Persuade means "to win someone over." (I *persuaded* him to take the day off.)

currently/presently

Currently means "the time now passing; belonging to the present time ' (The company is *currently* being formed.)

Presently means "shortly or before long." (She will arrive *presently*.)

deduction/induction

> *Deduction* refers to reasoning by moving from the general to the particular. (All computers accept some form of symbolic data; therefore, the XL100 should accept symbolic input.)
>
> *Induction* refers to reasoning by moving from the particular to the general. (Having read thousands of business letters, most of which have one or more grammatical errors, I believe that most business people need further education in basic English composition.)

defer/delay/postpone

> *Defer* means "to put off something until later." (He *deferred* his decision until next week.)
>
> *Delay* means "to set aside; to detain; to stop." (Let's *delay* further work on that project.)
>
> *Postpone* means "to put off something until later, with full intention of undertaking it at a specific time." (The director *postponed* the meeting until Wednesday, October 6.)

different from/different than/different to

> *Different from* is preferred by careful business writers. (My objective is *different from* yours.)
>
> *Different than* is sometimes used when followed by a clause. (The results were *different than* he had expected they would be.)
>
> *Different to* is a form of British usage.

differentiate/distinguish

> *Differentiate* means "to show in detail a difference in." (You can *differentiate* among the paper samples by weight and grain.)
>
> *Distinguish* also means "to show the difference in" but is used to point out general differences that separate one category from another. (You can easily *distinguish* radios from television sets.)

disinterested/uninterested

> *Disinterested* means "objective, free from selfish motive; unbiased." (The researchers remain *disinterested* while making their survey.)
>
> *Uninterested* means "indifferent, not interested." (He was *uninterested* in the new office decor.)

dissatisfied/unsatisfied

Dissatisfied means "unhappy; upset; displeased." (She is *dissatisfied* with her new position.)

Unsatisfied means "not content, not pleased; wanting something more or better to be done." (The supervisor was *unsatisfied* with the quality of the work.)

doubt if/doubt that/doubt whether

Doubt if should be avoided in business writing.

Doubt that is the preferred expression in negative or interrogative sentences when little doubt exists. (I *doubt that* we can meet the deadline.)

Doubt whether is usually limited to situations involving strong uncertainty. (I *doubt whether* anything will come of it.)

each other/one another

Each other is used when referring to two persons or objects. (The two attorneys consulted *each other* before taking action.)

One another is used when referring to three or more persons or objects. (The six candidates were debating with *one another* off camera as well as on camera.)

emigrate/immigrate

Emigrate means "to move from one place to another." (Feldman *emigrated* from Israel last year.)

Immigrate means "to enter a country to establish permanent residence." (O'Connell *immigrated* to the United States this spring.)

essentially/substantially

Essentially is used most often to mean "basically." (The new copier is *essentially* the same as the old one.) The word *essential* implies something indispensable. (Insurance is *essential*.)

Substantially is used in the same way to mean "basically," but the word *substantial* suggests a significant size or quantity. (The company showed a *substantial* net gain.)

farther/further

Farther refers to physical distance or spatial measurement. (Salespersons travel *farther* today, thanks to readily available air service.)

Further refers to quantity or degree. (This roll of film will go *further* than I expected). It also means "to promote." (He hopes to *further* his career.) Some business writers have stopped using both *farther* and *further* and are using only one of them (usually *further*) for all situations.

feasible/possible

Feasible means "capable of being done." (The suggestion sounds *feasible* to me.)

Possible means "within realistic limits; likely to occur." (An economic upturn next quarter is *possible*.)

frequent/recurring

Frequent means "habitual; persistent; occurring at short intervals." (He is a *frequent* customer.)

Recurring means "occurring again and again; occurring repeatedly." (Her *recurring* headaches suggest a serious problem.)

handle/manage

Handle means "to control or manage; to deal with" and is preferred over *manage* when physical action is involved. (He *handled* the controls like an expert.)

Manage also means "to control or handle; to deal with" and is preferred over *handle* when nonphysical action is involved. (She *managed* the office efficiently.)

happen/occur/transpire

Happen means "to occur by chance." (He *happened* to be in the neighborhood.)

Occur means "to take place, often unexpectedly" and usually refers to a specific event. (The computer breakdown *occurred* before closing.)

Transpire means "to pass off; to excrete as a vapor." (The leaves *transpired*.) Figuratively, it means "to become apparent." (The state of the company became clear as events *transpired*.)

if/whether

If is used to introduce one condition and often suggests doubt. (I'll meet you at the airport *if* the weather permits.)

Whether is used to introduce more than one condition. (Her client asked *whether* she should sue or accept the settlement.)

imply/infer

> *Imply* means "to suggest by inference or association." (The report *implies* that research was inadequate.)

imply/infer

> *Infer* means "to teach a conclusion from facts or circumstances." (The manager *inferred* from the report that research was inadequate.)

impracticable/impractical/unpractical

> *Impracticable* means "not capable of being used or accomplished." (The plan is *impracticable*.)

> *Impractical* means "not capable of dealing sensibly or practically with something." (Her approach is *impractical*.)

> *Unpractical* is an obsolete term for *impracticable*.

ineffective/ineffectual

> *Ineffective* means "not producing the intended effect; not effective" and often suggests incompetence in some particular area. (He is *ineffective* as a salesman.)

> *Ineffectual* also means "not producing the intended effect; not effective" and often suggests a general lack of competence. (He is *ineffectual*.)

know/realize

> *Know* means "to perceive; to understand." (I *know* a better route.)

> *Realize* means "to accomplish; to grasp fully" and implies a more thorough understanding than *know*. (I *realize* the implications of our action.)

lack/need/want

> *Lack*, as a noun, means "deficient or absent." (The program suffers from a *lack* of money.)

> *Need*, as a noun, refers to "a lack of something desirable or useful" and often is used in an emotional context. (The *need* was for security.)

> *Want*, as a noun, refers to "a lack of something needed or desired." (My *wants* seem to increase with age.)

> As verbs, *lack* suggests a deficiency; *need*, a necessity; and *want*, a desire.

lawful/legal

> *Lawful* means "to be in harmony with some form of law; rightful, ethical." (The directors considered the *lawful* implications of the amendment.)

Legal means "founded on the law; established by law." (The lottery is *legal* in New Hampshire.)

one's self/oneself

One's self is used less often than *oneself*, except when the emphasis is upon the *self*. (Psychologists say *one's self* is an amazing entity to be explored endlessly.)

Oneself is the preferred spelling in most general usage. (One has to discipline *oneself* in any position.)

part/portion/share

Part means "a subdivision of the whole." (This is one *part* of the proposal.)

Portion means "a part or share of something usually intended for a specific purpose." (This *portion* of the program is reserved for questions and answers.)

Share means "the part or portion of something belonging to or given by someone." (His *share* of the estate is being held in trust.)

persons/people

Persons is often preferred in references to a few individuals or when specific individuals are being discussed. (The president and the treasurer were the only *persons* there from the board.)

People is often preferred in references to large groups of indefinite numbers. (The *people* from Eastern cultures sometimes find it difficult to adjust to Western ways.)

practical/practicable

Practical means "sensible; useful; realistic." (He used a *practical* approach to the problem.)

Practicable means "usable; feasible." (It simply is not *practicable* to complete the project in two weeks.)

presumably/supposedly

Presumably means "taken for granted; reasonably assumed to be true." (*Presumably* he is correct since he ran all of the required tests.)

Supposedly means "believed, sometimes mistakenly, to be true; imagined to be true." (The order to halt production *supposedly* came from someone in the executive offices.)

principal/principle

> *Principal*, as a noun, means "chief participant or head" (the *principal* opponent) or "a sum of money." (The mortgage payment including the *principal* and interest.) As an adjective, it means "most important or consequential" (the *principal* reason).
>
> *Principle*, a noun, refers to "a rule, doctrine, or assumption" (the *principle* of universal sovereignty).

proved/proven

> *Proved* is the past tense of *prove*. (They *proved* their contention.)
>
> *Proven* is an adjective (the *proven* method) and a past participle. (The volunteers have *proven* their loyalty.)
>
> *Proved* is preferred. (The volunteers have *proved* their loyalty.)

reaction/reply/response

> *Reaction* means "a response to stimuli." (The injection caused a violent *reaction*.) It should not be used to mean "attitude, viewpoint, feeling, or opinion."
>
> *Reply* means "a response in words." (She sent her *reply* by messenger.)
>
> *Response* is "a reply; an answer." (The client's *response* was positive.)

shall/will

> *Shall*, traditionally, is used in the first person to express future time. (I *shall* be happy to go.) Some authorities believe *shall* sounds stuffy and snobbish and prefer to use *will*.
>
> *Will*, traditionally, is used in the second or third person to express future time. (He *will* be happy to go.) Contemporary usage shows an increasing preference for *will* in all instances (I *will*, you *will*, he/she *will*, they *will*.)

that/which

> *That* refers to persons, animals, or things and should be used in restrictive clauses where the clause introduced by *that* is essential to explain the preceding information. (The group *that* won last year came in first again.) The clause "that won last year" provides essential information about the group. It should *not* be set off with commas.
>
> *Which* refers to animals and things and should be used in nonrestrictive clauses where the clause introduced by *which* is not essential for the

reader to understand the meaning of the other information in the sentence. (The robin, *which* flies south in the winter, has a colorful orange breast.) The clause "which flies south in the winter" is not essential for the reader to understand that the robin has an orange breast. It *should* be set off with commas.

varied/various

Varied means "diverse; with numerous forms." (The logos on business letterheads are *varied*.)

Various means "dissimilar; separate; different." (The memo was sent to *various* divisions in the company.)

viable/workable

Viable means "capable of existence." (The new company is a *viable* entity.)

Workable means "practicable; feasible; capable of working or succeeding." (The plan seems *workable* to me.)

Source: Mary A. De Vries, *Guide to Better Business Writing* (Piscataway, N.J.: New Century Publishers, 1981). Reprinted with permission.

RULES OF CAPITALIZATION

Category	Rule	Examples
Education	Capitalize the official names of departments, schools, and colleges.	Columbia University; the university; Department of History; history department
	Capitalize the names of classes and the official titles of courses.	Senior Class; a senior; Geometry 102; a geometry course
	Capitalize degrees and honors that are part of a name or title.	Evan T. Wainwright Fellowship; the fellowship; Linda Schoenfeld, Ph.D.; a doctor of philosophy
Geography	Capitalize the divisions or major parts of the world, the divi-	Middle East; West Coast; North Atlantic states; Western

Category	Rule	Examples
	sions or major regions of continents and countries, and official topographical names.	world; the South (region); southern (direction, locality); the Orient; oriential culture; North Africa; northern Africa; Mississippi River; Mississippi and Arkansas rivers
	Capitalize proper names of regions and localities.	East Side (New York); Bay Area (San Francisco); Deep South (U.S.)
Government and politics	Capitalize the official titles of acts, bills, laws, amendments, and constitutions.	Pengraft Act; the act; Fourteenth Amendment (U.S. Constitution); the amendment; the Constitution (U.S.); the constitution (a state)
	Capitalize the names of political parties and the official titles of administrative, legislative, and deliberative bodies.	Communist party; Communists; communism; the party; the Left; left wing; the General Assembly (UN); the assembly; Nashville Board of Education; the board of education; Parliament (British); parliamentary
	Capitalize political divisions or units when they follow a name or when they are an accepted part of it.	Johnson County; the county of Johnson; New York State; the state of New York; Seventh Ward; the ward; the Union (U.S.); federal government
History	Capitalize the official names of important events, documents, early cultural periods, major geological periods, and movements derived from proper names.	World War II; Bill of Rights; Iron Age; space age; colonial period (U.S.); nineteenth century; Platonism; surrealism
Holidays, festivals, and seasons	Capitalize the names of religious seasons, religious and secular holidays, and calendar months and days of the week.	Passover; New Year's Day; election day; November; Monday, winter solstice

Category	Rule	Examples
The judiciary	Capitalize the official titles of courts and job titles when they precede a proper name, and capitalize all important words in legal cases.	U.S. Supreme Court, the Court (U.S.); Chicago Court of Civil Appeals; the court of civil appeals; American Bar Association; the bar; *L. Donovan Smith* v. *City of Milwaukee*; the *Smith* case; Justice Black; Mr. Justice Black; the justice

Listings and outlines	Capitalize the first word in each item of a list or outline.	I. Preliminaries
		  A. Copyright page
		    1. Copyright notice
		    2. Publishing history

The military	Capitalize military titles preceding a proper name and the full names of military groups, wars, craft and vessels, and awards.	Wayne Harrison, general; Gen. Wayne Harrison; the general; Allied forces; National Guard; the guard; U.S. Coast Guard; the Coast Guard; Royal Air Force; British air force; U.S. Army; the army; Pacific Fleet; the fleet; Korean War; the war; S.S. *United States*; ICBM; Purple Heart; John Jones, Admiral of the Fleet (Admiral of the Fleet and General of the Army are always capitalized)
Proper nouns	Capitalize the names of particular persons, places, and things, including peoples, races, tribes; epithets; fictitious names; trade names; and words that are personified.	South America; Great Depression; aurora borealis; Milky Way; Hodgkins disease, pneumonia; Orientals; blacks; Don Quixote; quixotic; Pacific standard time; central standard time; the Capitol; Romans; roman numerals
Religion	Capitalize names for the Bible; books and divisions of the Bible; other sacred religious works; references to the Deity in formal or religious writing;	Bible; biblical; Psalms; the Scriptures; the Gospels; the gospel truth; Talmud; talmudic; Greek gods; Resurrection; the Mass (the eucha-

Category	Rule	Examples
	special events, rites, and services; and official names of specific churches.	ristic sacrament); high mass (an individual celebration); bar mitzvah; Protestant church; the Second Presbyterian Church of Cincinnati
Titles of persons	Capitalize titles when they precede a person's name.	President Bush; George Bush, president of the United States; Rabbi Feldman; the rabbi; the Queen Mother; the queen of England; Her Majesty; Roland Farnsworth, first earl of Chestireshire; the earl of Chestireshire; the physician Donna Schoenfeld; Dr. Schoenfeld
Titles of works	Capitalize all important words, including verbs, in titles of written works, musical compositions, paintings and sculptures, television and radio programs, and motion pictures.	*Guide to Better Business Writing* (book); *Time* (magazine); "Reconstruction in the South" (dissertation); "Simon and Simon" (TV show); the *Emperor* Concerto, Piano Concerto no. 5 (musical composition); *The Thinker* (sculpture); *The Divine Comedy* (poem)

CORRECT USE OF NUMBERS AND FRACTIONS

Rule	Examples
Follow the practice in your profession for spelling out numbers: the two standard rules are (1) to spell out the numbers one through ten, except in paragraphs also having larger numbers; and (2) to spell out numbers under one hun-	*Rule 1*: one to eight people; 9 to 11 people; 12 to 14 people.

Rule 2: eighty to eighty-five people; one hundred to two hundred people; 200 to 215 people; 42 million adults |

Rule	Examples
dred as well as large round numbers such as two thousand, except in paragraphs having large uneven numbers.	and 31 million children; 6,793,211 adults and 5,000,000 children.
Spell out indefinite amounts.	a million ideas; a hundred times over; a thousand pardons.
Spell out numbers at the beginning of a sentence even when you would otherwise use figures.	Fifty percent of the audience left (*otherwise*: 50 percent).
Spell out nontechnical references to time but use figures in technical material.	ten years; seven hours; 20-year mortgage; 3-month note.
Use figures with A.M. and P.M.; use the words *o'clock* and *half past* in formal writing.	10:30 P.M.; 8 A.M.; 10 o'clock or ten o'clock; half past seven o'clock (*not* seven-thirty o'clock).
Write dates in general business writing in a month-day-year sequence (the military and some other organizations use a day-month-year sequence).	October 5, 1983 (*not* October 5th and *not* 10/5/83).
Enclose years in commas when both month and day are also given; otherwise omit the commas.	January 19, 1984, is his birthday; his next birthday is in January 1984.
Abbreviate numbers over 100 that are joined by a hyphen unless the first number ends in two zeros, unless the second number starts with different digits, and when different centuries are represented.	1977–78; 1877–1978; 24–34; 173–74; 180–85; 100–105; 901–1087; 207–8 (*but*: *from* 207 to 208; *from* 173 *to* 174).
Use figures for numbers referred to as numbers.	add 7 and 12; the winning number is 400; nos. 210 and 211.
Use figures in addresses for house and building numbers, except spell out the number 1; spell out one through ten in street names.	411 West Avenue; One Park Avenue; 2411 Fourth Avenue; 2411 12th Street.
Use numbers for ratios and proportions.	6:1 ratio; 1,000 to 1 odds; 50–50 chance.

Rule	Examples
Separate adjacent numbers with a comma.	In 1984, 195 companies . . . ; on page 11, 23 problems are . . .
Use a decimal point consistently in a paragraph with numbers.	$145 and $198; $145.50 and $198.00; $4.65 and $0.75.
Repeat the full amount in figure ranges involving dollars.	$8 million to $9 million (*not* $8 to $9 million).
Capitalize sums of money in checks and formal documents, names, or classifications with numbers; and in formal names containing numbers.	Five Hundred Dollars ($500); Eighty-ninth Congress; Ward 11; U.S. Route 71; Fifth Avenue; Third Reich; Local No. 21; nineteenth century; five o'clock; six pounds.
Hyphenate fractions when the numerator and denominator are both one-word forms but omit the hyphen when either the numerator or denominator already has a hyphen.	one-fourth; one-hundredth; one thirty-fourth; twenty-two twenty-fifths.
Avoid dividing numbers but if they must be divided, separate the parts only at the comma.	2,604,-590,000 (*not* 2,60-4,590,000)
Use an apostrophe in plural figures only if it might be confusing to omit it; otherwise add an *s* alone. Form the plural of spelled-out numbers by adding *s* or *es*.	1970s and 1980s; 6's and 7's; twos and threes; twenties and thirties.

Note: See also *Arabic and Roman Numerals* in Chapter 7.

RULES FOR USE OF ITALICS

Rule	Examples
Italicize sparingly for emphasis and avoid setting entire sentences or passages in italics.	Consider the impact of *impeding* voter registration.

Rule	Examples
Italicize only unfamiliar foreign words and do not use italics for proper names.	*quichet*; a priori; Tai-zhou (Chinese city)
Italicize words referred to as words and certain letters used as words or letters.	He repeated the word *stonewall* nine times; the sound *abad*; the letters *s* and *t*; B major; Mr. J; A-frame; *canvass*, meaning "to solicit votes or opinions."
Italicize newspaper, periodical, and book titles; titles of collections of poetry and long poems; titles of plays and motion pictures; titles of operas, oratorios, motets, tone poems, and other long musical compositions; descriptive titles of long musical works; and titles of paintings, drawings, statues, and other works of art.	*Business Week*; *The Divine Comedy*; *Chorus Line*; *Rear Window*; the *Emperor* Concerto; the *Messiah*; Rodin's *The Thinker*
Italicize legal cases; the *v* for *versus* may be roman or italic.	*Jones* v. *Lewis*; the *Jones* case
Italicize names of ships and other craft	SS *United States*; HMS *Divinity*
Italicize genera, subgenera, species, and subspecies but not phyla, classes, orders, families, tribes, and so on.	*Tsuga canadensis*; the family Leguminosae

Note: In typed material, underscore words you want to indicate as italicized.

PRINCIPAL MARKS OF PUNCTUATION

´	Accent, acute	^ or ⌢ or ˜	Circumflex
`	Accent, grave	:	Colon
' or '	Apostrophe	,	Comma
*	Asterisk	†	Dagger
{ }	Braces	¨ (ö)	Diaeresis
[ ]	Brackets	‡	Double dagger
˘	Breve	* * * or }	Ellipsis
^	Caret	. . .	
˛ (ç)	Cedilla	!	Exclamation point

˘ (č)	Haček	.	Period
-	Hyphen	?	Question mark (Interrogation
—	Em dash		point)
–	En dash	" "	Quotation marks
. . . . . .	Leaders	§	Section
¯ (ō)	Macron	;	Semicolon
¶	Paragraph	˜	Tilde
‖	Parallels	___	Underscore
( )	Parentheses	/	Virgule

RULES OF PROPER PUNCTUATION

Punctuation	Rule	Examples
Apostrophe	Use it to show possession, omission, some plurals; omit the apostrophe if the *s* can stand alone without confusion.	p's and q's; 2's and 3's; c.o.d.'s; 1980s; 60s; YWCAs.
	To show possession, add an apostrophe and an *s* to a singular word; add an apostrophe alone to a plural word that already ends in *s*.	army's strategy; boss's orders; four months' leave; the secretary's desk; teachers' lounge.
	With names, add an apostrophe and an *s* to a singular word and an apostrophe alone to a plural word; use the apostrophe to distinguish between joint and separate possession.	Henry Adams's house; the Adamses' house; Ellen and Louise's proposal (joint); Joe's and Paul's proposals (separate).
	Use the apostrophe alone to show omission.	He'll (he will); it's (it is); '70s (1970s).
Brackets	Use them to enclose comments and corrections that are not part of quoted material and	"Yes," he said, "the fall semester [1984] has the heaviest enrollment yet."

Punctuation	Rule	Examples
	to enclose parenthetical comments within parentheses.	The idea is going to be very productive (as his last [1983] idea was).
Colon	Use it after salutations in letters; to separate dates and pages and cities and publishers in citations; to show ratios and time; to introduce a list, quotation, or example. But do not use it after verbs such as *are* unless a formal listing follows.	Dear Ms. Henricks: *Time* 2 (1984): 14. New York: Business Books, 1981. 4:1 ratio. 10:30 A.M. Back matter consists of the following: appendixes, notes, glossary, bibliography, and indexes.
	Use it to indicate a pause between two closely related sentences that are not linked by a conjunction.	The manager had one objective: he wanted to fill as many program slots as possible.
Comma	Use it to separate three or more words or phrases in a series (*series comma*) and the clauses of a compound sentence. Set of *nonrestrictive* clauses (those not essential to the sentence), introductory and transitional words and phrases, words in apposition, parenthetical expressions, and quoted material.	apples, oranges, and pears. Five people worked on Thanksgiving last year; two, this year. The minibus, which holds 12 people, is ready for loading now. When you've finished, let me see the report, please. therefore, we need . . the secretary, Ms. Jones, is . . . "It's true," she said, "that this job is difficult." In 1984, 56 employees . . . The day before, they had a trial run.

Punctuation	Rule	Examples
Dash	Use it to show a sudden interruption or to set off and emphasize clauses of explanation; do not use with other punctuation marks in succession (*not* "today,—it is said—the real test begins").	Pencils, paper clips, tape—these are the tools of a secretary. His new car—new to him, that is—is outside. Lunch—who has time for it?
Ellipsis points	Use them to show the omission of words: three dots to show words omitted in the middle of a sentence; four dots to show words, sentences, and paragraphs omitted at the end of a sentence.	According to the company president, "Sales declined . . . last quarter. . . . But an upturn is expected next year."
Exclamation point	Use it to show surprise, irony, or strong feeling; words alone are usually insufficient to express these thoughts and emotions.	Oh, no! The file is missing. Hurry! They close the gate at noon. Bargain Sale! Order Now!
Hyphen	Use it to divide words at the end of a line and to separate compound words; also use it in fractions, with prefixes before a proper name, and in various numbers such as telephone numbers. (See also *Proper Use of Compound Adjectives*, *General Rules for Writing Compounds*, and *Rules of Word Division* in this chapter.)	self-centered politicians; 80-foot tower; one-fourth; secretary-treasurer; vice-president; quasi-public corporation; 3-by 5-inch index cards; anti-American; 555-1212; well-managed campaign
Parentheses	Use them to enclose incidental comments and figures or letters in lists run into the text.	The report disagreed with his thesis (see page 41). The office is closed for inventory on January 30 (?). We need (1) note pads, (2) paperclips, and (3) erasers.

Punctuation	Rule	Examples
Period	Use it at the end of a sentence, after numbers and letters in a list, after certain abbreviations, and as decimals. (See also *Ellipsis points*.)	It's time to go. 14.793 a. Introduction b. Body c. Conclusions
Question mark	Use it to end a direct question and to show doubt.	Is the letter finished? Would you prefer to meet on Monday? Tuesday? Friday? The remittance copy is yellow (?) and the regular file copies are white.
Quotation marks	Use them to enclose precise quotations; single marks are used for quotations within a quotation. Also use them for titles of articles, unpublished material, essays, TV shows, short poems, and short musical works. Do not enclose indented (extract) quotations, slang, general use of the words *yes* and *no*, or words following *so-called*. (See also *Rules for Use of Italics* in this chapter.)	"I agree," he added. Look at the chapter "Grammar." Jimmy "Red" Anderson "Today," he began, "we want to consider our president's remarks: 'Happy employees are more productive.' "
Semicolon	Use it to separate clauses that do not have a connecting conjunction and to separate items in a series that already have commas.	It's time to streamline the files; in fact, it's past time. The tour will pass through Los Angeles, California; Las Vegas, Nevada; and Phoenix, Arizona. The winners are John Davis, treasurer; Annette Jenkins, secretary; and Tom McHenry, project supervisor.

DIACRITICAL MARKS

´	Acute accent
`	Grave accent
˘	Breve
ˇ	Hač̌ek
¨	Diaeresis
ˆ or ⌢ or ˜	Circumflex
˜	Tilde
¯	Macron
¸	Cedilla

RULES OF WORD DIVISION

Rule	Examples
Use pronunciation as a guide to word division.	pre-sent (to introduce); pres-ent (now existing); knowl-edge (*not* know-ledge)
Do not divide one-syllable words.	through (*not* th-rough); filled (*not* fil-led or fill-ed)
Avoid dividing words with fewer than six letters.	glory (*not* glo-ry); noel (*not* no-el)
Avoid dividing a word before or after a single letter.	aban-don (*not* a-bandon); cafete-ria (*not* cafeteri-a)
Do not divide a word unless three or more characters, including the hyphen, remain on the top line or are carried to the bottom line.	re-design (re-); baroni-al? (al?)
Do not divide prefixes and suffixes; divide a word before or after its prefix or suffix.	anti-climax (*not* an-ticlimax); per-missible (*not* permissi-ble)
When a consonant is doubled before an *-ing* ending, divide the word between the two consonants. *Exception*:	deter-ring (*not* deterr-ing); travel-ling (*not* travell-ing); thrill-ing (*not* thril-ling)

Rule	Examples
Some words already have a double consonant and should be divided after the double letters.	
Avoid dividing a word *before* a single syllable.	generali-zation (*not* general-iza-tion); mili-tary (*not* mil-itary)
Divide compound words that are already hyphenated only at the hyphen.	father-in-law (*not* fa-ther-in-law); vice-president (*not* vice-presi-dent)
Avoid dividing proper names; if necessary, divide only between first and last names.	Edna/Davidson (*not* Edna David-son); J. T./Parker (*not* J./T. Parker
Avoid dividing figures; if necessary, divide only at the comma	1,802,-534,611 (*not* 1,80-2,534,611)
Do not divide contractions, acronyms, and organization abbreviations.	UNICEF (*not* UNI-CEF; isn't (*not* is-n't)
Avoid separating figures from abbreviations, days and years, and other word groups; if necessary, separate a date only between day and year.	page 5 (*not* page / 5); 80 km (*not* 80 / km); September 16, / 1937 (*not* September / 16, 1937)
Separate numbered or lettered lists only before the number or letter.	Words are (1) spelled, / (2) divided, and (3) accented (*not* Words are [1] spelled, [2] / divided, and [3] accented).
Do not separate addresses between numbers and words.	1200 West / Avenue (*not* 1200 / West Avenue)
Always keep a dash at the point of division on the top line.	today— / or yesterday (*not* today / —or yesterday)

Note: See also in this chapter *Correct Use of Numbers and Fractions*; *General Rules for Writing Compounds*; and *Rules of Proper Punctuation*, Hyphen.

SPELLING RULES

FORMING PLURALS

Rules	Examples
The plural of most singular nouns is formed by adding *s*.	table, tables; house, houses
When a word ends with a consonant followed by *y*, change the *y* to *i* and add *es*; when the *y* follows a vowel, add *s*.	mortuary, mortuaries; attorney, attorneys
When a word ends in *ch*, *sh*, *ss*, or *x*, add *es*.	porch, porches; fish, fishes; mass, masses; fox, foxes
When a word ends in *f*, *ff*, or *fe*, add *s* or change the *f* to *v* and add *es*; however, no clear-cut rule exists to indicate when to change the *f* to *v*.	spoof, spoofs; cliff, cliffs; safe, safes; loaf, loaves; wife, wives; shelf, shelves
When a word ends with a vowel followed by *o*, add *s*; when it ends with a consonant followed by *o*, add *es* in most cases, *s* in a few cases, and occasionally either *s* or *es*.	folio, folios; hero, heroes; memo, memos; zero, zeros, zeroes
Generally, add *s* to the most important part of a compound noun; in a few cases, both parts take an *s*. When a word ends in *-ful*, add *s* to the end of it.	sister-in-law; sisters-in-law; senator-elect, senators-elect; right-of-way, rights-of-way; trade union, trade unions; bill of sale, bills of sale; notary public, notaries public; woman volunteer, women volunteers; coat of arms, coats of arms; cupfuls
Some words form the plural by a change in spelling or they retain the same form in the plural.	child, children; corps, corps; economics, economics

PREFIXES

Rules	Examples
Write most prefixes closed (no hyphen).	predetermined; antinuclear; deemphasize; pro-American

Rules	Examples
Words that begin with *s* will have a double *s* after adding a prefix *mis-* or *dis-*.	spell, misspell; satisfied, dissatisfied

SUFFIXES AND VERB ENDINGS

Rules	Examples
When a one-syllable word ends with one vowel followed by one consonant, double the final consonant before adding a word ending that starts with a vowel.	stop, stopped; hot, hotter
When a one-syllable word ends with one vowel followed by one consonant, do not double the final consonant before adding an -ly ending.	sad, sadly; glad, gladly
When a multisyllable word ends with one vowel followed by one consonant and the accent falls on the last syllable, double the final consonant before adding a word ending starting with a vowel.	deter, deterring; occur, occurrence
When a multisyllable word ends with one vowel followed by one consonant and the accent does not fall on the last syllable, do not double the final consonant before adding a word ending starting with a vowel.	revel, reveling; differ, difference
When a multisyllable word ends with more than one vowel followed by a consonant, do not double the final consonant before adding a word ending.	congeal, congealed; appeal, appealing
When a multisyllable word ends with more than one consonant, do not double the final consonant before adding a word ending.	element, elemental; gallivant; gallivanting
When a word ends with a silent *e*, drop the *e* before adding a word ending that starts with a vowel.	care, caring; use, usage

Rules	Examples
When a word ends with a silent *e*, retain the *e* before a word ending that starts with a consonant unless another vowel precedes the final *e*.	manage, management; argue, argument
When a word ends in *ce* or *ge*, retain the *e* before adding a word ending that starts with *a*, *o*, or *u*.	courage, courageous; manage, manageable
When a word ends in *ce* or *ge*, retain the final *e* before adding *-able* or *-ous*; drop it before adding *-ible*.	change, changeable; deduce, deducible
When a word ends in *ie*, change the *ie* to *y* before adding *-ing*; in most cases, the rule for *ie* words is "*i* before *e* except after *c* or when sounded like *a* as in *neighbor* and *weigh*."	die, dying; retrieve (*i* before *e*); deceive (except after *c*); freight (*when sounded like a*)
When a word ends in *-ation*, change it to *-able*; generally, no clear-cut rule exists for using *-able* and *-ible*.	reputation, reputable; application, applicable
Only one word ends in *-sede*; three words end in *-ceed*; any others end in *-cede*.	supersede; proceed, exceed, succeed; intercede, concede, precede
Usually, one should use *-ance*, *-ancy*, and *-ant* when a word has a *c* that sounds like *k* or has a *g* with a hard sound.	significant; extravagant
Usually, one should use *-ence*, *-ency*, and *-ent* when a word has a *c* that sounds like *s* or a *g* that sounds like *j*.	convalescence; negligent
No rule exists for using *-ize*, *ise*, and *-yze*, although most words end in *-ize*, some in *-ise*, very few in *-yze*.	apologize; advertise; analyze
When a word ends in a consonant followed by *y*, change the *y* to *i* before all word endings except those starting with *i*. *Exception*: one-syllable adjectives such as *dry* and certain words such as *ladylike*.	happy, happiness; spy, spying; shy, shyness; secretary, secretaryship

Rules	Examples
When a word ends in a vowel followed by *y*, keep the *y* before adding a word ending.	annoy, annoyed; employ, employment

Note: Because of the numerous exceptions to many of the rules of spelling, consult a modern dictionary when in doubt. See also in this chapter *Rules of Word Division*; *General Rules for Writing Compounds*; *Abbreviation Guidelines*; and the various lists of abbreviations.

CHAPTER 5

Correspondence

FULL-BLOCK LETTER FORMAT

YOUR LETTERHEAD

January 2, 19___

CONFIDENTIAL

Mr. Donald Clarke
Computer Time-Sharing, Inc.
14 Orange Avenue
Augusta, GA 30901

Dear Mr. Clarke:

Subject: Full-Block Format

This letter is an example of the full-block format. The
simple, clean look is preferred in many modern offices.

All principal parts of a full-block letter are typed flush
left, with a double space between paragraphs and most
basic parts of the letter. The subject line is positioned
immediately below the salutation.

This letter format is especially popular as a time-saver.
Since all parts are typed against the left margin, typists
do not have to set up and use tabular stops.

Sincerely,

Sonja Forrestor
Office Manager

mr

Enc.

cc: H. V. McKenzie

BLOCK LETTER FORMAT

YOUR LETTERHEAD

> January 2, 19___
> Our file 055–1

Modern Secretarial Services
2114 West End Boulevard
Louisville, KY 40219

Attention: Ms. Lynda Parnelli

Ladies and Gentlemen:

This is an example of the block letter format. Unlike the full-block style, not all parts are positioned flush left in this letter.

The dateline and the reference line are typed against the right margin, and the complimentary close and signature line are typed just to the right of center page. All other elements are typed flush left.

Many companies prefer this format because it is easy to set up like the block format but is less extreme.

> Sincerely,
>
> Paul Gonzales
> Business Manager

oc

P.S. If you would like additional information, please let me know. PG

MODIFIED-BLOCK FORMAT

YOUR LETTERHEAD

January 2, 19___
Your ref. XYZ

Mrs. Jeanne Wyatt
Cole Industries
623 Fifth Street
Paterson, NJ 07524

Dear Mrs. Wyatt:

   Subject: Modified-Block Letter Format

   This is an example of the modified-block letter format. With this style, paragraphs are indented.

   As with the block style, the dateline and reference line in this letter are typed against the right margin. The complimentary close and signature line are typed just to the right of center page. Both the subject line and the postscript are indented the same as each paragraph.

   Even though the trend is toward more modern styles such as the block letter and the simplified letter, the traditional modified-block format will remain a favorite in many offices.

Sincerely,

Mary Newsome
Corresponding Secretary

jt

   P.S. Let me know if I can send you further information.
MN

SIMPLIFIED LETTER FORMAT

YOUR LETTERHEAD

January 2, 19___

Mr. Benjamin Solomon
Solomon Manufacturing Co.
One Washington Avenue
Oklahoma City, OK 73314

SIMPLIFIED FORMAT

This is an example of the simplified letter format, Mr. Solomon. It's a clean, easy-to-type format that appeals to both executives and secretaries.

Unlike the other styles, this one does not use a salutation or complimentary close. In other respects, it resembles the block format. The subject line is typed in all capitals without the word "Subject," and the signature is also typed in capital letters—on one line.

To avoid an impersonal appearance without a salutation or complimentary close, Mr. Solomon, this format mentions the addressee's name in the opening and closing paragraphs.

JOSEPH STARK—DIRECTOR OF BUSINESS SERVICES
dm

OFFICIAL LETTER FORMAT

YOUR LETTERHEAD

January 2, 19—

Dear Miss Brownley:

This is an example of the official letter format, used by many persons for personal as well as official letters. It looks exceptionally well on executive-size letterhead.

Like the modified-block format, this style indents paragraphs and shows the dateline typed flush right. The complimentary close and signature line are typed just to the right of center page. Unlike the other letter formats, this style places the inside address flush left from two to five spaces beneath the final line of the signature. The enclosure notation would appear two spaces below the address. The dictator's name is typed in the signature, so an identification line is unnecessary. The typist's initials may be typed on the carbon copy but should be omitted from the original.

Sincerely yours,

Nadine Ratcliff
Communications Consultant

Miss Anita Brownley
Midwestern Business College
1900 Bennington Road
Washington, DC 20012

NOTE MEMO FORMAT

M E M O from Jane Doe

The simplest memo format is the note style, often printed and bound in small pads. This type of note is used primarily for brief, informal (sometimes handwritten) messages to coworkers and colleagues. A variety of memo and note pads are available in office supply and stationery stores.

STANDARD MEMO FORMAT

YOUR LETTERHEAD

To: John Jones   From: Helen Malone

Subject: Standard Memo Format   Date: Jan. 2, 19__

The standard memo format varies from preprinted multiple-copy sets and speed-message pads to company-designed memo letterhead. Unlike the brief note pad, this standard format contains several guide words (*To, From, Subject, Date, Our Ref., Your Ref.*, and so on) positioned at the top of the page. Some designs add a line for the signature at the bottom of the sheet. Others divide the memo page into two parts, so the receiver may write his or her reply on the second half.

This format resembles an informal letter. Regular paragraphs are indented or typed flush left, but there is no signature line. However, some writers type or write their initials below the last line of the body. Miscellaneous notations such as *Enc.* are positioned flush left below the last line, the same as they appear in a traditional letter.

These memos, once used only for interoffice correspondence, are now commonly used for informal external correspondence too (quick messages to associates, transmittal messages, purchase orders and replies, and so on).

HM

pk

cc: Lee Alexander

PRINCIPAL PARTS OF LETTERS

Principal Part	Description
Attention line	Attention lines in letters addressed to a firm ensure that, if that person is absent, someone else will open the letter. Place this line two spaces below the inside address. (See *Block Letter Format* in this chapter.) On the envelope place it left of the address block on any line above the second line from the bottom of the address or immediately beneath the company name within the address block.
Body	The body of a letter usually begins after the salutation or subject line; in the simplified format, after the inside address or subject line. (See the various letter formats in this chapter.) Paragraphs are single spaced, with a line space between them, and are indented or flush left, depending on the letter format being used.

Principal Part	Description
Complimentary close	The closing follows the last line of the last paragraph in a letter. (See the various letter formats in this chapter for position.) The trend is toward a personal, informal closing (*Sincerely, Cordially, Best regards, Best wishes*). Formal closings such as *Yours very truly* and *Respectfully* are used only in legal and offical correspondence. The closing phrase I *remain* is no longer used in contemporary correspondence. (See *Table of Complimentary Closes* in this chapter.)
Continuation page	Any page after the first page of a letter is a continuation page. Do *not* use the word *continued* or abbreviation *cont.* Head the continuation page with the addressee's name, the date, and the page number. These items may be placed on one line or stacked, flush left: Daniel Collins January 2, 19__ page two
Copy notation	A copy notation (cc = carbon copy; pc = photocopy; copy = noncarbon copy) indicates who will receive copies of the letter. (See *Full-Block Letter Format.*) A blind-copy notation (*bcc*) is placed in the upper left corner of a letter *only* on that particular copy and on your file copy. It is used when you don't want the addressee to know that you are sending a copy elsewhere.
Dateline	The date is typed at the top of the page. See the various letter formats in this chapter. The traditional style is *January 2, 19__*. The military and some other organizations use *2 January 19__*.
Enclosure notation	This notation is positioned at the bottom of the letter beneath the reference notation. (See *Full-Block Letter Format* in this chapter.) Styles vary: Enclosure Enc. Encs. 2 Enclosures: Check Invoice

Principal Part	Description
	Enc. Under separate cover: Price List
Identification line	The initials in an identification line indicate who dictated and typed the letter. They are usually placed two spaces below the signature, flush left. (See *Block Letter Format* in this chapter.) Some companies omit the initials on the original, adding them only on the file copy. Some companies also omit the initials of the dictator when the dictator's name appears in the signature line. When all initials are to appear, the person signing the letter comes first, next the dictator, and then the typist (*KG:RF:cm*). All capital letters are used for the dictator and the signer.
Inside address	The inside address is placed flush left. See the various letter formats in this chapter. If the addressee's name is unknown, use a job title (*Sales Manager*) if possible. When the addressee's name is used, omit the job title if it makes the address run over four lines. Use the same data on the envelope. (See *Envelope Addressing Requirements for Automated Sorting* in Chapter 2.) Use the two-letter postal abbreviations for states and use the five- or nine-digit zip codes on the inside address as well as on the envelope address.
Mail notation	Notations such as *Special Delivery* are placed above the inside address only on the copies. For envelope placement, put the notation two to four spaces beneath the postage.
Personal or confidential notation	Place the words *Personal* or *Confidential*, underscored, beneath the dateline against the left margin two to four spaces above the inside address. On the envelope place the notation in all capitals to the left and two lines below the address block.
Postscript	Place comments unrelated to the message of the letter beneath the last notation of the letter and add the sender's initials immediately after the postscript message. (See *Block Letter Format* and *Modified-Block Letter Format* in this chapter.)
Reference line	Instructions such as *Please refer to* and *In reply, please refer to* are often printed on the letterhead.

Principal Part	Description
	Otherwise, the information, with or without the instructional phrase, is added under the dateline. (See *Block Letter Format* and *Modified-Block Letter Format* in this chapter.)
Salutation	Salutations follow the inside address, flush left. (See the various letter formats in this chapter.) The trend is toward informality (*Dear Joe* or *Dear Mr. Barnes*). Formal greetings such as *Sir* or *My dear Mrs. Adams* are reserved for official correspondence. (See *Guide to Correct Letter Salutations* in this chapter.)
Signature	The signature follows the complimentary close. (See the various letter formats in this chapter.) Women may, but need not, put *Miss* or *Mrs.* in parentheses before their names. (Do not put *Mr.* or *Ms.* before a signature.) Professional persons may add initials such as *M.D.* after their names. Company names are usually in all capitals. (See *Guide to Correct Signature Lines* in this chapter.)
Subject line	The correct position for a subject line is *after* the salutation. (Attorneys frequently use the words *In re* or *Re* instead of *Subject* and place the line *above* the salutation.) (See *Full-Block Letter Format*, *Modified-Block Letter Format*, and *Simplified Letter Format* in this chapter.) The trend is away from underscoring and the use of all capitals.

PRINCIPAL PARTS OF MEMOS

Principal Part	Description
Heading	The traditional memo format has headings printed at the top of the page beneath the letterhead: *DATE*, *TO*, *FROM*, *SUBJECT*, and so on. The appropriate information is then added on each letter after those guide words. All major words in the subject line are capitalized. (See *Standard Memo Format* in this chapter.)

Principal Part	Description
Body	The body of a memo is prepared much the same as a letter, with paragraphs that may or may not be indented (flush-left paragraphs are more common in memos than indented paragraphs.) (See *Standard Memo Format* in this chapter.) Since there is no salutation, the first paragraph begins at least two spaces after the heading guide words.
Notations	Miscellaneous notations such as the identification line, enclosure line, and postscript are positioned the same as in a traditional letter. (See *Standard Memo Format* in this chapter.)
Envelope	Although the memo has no inside address, the envelope should be addressed the same as it would be for a traditional letter. (See *Envelope Addressing Requirements for Automated Sorting* in Chapter 2 and various references to envelope addressing in *Principal Parts of Letters* in this chapter.)

CORRECT FORMS OF ADDRESS

Correct Form	Examples
Titles: A title should precede a name unless *Esq.* or initials such as *M.D.* follow the name. A title is used with initials only when the two are not synonymous (e.g., *not Dr.* and *M.D.* together); see *Scholastic degrees*, below. Religious orders may be listed after a name along with the religious title of *father*, *sister*, and so on.	*Ms.* Jennifer Henderson: *Mr.* K. C. Phillips III; *Professor* Janet Kline; *Dr.* Jacob Feldman; Lois Walker, *M.D.*; *Father* James Billingsly, *S.J.*
Scholastic degrees: Generally, avoid use in an inside address. If a professional person such as a medical doctor, prefers their use, omit *Dr.*, *Miss*, *Mrs.*, *Ms.*, or *Mr.* before the name. But you may use a descriptive title such as *Pro-*	Michael Depora, *D.V.M.*; *The Reverend* David Caine, *D.D.*, *Ph.D.*

Correct Form	Examples

fessor or *Reverend* before the name with degrees after it. If a person has several degrees, list the one pertaining to his or her profession/occupation first.

Esquire: The abbreviation *Esq.* may be used in addressing prominent attorneys and other high-ranking officials who do not have other titles. No other title, such as *Mr.* or *Honorable*, should be used with *Esq.* (In Britain *Esq.* is used more widely than in America.

Madeline Fontaine, *Esq.*; *The Honorable* Madeline Fontaine

Firms: Do not use single-sex designations for firms consisting of both men and women. Do not use single-sex designations with impersonal business organization names.

Ladies or *Mesdames* (women alone); *Gentlemen* or *Messrs.* (men alone); *Ladies and Gentlemen* (both men and women); *Messrs.* Johnson, Clarke, and Skinner (all men), *not Messrs.* Johnson Manufacturing Company

Single women: In *business*, use *Ms.* for a single woman unless you know that she prefers *Miss*. *Socially*, address a single woman as *Miss*. For *social-business* and *informal social occasions*, follow the guidelines for business use.

Business, social-business, and informal social use: *Ms.* Joan Maderia; *Miss* Joan Maderia

Formal social use: *Miss* Joan Maderia

Married and widowed women: In *business*, use *Ms.* for a married or widowed woman unless you know that she prefers *Mrs.* Use her first name and married last name, unless you know that professionally she uses her maiden name (with *Miss* or *Ms.*) or maiden and married names combined (with *Mrs.* or *Ms.*). *Socially*, address a married or widowed woman as *Mrs.* with her husband's full name. For *social-business* and *informal social occasions*, follow the guidelines for business use.

Business, social-business, and informal social use: *Ms.* Susan Gregory; *Mrs.* Susan Gregory; *Mrs.* Susan Sloane-Gregory; *Ms.* Susan Sloane-Gregory; *Miss* Susan Sloane; *Ms.* Susan Sloane

Formal social use: *Mrs.* Henry Gregory

Correct Form	Examples

Divorced women: In *business*, use *Ms.* for a divorced woman with her first name and married last name, unless she has returned to her maiden name or uses her maiden and married names combined. Use *Mrs.* with her married name or *Miss* with her maiden name only if you know that she prefers it. *Socially*, address a divorced woman who retains her married name as *Mrs.* with her maiden and married names combined. If she uses her maiden name only, address her as *Miss.* If she uses her maiden and married names combined, address her as *Mrs.* In *social-business* and *informal social occasions*, follow the guidelines for business use.

Business, social-business, and informal social use: *Ms.* Helen Parker; *Ms.* Helen Oresto; *Miss* Helen Oresto; *Ms.* Helen Oresto-Parker; *Mrs.* Helen Parker; *Mrs.* Helen Oresto-Parker

Formal social use: *Mrs.* Oresto-Parker; *Mrs.* Helen Parker; *Miss* Helen Oresto; *Mrs.* Helen Oresto-Parker

Professional women: Address a woman by her professional title and her first and last (married) names (or maiden or maiden-married name combination if she prefers it).

Dr. Louise Faulkner; *Professor* Mary Salk; *Senator* Judith Flagg

Husbands and wives: Retain professional titles for both parties in addressing husbands and wives. When there is no title, use *Mr.* and *Mrs.* When married women are addressed individually, follow the guidelines in *Married and widowed women*, above.

Mr. and *Mrs.* Jeffrey Lewis; *Dr.* and *Mrs.* Jeffrey Lewis; *Drs.* Pauline and Jeffrey Lewis; *Dr.* Pauline and *Mr.* Jeffrey Lewis; *Dr.* Pauline Lewis and *Mr.* Jeffrey Lewis

Gender unknown: Omit the title in a letter salutation when the gender is unknown.

Dear Leslie Briarwood; Dear M. C. Baker

Name unknown: Use a title, if known; otherwise, *Sir* or *Madam*

Acting Mayor of Louisville; *The Lieutenant Governor* of Idaho; *Sir*; *Madam*

Name, gender, and title unknown: Use *Sir* or *Madam* together

Sir or Madam

Retired officials: A person who held an official title may be addressed as

The Honorable John Smith/*Dear Sir* or *Dear Mr.* Smith (former governor);

Correct Form	Examples
The Honorable after retirement. Former titles such as *Senator* and *President* are not used in the inside address or salutation after retirement, except for the title of *Judge* and titles of officers retired from the armed forces.	*The Honorable* Joseph Feinstein/*Sir* or *Dear Judge* Feinstein; *General* Carl Saxon, *U.S.A., Retired/Dear General* Saxon

Note: See *Forms of Address for Official or Honorary Positions* in this chapter.

CORRECT FORMS OF ADDRESS

United States Government Officials

Personage	Envelope and Inside Address (Add City, State, Zip)	Formal Salutation	Informal Salutation	Formal Close	Informal Close	1. Spoken Address 2. Informal Introduction or Reference
The President	The President The White House	Mr. President	Dear Mr. President:	Respectfully yours,	Very respectfully yours, *or* Sincerely yours,	1. Mr. President 2. Not introduced (The President)
Former President of the United States[1]	The Honorable William R. Blank (local address)	Sir:	Dear Mr. Blank:	Respectfully yours,	Sincerely yours,	1. Mr. Blank 2. Former President Blank *or* Mr. Blank
The Vice-President of the United States	The Vice-President of the United States The White House	Mr. Vice-President:	Dear Mr. Vice-President	Very truly yours,	Sincerely yours,	1. Mr. Vice-President *or* Mr. Blank The Vice-President
The Chief Justice of the United States Supreme Court	The Chief Justice of the United States The Supreme Court of the United States	Sir:	Dear Mr. Chief Justice:	Very truly yours,	Sincerely yours,	1. Mr. Chief Justice 2. The Chief Justice
Associate Justice of the United States Supreme Court	Mr. Justice Blank The Supreme Court of the United States	Sir:	Dear Mr. Justice: *or* Dear Justice Blank:	Very truly yours,	Sincerely yours,	1. Mr. Justice Blank *or* Justice Blank 2. Mr. Justice Blank

Note: In this chart the form of address for a man is used throughout except where not applicable. To use the form of address for a woman in any of these positions, use the substitution Madam for Sir and Mrs., Miss, or Ms. for Mr. Thus Dear Madam; Mrs. Blank, Respresentative from New York; The Lieutenant Governor of Iowa, Miss Blank; The American Minister, Ms. Blank. The Mr. preceding a title becomes Madam. Thus Madam Secretary; Madam Ambassador. Use Esquire or Esq. in addressing a man or woman where appropriate. (For additional information see Chapter 11, page 327.)

1. If a former president has a title, such as General of the Army, address him by it.

United States Government Officials *continued*

Personage	Envelope and Inside Address (Add City, State, Zip)	Formal Salutation	Informal Salutation	Formal Close	Informal Close	1. Spoken Address 2. Informal Introduction or Reference
Retired Justice of the United States Supreme Court	The Honorable William R. Blank (local address)	Sir:	Dear Justice Blank:	Very truly yours,	Sincerely yours,	1. Mr. Justice Blank *or* Justice Blank 2. Mr. Justice Blank
The Speaker of the House of Representatives	The Honorable William R. Blank Speaker of the House of Representatives	Sir:	Dear Mr. Speaker: *or* Dear Mr. Blank:	Very truly yours,	Sincerely yours,	1. Mr. Speaker *or* Mr. Blank 2. The Speaker, Mr. Blank (The Speaker *or* Mr. Blank)
Former Speaker of the House of Respresentatives	The Honorable William R. Blank (local address)	Sir:	Dear Mr. Blank:	Very truly yours,	Sincerely yours,	1. Mr. Blank 2. Mr. Blank
Cabinet Officers addressed as "Secretary"[2]	The Honorable William R. Blank Secretary of State The Honorable William R. Blank Secretary of State of the United States of America (if written from abroad)	Sir:	Dear Mr. Secretary:	Very truly yours,	Sincerely yours,	1. Mr. Secretary *or* Secretary Blank 2. Mr. Blank The Secretary of State Mr. Blank (Mr. Blank or The Secretary)
Former Cabinet Officer	The Honorable William R. Blank (local address)	Dear Sir:	Dear Mr. Blank:	Very truly yours,	Sincerely yours,	1. Mr. Blank 2. Mr. Blank

2. Titles for cabinet secretaries are Secretary of State; Secretary of the Treasury; Secretary of Defense; Secretary of Education; Secretary of Energy; Secretary of the Interior; Secretary of Agriculture; Secretary of Commerce; Secretary of Labor; Secretary of Health and Human Services; Secretary of Housing and Urban Development; Secretary of Transportation.

United States Government Officials *continued*

Personage	Envelope and Inside Address (Add City, State, Zip)	Formal Salutation	Informal Salutation	Formal Close	Informal Close	1. Spoken Address 2. Informal Introduction or Reference
Postmaster General	The Honorable William R. Blank Postmaster General,	Sir:	Dear Mr. Postmaster General:	Very truly yours,	Sincerely yours,	1. Mr. Postmaster General *or* Postmaster General Blank or Mr. Blank 2. The Postmaster General, Mr. Blank (Mr. Blank or The Postmaster General)
The Attorney General	The Honorable William R. Blank Attorney General of the United States	Sir:	Dear Mr. Attorney General:	Very truly yours,	Sincerely yours,	1. Mr. Attorney General *or* Attorney General Blank 2. The Attorney General, Mr. Blank (Mr. Blank or The Attorney General)
Under Secretary of a Department	The Honorable William R. Blank Under Secretary of Labor	Sir:	Dear Mr. Under Secretary: *or* Dear Mr. Blank:	Very truly yours,	Sincerely yours,	1. Mr. Blank 2. Mr. Blank
United States Senator	The Honorable William R. Blank United States Senate	Sir:	Dear Senator Blank:	Very truly yours,	Sincerely yours,	1. Senator Blank *or* Senator 2. Senator Blank
Former Senator	The Honorable William R. Blank (local address)	Dear Sir:	Dear Mr. Blank:	Very truly yours,	Sincerely yours,	1. Mr. Blank 2. Mr. Blank

United States Government Officials *continued*

Personage	Envelope and Inside Address (Add City, State, Zip)	Formal Salutation	Informal Salutation	Formal Close	Informal Close	1. Spoken Address 2. Informal Introduction or Reference
Senator-elect	The Honorable William R. Blank Senator-elect United States Senate	Dear Sir:	Dear Mr. Blank:	Very truly yours,	Sincerely yours,	1. Mr. Blank 2. Senator-elect Blank *or* Mr. Blank
Committee Chairman— United States Senate	The Honorable William R. Blank, Chairman Committee on Foreign Affairs United States Senate	Dear Mr. Chairman:	Dear Mr. Chairman: *or* Dear Senator Blank:	Very truly yours,	Sincerely yours,	1. Mr. Chairman *or* Senator Blank *or* Senator 2. The Chairman *or* Senator Blank
Subcommittee Chairman— United States Senate	The Honorable William R. Blank, Chairman, Subcommittee on Forgeign Affairs United States Senate	Dear Senator Blank:	Dear Senator Blank:	Very truly yours,	Sincerely yours,	1. Senator Blank *or* Senator 2. Senator Blank
United States Representative or Congressman[3]	The Honorable William R. Blank House of Representatives The Honorable William R. Blank Representative in Congress (local address) (when away from Washington, DC)	Sir:	Dear Mr. Blank:	Very truly yours,	Sincerely yours,	1. Mr. Blank 2. Mr. Blank, Representative (Congressman) from New York *or* Mr. Blank

3. The official title of a "congressman" or "congresswoman" is *Representative*. Senators are also congressmen or congresswomen.

United States Government Officials *continued*

Personage	Envelope and Inside Address (Add City, State, Zip)	Formal Salutation	Informal Salutation	Formal Close	Informal Close	1. Spoken Address 2. Informal Introduction or Reference
Former Representative	The Honorable William R. Blank (local address)	Dear Sir: *or* Dear Mr. Blank:	Dear Mr. Blank:	Very truly yours,	Sincerely yours,	1. Mr. Blank 2. Mr. Blank
Territorial Delegate	The Honorable William R. Blank Delegate of Puerto Rico House of Representatives	Dear Sir: *or* Dear Mr. Blank:	Dear Mr. Blank:	Very truly yours,	Sincerely yours,	1. Mr. Blank 2. Mr. Blank
Resident Commissioner	The Honorable William R. Blank Resident Commissioner of (Territory) House of Representatives	Dear Sir: *or* Dear Mr. Blank:	Dear Mr. Blank:	Very truly yours,	Sincerely yours,	1. Mr. Blank 2. Mr. Blank
Directors or Heads of Independent Federal Offices, Agencies, Commissions, Organizations, etc.	The Honorable William R. Blank Director Mutual Security Agency	Dear Mr. Director (Commissioner, etc.):	Dear Mr. Blank:	Very truly yours,	Sincerely yours,	1. Mr. Blank 2. Mr. Blank
Other High Officials of the United States, in general: Public Printer, Comptroller General	The Honorable William R. Blank Public Printer The Honorable William R. Blank Comptroller General of the United States	Dear Sir: *or* Dear Mr. Blank:	Dear Mr. Blank:	Very truly yours,	Sincerely yours,	1. Mr. Blank 2. Mr. Blank

United States Government Officials *continued*

Personage	Envelope and Inside Address (Add City, State, Zip)	Formal Salutation	Informal Salutation	Formal Close	Informal Close	1. Spoken Address 2. Informal Introduction or Reference
Secretary to the President	The Honorable William R. Blank Secretary to the President The White House	Dear Sir: *or* Dear Mr. Blank:	Dear Mr. Blank:	Very truly yours,	Sincerely yours,	1. Mr. Blank 2. Mr. Blank
Assistant Secretary to the President	The Honorable William R. Blank Assistant Secretary to the President The White House	Dear Sir: *or* Dear Mr. Blank:	Dear Mr. Blank:	Very truly yours,	Sincerely yours,	1. Mr. Blank 2. Mr. Blank
Press Secretary to the President	Mr. William R. Blank Press Secretary to the President The White House	Dear Sir: *or* Dear Mr. Blank:	Dear Mr. Blank:	Very truly yours,	Sincerely yours,	1. Mr. Blank 2. Mr. Blank

State and Local Government Officials

	Envelope and Inside Address (Add City, State, Zip)	Formal Salutation	Informal Salutation	Formal Close	Informal Close	1. Spoken Address 2. Informal Introduction or Reference
Governor of a State or Territory[1]	The Honorable William R. Blank Governor of New York	Sir:	Dear Governor Blank:	Very truly yours,	Sincerely yours,	1. Governor Blank *or* Governor 2. a) Governor Blank b) The Governor c) The Governor of New York (used only outside his or her own state)

1. The form of addressing governors varies in the different states. The form given here is the one used in most states. In Massachusetts by law and in some other states by courtesy, the form is *His (Her) Excellency, the Governor of Massachusetts.*

State and Local Government Officials *continued*

Personage	Envelope and Inside Address (Add City, State, Zip)	Formal Salutation	Informal Salutation	Formal Close	Informal Close	1. Spoken Address 2. Informal Introduction or Reference
Acting Governor of a State or Territory	The Honorable William R. Blank Acting Governor of Connecticut	Sir:	Dear Mr. Blank:	Very truly yours,	Sincerely yours,	1. Mr. Blank 2. Mr. Blank
Lieutenant Governor	The Honorable William R. Blank Lieutenant Governor of Iowa	Sir:	Dear Mr. Blank:	Very truly yours,	Sincerely yours,	1. Mr. Blank 2. The Lieutenant Governor of Iowa, Mr. Blank *or* The Lieutenant Governor
Secretary of State	The Honorable William R. Blank Secretary of State of New York	Sir:	Dear Mr. Secretary:	Very truly yours,	Sincerely yours,	1. Mr. Blank 2. Mr. Blank
Attorney General	The Honorable William R. Blank Attorney General of Massachusetts	Sir:	Dear Mr. Attorney General:	Very truly yours,	Sincerely yours,	1. Mr. Blank 2. Mr. Blank
President of the Senate of a State	The Honorable William R. Blank President of the Senate of the State of Virginia	Sir:	Dear Mr. Blank:	Very truly yours,	Sincerely yours,	1. Mr. Blank 2. Mr. Blank
Speaker of the Assembly or The House of Representatives.[2]	The Honorable William R. Blank Speaker of the Assembly of the State of New York	Sir:	Dear Mr. Blank:	Very truly yours,	Sincerely yours,	1. Mr. Blank 2. Mr. Blank

2. In most states the lower branch of the legislature is the House of Representatives. The exceptions to this are: New York, California, Wisconsin, and Nevada, where it is known as the Assembly; Maryland, Virginia, and West Virginia—the House of Delegates; New Jersey—the House of General Assembly.

State and Local Government Officials *continued*

Personage	Envelope and Inside Address (Add City, State, Zip)	Formal Salutation	Informal Salutation	Formal Close	Informal Close	1. Spoken Address 2. Informal Introduction or Reference
Treasurer, Auditor, or Comptroller of a State	The Honorable William R. Blank Treasurer of the State of Tennessee	Dear Sir:	Dear Mr. Blank:	Very truly yours,	Sincerely yours,	1. Mr. Blank 2. Mr. Blank
State Senator	The Honorable William R. Blank The State Senate	Dear Sir:	Dear Senator Blank:	Very truly yours,	Sincerely yours,	1. Senator Blank *or* Senator 2. Senator Blank
State Representative, Assemblyman, or Delegate	The Honorable William R. Blank House of Delegates	Dear Sir:	Dear Mr. Blank:	Very truly yours,	Sincerely yours,	1. Mr. Blank 2. Mr. Blank *or* Delegate Blank
District Attorney	The Honorable William R. Blank District Attorney, Albany county Country Courthouse	Dear Sir:	Dear Mr. Blank:	Very truly yours,	Sincerely yours,	1. Mr. Blank 2. Mr. Blank
Mayor of a city	The Honorable William R. Blank Mayor of Detroit	Dear Sir:	Dear Mr. Mayor: *or* Dear Mayor Blank:	Very truly yours,	Sincerely yours,	1. Mayor Blank *or* Mr. Mayor 2. Mayor Blank
President of a Board of Commissioners	The Honorable William R. Blank, President Board of commissioners of the City of Buffalo	Dear Sir:	Dear Mr. Blank:	Very truly yours,	Sincerely yours,	1. Mr. Blank 2. Mr. Blank

State and Local Government Officials *continued*

Personage	Envelope and Inside Address (Add City, State, Zip)	Formal Salutation	Informal Salutation	Formal Close	Informal Close	1. Spoken Address 2. Informal Introduction or Reference
City Attorney, City Counsel, Corporation Counsel	The Honorable William R. Blank, City Attorney (City Counsel, Corporation Counsel)	Dear Sir:	Dear Mr. Blank:	Very truly yours,	Sincerely yours,	1. Mr. Blank 2. Mr. Blank
Alderman	Alderman William R. Blank City Hall	Dear Sir:	Dear Mr. Blank:	Very truly yours,	Sincerely yours,	1. Mr. Blank 2. Mr. Blank

Court Officials

Personage	Envelope and Inside Address (Add City, State, Zip)	Formal Salutation	Informal Salutation	Formal Close	Informal Close	1. Spoken Address 2. Informal Introduction or Reference
Chief Justice[1] of a State Supreme Court	The Honorable William R. Blank Chief Justice of the Supreme Court of Minnesota[2]	Sir:	Dear Mr. Chief Justice:	Very truly yours,	Sincerely yours,	1. Mr. Chief Justice *or* Judge Blank 2. Mr. Chief Justice Blank *or* Judge Blank
Associate Justice of a Supreme Court of a State	The Honorable William R. Blank Associate Justice of the Supreme Court of Minnesota	Sir:	Dear Justice: *or* Dear Justice Blank:	Very truly yours,	Sincerely yours,	1. Mr. Justice Blank 2. Mr. Justice Blank
Presiding Justice	The Honorable William R. Blank Presiding Justice, Appellate Division Supreme Court of New York	Sir:	Dear Justice: *or* Dear Justice Blank:	Very truly yours,	Sincerely yours,	1. Mr. Justice (or Judge) Blank 2. Mr. Justice (or Judge) Blank

1. If his or her official title is *Chief Judge* substitute *Chief Judge* for *Chief Justice*, but never use *Mr., Mrs., Miss,* or *Ms.* with *Chief Judge* or *Judge.*
2. Substitute here the appropritae name of the court. For example, the highest court in New York State is called the Court of Appeals.

Court Officials *continued*

Personage	Envelope and Inside Address (Add City, State, Zip)	Formal Salutation	Informal Salutation	Formal Close	Informal Close	1. Spoken Address 2. Informal Introduction or Reference
Judge of a Court[3]	The Honorable William R. Blank Judge of the United States District Court for the Southern District of California	Sir:	Dear Judge Blank:	Very truly yours,	Sincerely yours,	1. Judge Blank 2. Judge Blank
Clerk of a Court	William R. Blank, Esq. Clerk of the Superior Court of Massachusetts	Dear Sir:	Dear Mr. Blank:	Very truly yours,	Sincerely yours,	1. Mr. Blank 2. Mr. Blank

3. Not applicable to judges of the United States Supreme Court.

United States Diplomatic Representatives

Personage	Envelope and Inside Address (Add City, State, Zip)	Formal Salutation	Informal Salutation	Formal Close	Informal Close	1. Spoken Address 2. Informal Introduction or Reference
American Ambassador	The Honorable William R. Blank American Ambassador[1]	Sir:	Dear Mr. Ambassador: *or* Dear Ambassador Blank:	Very truly yours,	Sincerely yours,	1. Mr. Ambassador *or* Mr. Blank 2. The American Ambassador[2] (The Ambassador or Mr. Blank)
American Minister	The Honorable William R. Blank American Minister to Rumania	Sir:	Dear Mr. Minister: *or* Dear Minister Blank:	Very truly yours,	Sincerely yours,	1. Mr. Minister or Mr. Blank 2. The American Minister, Mr. Blank (The Minister or Mr. Blank)

1. When an ambassador or minister is not at his or her post, the name of the country to which he or she is accredited must be added to the address. For example: *The American Ambassador to Great Britain.* If he or she holds military rank, the diplomatic complimentary title *The Honorable* should be omitted, thus *General William R. Blank, American Ambassador* (or *Minister*).
2. With reference to ambassadors and ministers to Central or South American countries, substitute *The Ambassador of the United States* for *American Ambassador or American Minister.*

United States Diplomatic Representatives *continued*

Personage	Envelope and Inside Address (Add City, State, Zip)	Formal Salutation	Informal Salutation	Formal Close	Informal Close	1. Spoken Address 2. Informal Introduction or Reference
American Chargé d'Affaires, Consul General, Consul, or Vice Consul	William R. Blank, Esq. American Chargé d'Affaires ad interim (Consul General, Consul, Vice Consul)	Sir:	Dear Mr. Blank:	Very truly yours,	Sincerely yours,	1. Mr. Blank 2. Mr. Blank
High Commissioner	The Honorable William R. Blank United States High Commissioner to Argentina	Sir:	Dear Mr. Blank:	Very truly yours,	Sincerely yours,	1. Commissioner Blank or Mr. Blank 2. Commissioner Blank or Mr. Blank

Foreign Officials and Representatives

Personage	Envelope and Inside Address (Add City, State, Zip)	Formal Salutation	Informal Salutation	Formal Close	Informal Close	1. Spoken Address 2. Informal Introduction or Reference
Foreign Ambassador[1] in the United States	His Excellency,[2] Erik Rolf Blankson Ambassador of Norway	Excellency:	Dear Mr. Ambassador:	Very truly yours,	Sincerely yours,	1. Mr. Ambassador or Mr. Blankson 2. The Ambassador of Norway (The Ambassador or Mr. Blankson)

1. The correct title of all ambassadors and ministers of foreign countries is Ambassador (Minister of _____ (name of country), with the exception of Great Britain. The adjective form is used with reference to representatives from Great Britain—*British Ambassador, British Minister.*
2. When the representative is British or a member of the British Commonwealth, it is customary to use *The Right Honorable* and *The Honorable* in addition to *His (Her) Excellency*, whenever appropriate.

Foreign Officials and Representatives *continued*

Personage	Envelope and Inside Address (Add City, State, Zip)	Formal Salutation	Informal Salutation	Formal Close	Informal Close	1. Spoken Address 2. Informal Introduction or Reference
Foreign Minister[3] *in the United States*	The Honorable George Macovescu Minister of Rumania	Sir:	Dear Mr. Minister:	Very truly yours,	Sincerely yours,	1. Mr. Minister or Mr. Macovescu 2. The Minister of Rumania (The Minister or Mr. Macovescu)
Foreign Diplomatic Representative with a Personal Title[4]	His Excellency,[5] Count Allesandro de Bianco Ambassador of Italy	Excellency:	Dear Mr. Ambassador:	Very truly yours,	Sincerely yours,	1. Mr. Ambassador or Count Bianco 2. The Ambassador of Italy (The Ambassador or Count Bianco)
Prime Minister	His Excellency, Christian Jawaharal Blank Prime Minister of India	Excellency:	Dear Mr. Prime Minister:	Respectfully yours,	Sincerely yours,	1. Mr. Blank 2. Mr. Blank or The Prime Minister
British Prime Minister	The Right Honorable Godfrey Blanc, K.G., M.C., M.P. Prime Minister	Sir:	Dear Mr. Prime Minister: or Dear Mr. Blanc:	Respectfully yours,	Sincerely yours,	1. Mr. Blanc 2. Mr. Blanc or The Prime Minister
Canadian Prime Minister	The Right Honorable Claude Louis St. Blanc, C.M.G. Prime Minister of Canda	Sir:	Dear Mr. Prime Minister: or Dear Mr. St. Blanc:	Respectfully yours,	Sincerely yours,	1. Mr. St. Blanc 2. Mr. St. Blanc or The Prime Minister

3. The correct title of all ambassadors and ministers of foreign countries is Ambassador (Minister) of ——————— (name of country), with the exception of Great Britain. The adjective form is used with reference to representatives from Great Britain— *British Ambassador, British Minister.*

4. If the personal title is a royal one, such as *His (Her) Highness* or *Prince,* the diplomatic title *His (Her) Excellency* or *The Honorable* is omitted.

5. *Dr., Señor, Don,* and other titles of special courtesy in Spanish-speaking countries may be used with the diplomatic title *His (Her) Excellency* or *The Honorable.*

Foreign Officials and Representatives *continued*

Personage	Envelope and Inside Address (Add City, State, Zip)	Formal Salutation	Informal Salutation	Formal Close	Informal Close	1. Spoken Address 2. Informal Introduction or Reference
President of a Republic	His Excellency, Juan Cuidad Blanco President of the Dominican Republic	Excellency:	Dear Mr. President:	Respectfully yours,	Sincerely yours,	1. Your Excellency 2. Not introduced (President Blanco or the President)
Premier	His Excellency, Charles Yves de Blanc Premier of the French Republic	Excellency:	Dear Mr. Premier:	Respectfully yours,	Sincerely yours,	1. Mr. de Blanc 2. Mr. de Blanc or The Premier
Foreign Chargé d'Affaires (de missi)[6] in the United States	Mr. Jan Gustaf Blanc Chargé d'Affaires of Sweden	Sir:	Dear Mr. Blanc:	Very truly yours,	Sincerely yours,	1. Mr. Blanc 2. Mr. Blanc
Foreign Chargé d'Affaires ad interim in the United States	Mr. Edmund Blank Chargé d'Affaires ad interim[7] of Ireland	Sir:	Dear Mr. Blank:	Very truly yours,	Sincerely yours,	1. Mr. Blank 2. Mr. Blank

6. The full title is usually shortened to *Chargé d'Affaires.*
7. The words *ad interim* should not be omitted in the address.

The Armed Forces/Army

Personage	Envelope and Inside Address (Add City, State, Zip)	Formal Salutation	Informal Salutation	Formal Close	Informal Close	1. Spoken Address 2. Informal Introduction or Reference
General of the Army	General of the Army William R. Blank, USA Department of the Army	Sir:	Dear General Blank:	Very truly yours,	Sincerely yours,	1. General Blank 2. General Blank
General, Lieutenant General, Major General, Brigadier General	General (Lieutenant General, Major General, or Brigadier General) William R. Blank, USA[1]	Sir:	Dear General (Lieutenant General, Major General, Brigadier General) Blank:	Very truly yours,	Sincerely yours,	1. General Blank 2. General Blank
Colonel, Lieutenant Colonel	Colonel (Lieutenant Colonel) William R. Blank, USA	Dear Colonel (Lieutenant Colonel) Blank:	Dear Colonel (Lieutenant Colonel) Blank:	Very truly yours,	Sincerely yours,	1. Colonel Blank 2. Colonel Blank
Major	Major William R. Blank, USA	Dear Major Blank:	Dear Major Blank:	Very truly yours,	Sincerely yours,	1. Major Blank 2. Major Blank
Captain	Captain William R. Blank, USA	Dear Captain Blank:	Dear Captain Blank:	Very truly yours,	Sincerely yours,	1. Captain Blank 2. Captain Blank
First Lieutenant, Second Lieutenant[2]	Lieutenant William R. Blank, USA	Dear Lieutenant Blank:	Dear Lieutenant Blank:	Very truly yours,	Sincerely yours,	1. Lieutenant Blank 2. Lieutenant Blank
Chief Warrant Officer, Warrant Officer	Chief Warrant Officer (Warrant Officer) William R. Blank, USA	Dear Mr. Blank:	Dear Mr. Blank:	Very truly yours,	Sincerely yours,	1. Mr. Blank 2. Mr. Blank
Chaplain in the U.S. Army[3]	Chaplain William R. Blank, Captain, USA	Dear Chaplain Blank:	Dear Chaplain Blank:	Very truly yours,	Sincerely yours,	1. Chaplain Blank 2. Chaplain Blank (Chaplain Blank)

Note: Although civilian writers traditionally spell out the rank for all branches of the service, military writers use abbreviations such as CPT for Captain and 1LT for first Lieutenant.

1. *USA indicates regular service, USAR signifies the reserve.*
2. *In all official correspondence, the full rank should be included in both the envelope and the inside address, but not in the salutation.*
3. *Roman Catholic chaplains and certain Anglican priests are introduced as Chaplain Blank but are spoken to and referred to as Father Blank.*

The Armed Forces/Navy

Personage	Envelope and Inside Address (Add City, State, Zip)	Formal Salutation	Informal Salutation	Formal Close	Informal Close	1. Spoken Address 2. Informal Introduction or Reference
Fleet Admiral	Admiral William R. Blank, USN Chief of Naval Operations, Department of the Navy	Sir:	Dear Admiral Blank:	Very truly yours,	Sincerely yours,	1. Admiral Blank 2. Admiral Blank
Admiral, Vice Admiral, Rear Admiral	Admiral (Vice Admiral or Rear Admiral) William R. Blank, USN United States Naval Academy[1]	Sir:	Dear Admiral (Vice Admiral, Rear Admiral) Blank:	Very truly yours,	Sincerely yours,	1. Admiral Blank 2. Admiral Blank
Commodore, Captain, Commander, Lieutenant Commander	Commodore (Captain, Commander, Lieutenant Commander) William R. Blank, USN USS Mississippi	Dear Commodore (Captain, Commander) Blank:	Dear Commodore (Captain, Commander, Lieutenant Commander) Blank:	Very truly yours,	Sincerely yours,	1. Commodore (etc.) Blank 2. Commodore (etc.) Blank
Junior Officers: Lieutenant, Lieutenant Junior Grade, Ensign	Lieutenant (Lieutenant Junior Grade, Ensign) William R. Blank, USN USS Wyoming	Dear Mr. Blank:	Dear Mr. Blank:	Very truly yours,	Sincerely yours,	1. Mr. Blank[2] 2. Lieutenant (etc.) Blank (Mr. Blank)

1. *USN* signifies regular service; *USNR* indicates the reserve.
2. Junior officers in the medical or dental corps are spoken to and referred to as *Dr.* but are introduced by their rank.

The Armed Forces/Navy continued

Personage	Envelope and Inside Address (Add City, State, Zip)	Formal Salutation	Informal Salutation	Formal Close	Informal Close	1. Spoken Address 2. Informal Introduction or Reference
Chief Warrant Officer, Warrant Officer	Chief Warrant Officer (Warrant Officer) William R. Blank, USN USS Texas	Dear Mr. Blank:	Dear Mr. Blank:	Very truly yours,	Sincerely yours,	1. Mr. Blank 2. Mr. Blank
Chaplain	Chaplain William R. Blank, Captain, USN Department of the Navy	Dear Chaplain Blank:	Dear Chaplain Blank:	Very truly yours,	Sincerely yours,	1. Chaplain Blank 2. Captain Blank (Chaplain Blank)

The Armed Forces—Air Force

Air force titles are the same as those in the army *USAF* is used instead of *USA*, and *USAFR* is used to indicate the reserve.

The Armed Forces—Marine Corps

Marine Corps titles are the same as those in the army, except that the top rank is *Commandant of the Marine Corps*. *USMC* indicates regular service, *USMCR* indicates the reserve.

The Armed Forces—Coast Guard

Coast Guard titles are the same as those in the navy, except that the top rank is *Admiral*, *USCG* indicates regular service; *USCGR* indicates the reserve.

Church Dignitaries/Catholic Faith

Personage	Envelope and Inside Address (Add City, State, Zip)	Formal Salutation	Informal Salutation	Formal Close	Informal Close	1. Spoken Address 2. Informal Introduction or Reference
The Pope	His Holiness, The Pope or His Holiness, Pope ——— Vatican City	Your Holiness: Most Holy Father:	Always *Formal*	Respectfully yours,	Always *Formal*	1. Your Holiness 2. Not introduced (His Holiness or The Pope)
Apostolic Pro-Nuncio	His Excellency, The Most Reverend William R. Blank Titular Archbishop of ——— The Apostolic Pro-Nuncio	Your Excellency:	Dear Archbishop Blank:	Respectfully yours,	Sincerely yours,	1. Your Excellency 2. Not introduced (The Apostolic Delegate)
Cardinal in the United States	His Eminence, William Cardinal Blank Archbishop of New York	Your Eminence:	Dear Cardinal Blank:	Respectfully yours,	Sincerely yours,	1. Your Eminence or less formally Cardinal Blank 2. Not introduced (His Eminence or Cardinal Blank)
Bishop and Archbishop in the United States	The Most Reverend William R. Blank, D.D. Bishop (Archbishop) of Baltimore	Your Excellency:	Dear Bishop (Archbishop) Blank:	Respectfully yours,	Sincerely yours,	1. Bishop (Archbishop) Blank 2. Bishop (Archbishop) Blank
Bishop in England	The Right Reverend William R. Blank Bishop of Sussex (local address)	Right Reverend Sir:	Dear Bishop:	Respectfully yours,	Sincerely yours,	1. Bishop Blank 2. Bishop Blank
Abbot	The Right Reverend William R. Blank Abbot of Westmoreland Abbey	Dear Father Abbot:	Dear Father Blank:	Respectfully yours,	Sincerely yours,	1. Father Abbot 2. Father Blank

Church Dignitaries/Catholic Faith *continued*

Personage	Envelope and Inside Address (Add City, State, Zip)	Formal Salutation	Informal Salutation	Formal Close	Informal Close	1. Spoken Address / 2. Informal Introduction or Reference
Monsignor	Reverend Msgr. William R. Blank	Reverend Monsignor:	Dear Monsignor Blank:	Respectfully yours,	Sincerely yours,	1. Monsignor Blank 2. Monsignor Blank
Superior of a Brotherhood and Priest[1]	The Very Reverend William R. Blank, M.M. Director	Dear Father Superior:	Dear Father Superior:	Respectfully yours,	Sincerely yours,	1. Father Blank 2. Father Blank
Priest	*With scholastic degree:* The Reverend William R. Blank, Ph.D. Georgetown University	Dear Dr. Blank:	Dear Dr. Blank:	Very truly yours,	Sincerely yours,	1. Doctor (Father) Blank 2. Doctor (Father) Blank
	Without scholastic degree (but member of religious order) The Reverend William R. Blank, S.J.[2] St. Vincent's Church	Dear Father Blank:	Dear Father Blank:	Very truly yours,	Sincerely yours,	1. Father Blank 2. Father Blank
Brother	Brother John Blank 932 Maple Avenue	Dear Brother:	Dear Brother John:	Very truly yours,	Sincerely yours,	1. Brother John 2. Brother John

1. The address for the superior of a Brotherhood depends on whether or not he is a priest or has a title other than superior. Consult the *Official Catholic Directory*.
2. When the order is known, the initials immediately follow the person's name, preceded by a comma.

Church Dignitaries/Catholic Faith *continued*

Personage	Envelope and Inside Address (Add City, State, Zip)	Formal Salutation	Informal Salutation	Formal Close	Informal Close	1. Spoken Address 2. Informal Introduction or Reference
Mother Superior of a Sisterhood (Catholic or protestant)[3]	The Reverend Mother Superior, O.C.A. Convent of the Sacred Heart	Dear Reverend Mother: *or* Dear Mother Superior:	Dear Reverend Mother: *or* Dear Mother Superior:	Respectfully yours,	Sincerely yours,	1. Reverend Mother 2. Reverend Mother
Sister Superior	The Reverend Sister Superior (order, if used)[4] Convent of the Sacred Heart	Dear Sister Superior:	Dear Sister Superior:	Respectfully yours,	Sincerely yours,	1. Sister Blank *or* Sister St. Teresa 2. The Sister Superior or Sister Blank (Sister St. Teresa)
Sister[5]	Sister Mary Blank St. John's High School	Dear Sister: *or* Dear Sister Blank:	Dear Sister Mary:	Very truly yours,	Sincerely yours,	1. Sister Mary 2. Sister Mary

3. Many religious congregations no longer use the title *Superior.* The head of a congregation is known instead by another title such as *President.*
4. The address of the superior of a Sisterhood depends on the order to which she belongs. The abbreviation of the order is not always used. Consult the *Official Catholic Directory.*
5. Use the form of address preferred by the person if you know it. Some women religious prefer to be addressed as "Sister Blank" rather than "Sister Mary" in business situations, but others object to the use of the last name.

Church Dignitaries/Jewish Faith

Personage	Envelope and Inside Address (Add City, State, Zip)	Formal Salutation	Informal Salutation	Formal Close	Informal Close	1. Spoken Address 2. Informal Introduction or Reference
Rabbi	*With scholastic degree:* Rabbi William R. Blank, Ph.D.	Sir:	Dear Dr. Blank: *or* Dear Rabbi Blank:	Very truly yours,	Sincerely yours,	1. Rabbi Blank *or* Dr. Blank 2. Rabbi Blank *or* Dr. Blank
	Without scholastic degree: Rabbi William R. Blank	Sir:	Dear Rabbi Blank:	Very truly yours,	Sincerely yours,	1. Rabbi Blank 2. Rabbi Blank

Church Dignitaries/Protestant Faith

Personage	Envelope and Inside Address (Add City, State, Zip)	Formal Salutation	Informal Salutation	Formal Close	Informal Close	1. Spoken Address 2. Informal Introduction or Reference
Archbishop (Anglican)	The Most Reverend Archbishop of Canterbury *or* The Most Reverend John Blank Archbishop of Canterbury	Your Grace:	Dear Archbishop Blank:	Respectfully yours,	Sincerely yours,	1. Your Grace 2. Not introduced (His Grace or The Archbishop)
Presiding Bishop of the Protestant Episcopal Church in America	The Right Reverend William R. Blank, D.D., L.L.D. Presiding Bishop of the Protestant Episcopal Church in America Northwick House	Right Reverend Sir:	Dear Bishop Blank:	Respectfully yours,	Sincerely yours,	1. Bishop Blank 2. Bishop Blank

Church Dignitaries/Protestant Faith *continued*

Personage	Envelope and Inside Address (Add City, State, Zip)	Formal Salutation	Informal Salutation	Formal Close	Informal Close	1. Spoken Address 2. Informal Introduction or Reference
Anglican Bishop	The Right Reverend The Lord Bishop of London	Right Reverend Sir:	Dear Bishop Blank:	Respectfully yours,	Sincerely yours,	1. Bishop Blank 2. Bishop Blank
Methodist Bishop	The Reverend William R. Blank Methodist Bishop	Reverend Sir:	Dear Bishop Blank:	Respectfully yours,	Sincerely yours,	1. Bishop Blank 2. Bishop Blank
Protestant Episcopal Bishop	The Right Reverend William R. Blank, D.D., L.L.D. Bishop of Denver	Right Reverend Sir:	Dear Bishop Blank:	Respectfully yours,	Sincerely yours,	1. Bishop Blank 2. Bishop Blank
Archdeacon	The Venerable William R. Blank Archdeacon of Baltimore	Venerable Sir:	Dear Archdeacon Blank:	Respectfully yours,	Sincerely yours,	1. Archdeacon Blank 2. Archdeacon Blank
Dean[1]	The Very Reverend William R. Blank, D.D. Dean of St. John's	Very Reverend Sir:	Dear Dean Blank:	Respectfully yours,	Sincerely yours,	1. Dean Blank or Dr. Blank 2. Dean Blank or Dr. Blank
Canon	The Reverend William R. Blank, D.D. Canon of St. Andrew's Cathedral	Reverend Sir:	Dear Canon Blank:	Respectfully yours,	Sincerely yours,	1. Canon Blank 2. Canon Blank
Protestant Minister	*With scholastic degree:* The Reverend William R. Blank, D.D., Litt.D. *or* The Reverend Dr. William R. Blank	Dear Dr. Blank:	Dear Dr. Blank:	Very truly yours,	Sincerely yours,	1. Dr. Blank 2. Dr. Blank
	Without scholastic degree: The Reverend William R. Blank	Dear Mr. Blank:	Dear Mr. Blank:	Very truly yours,	Sincerely yours,	1. Mr. Blank 2. Mr. Blank

1. Applies only to the head of a cathedral or of a theological seminary.

Church Dignitaries/Protestant Faith *continued*

Personage	Envelope and Inside Address (Add City, State, Zip)	Formal Salutation	Informal Salutation	Formal Close	Informal Close	1. Spoken Address 2. Informal Introduction or Reference
Episcopal Priest (High Church)	*With scholastic degree:* The Reverend William R. Blank, D.D., Litt.D. All Saint's Cathedral *or* The Reverend Dr. William R. Blank	Dear Dr. Blank:	Dear Dr. Blank:	Very truly yours,	Sincerely yours,	1. Dr. Blank 2. Dr. Blank
	Without scholastic degree: The Reverend William R. Blank St. Paul's Church	Dear Father Blank: *or* Dear Mr. Blank	Dear Father Blank: *or* Dear Mr. Blank:	Very truly yours,	Sincerely yours,	1. Father Blank *or* Mr. Blank 2. Father Blank *or* Mr. Blank

College and University Officials

Personage	Envelope and Inside Address (Add City, State, Zip)	Formal Salutation	Informal Salutation	Formal Close	Informal Close	1. Spoken Address 2. Informal Introduction or Reference
President of a College or University	*With a doctorate:* Dr. William R. Blank *or* William R. Blank, L.L.D., Ph.D. President Amherst College	Sir:	Dear Dr. Blank:	Very truly yours,	Sincerely yours,	1. Dr. Blank 2. Dr. Blank

College and University Officials *continued*

Personage	Envelope and Inside Address (Add City, State, Zip)	Formal Salutation	Informal Salutation	Formal Close	Informal Close	1. Spoken Address 2. Informal Introduction or Reference
President of a College or University	*Without a doctorate:* Mr. William R. Blank President Columbia University	Sir:	Dear President Blank:	Very truly yours,	Sincerely yours,	1. Mr. Blank 2. Mr. Blank *or* Mr. Blank, President of the College
	Catholic priest: The Reverend William R. Blank, S.J., D.D., Ph.D. President Fordham University	Sir:	Dear Dr. Blank:	Very truly yours,	Sincerely yours,	1. Doctor (Father) Blank 2. Doctor (Father) Blank
University Chancellor	Dr. William R. Blank Chancellor University of Alabama	Sir:	Dear Dr. Blank:	Very truly yours,	Sincerely yours,	1. Dr. Blank 2. Dr. Blank
Dean or Assistant Dean of a College or Graduate School	Dean (Assistant Dean) William R. Blank School of Law	Dear Sir: *or* Dear Dean Blank:	Dear Dean Blank:	Very truly yours,	Sincerely yours,	1. Dean (Assistant Dean) Blank 2. Dean (Assistant Dean) *or* Dr. Blank, the Dean (Assistant Dean) of the School of Law
	(If he holds a doctorate) Dr. William R. Blank Dean (Assistant Dean), School of Law University of Virginia	Dear Sir: *or* Dear Dean Blank:	Dear Dean Blank:			
Professor	Professor William R. Blank	Dear Sir: *or* Dear Professor Blank:	Dear Professor Blank:	Very truly yours,	Sincerely yours,	1. Professor (Dr.) Blank
	(If he holds a doctorate) Dr. William R. Blank *or* William R. Blank, Ph.D. Yale University	Dear Sir: *or* Dear Dr. (or Professor) Blank:	Dear Dr. (or Professor) Blank:			2. Professor (Dr.) Blank

College and University Officials *continued*

Personage	Envelope and Inside Address (Add City, State, Zip)	Formal Salutation	Informal Salutation	Formal Close	Informal Close	1. Spoken Address 2. Informal Introduction or Reference
Associate or Assistant Professor	Mr. William R. Blank or *(If he holds a doctorate)* Dr. William R. Blank or William R. Blank, Ph.D. Associate (Assistant) Professor Department of Romance Languages Williams College	Dear Sir: or Dear Professor Blank: Dear Sir: or Dear Dr. (or Professor) Blank:	Dear Professor Blank: Dear Dr. (or Professor) Blank:	Very truly yours,	Sincerely yours,	1. Professor (Dr.) Blank 2. Professor (Dr.) Blank
Instructor	Mr. William R. Blank or *(If he holds a doctorate)* Dr. William R. Blank or William R. Blank, Ph.D. Department of Economics University of California	Dear Sir: Dear Sir: or Dear Dr. Blank:	Dear Mr. Blank: Dear Dr. Blank:	Very truly yours,	Sincerely yours,	1. Mr. (Dr.) Blank 2. Mr. (Dr.) Blank

College and University Officials *continued*

Personage	Envelope and Inside Address (Add City, State, Zip)	Formal Salutation	Informal Salutation	Formal Close	Informal Close	1. Spoken Address 2. Informal Introduction or Reference
Chaplain of a College or University	Chaplain William R. Blank Trinity College *or* (If he holds a doctorate) The Reverend William R. Blank, D.D. Chaplain Trinity College	Dear Chaplain Blank: *or* Dear Dr. Blank:	Dear Chaplain (Dr.) Blank:	Very truly yours,	Sincerely yours,	1. Chaplain Blank 2. Chaplain Blank *or* Dr. Blank

United Nations Officials[1]

Personage	Envelope and Inside Address (Add City, State, Zip)	Formal Salutation	Informal Salutation	Formal Close	Informal Close	1. Spoken Address 2. Informal Introduction or Reference
Secretary General	His Excellency, William R. Blank Secretary General of the United Nations	Excellency:[2]	Dear Mr. Secretary General:	Very truly yours,	Sincerely yours,	1. Mr. Blank *or* Sir 2. The Secretary General of the United Nations *or* Mr. Blank
Under Secretary	The Honorable William R. Blank Under Secretary of the United Nations The Secretariat United Nations	Sir:	Dear Mr. Under Secretary: *or* Dear Mr. Blank:	Very truly yours,	Sincerely yours,	1. Mr. Blank 2. Mr. Blank

1. The six principal branches through which the United Nations functions are The General Assembly, The Security Council, The Economic and Social Council, The Trusteeship Council, The International Court of Justice, and The Secretariat.
2. An American citizen should never be addressed as "Excellency."

United Nations Officials *continued*

Personage	Envelope and Inside Address (Add City, State, Zip)	Formal Salutation	Informal Salutation	Formal Close	Informal Close	1. Spoken Address 2. Informal Introduction or Reference
Foreign Representative (with ambassadorial rank)	His Excellency, William R. Blank Representative of Spain to the United Nations	Excellency:	Dear Mr. Ambassador:	Very truly yours,	Sincerely yours,	1. Mr. Ambassador *or* Mr. Blank 2. Mr. Ambassador *or* The Representative of Spain to the United Nations (The Ambassador or Mr. Blank)
United States Representative (with ambassadorial rank)	The Honorable William R. Blank United States Representative to the United Nations	Sir: *or* Dear Mr. Ambassador.	Dear Mr. Ambassador:	Very truly yours,	Sincerely yours,	1. Mr. Ambassador *or* Mr. Blank 2. Mr. Ambassador *or* The United States Representative to the United Nations (The Ambassador or Mr. Blank)

NATIONAL DEPARTMENTS, AGENCIES. AND OFFICES

EXECUTIVE BRANCH

Office of the President
The White House
1600 Pennsylvania Ave., N.W.
Washington, DC 20500

Office of the Vice-President
Old Executive Office Building
Washington, DC 20501

Office of the First Lady
The White House
1600 Pennsylvania Ave., N.W.
Washington, DC 20500

Central Intelligence Agency
Washington, DC 20505

Counsil of Economic Advisers
Old Executive Office Building
Washington, DC 20506

Council on Environmental
   Quality
722 Jackson Place, N.W.
Washington, D.C. 20006

National Security Council
Old Executive Office Building
Washington, DC 20506

Office of Administration
Old Executive Office Building
Washington, DC 20500

Office of Management and
   Budget
Old Executive Office Building
Washington, DC 20503

Office of Policy Development
Old Executive Office Building
Washington, D.C. 20503

Office of Science and
   Technology
Old Executive Office Building
Washington, DC 20500

Regulatory Information Service
   Center
2100 M Street, N.W.
Washington, DC 20037

Department of Agriculture
14th Street and Independence
   Ave., S.W.
Washington, D.C. 20250

Department of Commerce
14th and E Streets, S.W.
Washington, DC 20230

Department of Defense
The Pentagon
Washington, DC 20301

Department of Education
400 Maryland Ave., S.W.
Washington, DC 20202

Department of Energy
1000 Independence Ave., S.W.
Washington, DC 20585

Department of Health and
   Human Services
200 Independence Ave., S.W.
Washington, DC 20201

Department of Housing and
   Urban Development
451 Seventh Street, S.W.
Washington, DC 20410

Department of the Interior
C and 19th Streets, N.W.
Washington, DC 20240

Department of Justice
Tenth Street and Constitution
 Ave., N.W.
Washington, D.C. 20530

Department of Labor
200 Constitution Ave., N.W.
Washington, D.C. 20210

Department of State
2201 C Street, N.W.
Washington, DC 20520

Department of Transportation
400 Seventh Street, S.W.
Washington, DC 20590

Department of the Treasury
1500 Pennsylvania Ave., N.W.
Washington, D.C. 20220

LEGISLATIVE BRANCH

The Senate
Capitol Building
Washington, DC 20510

The House of Representatives
Capitol Building
Washington, DC 20515

Congressional Budget Office
300 D Street, S.W.
Washington, DC 20515

Copyright Royalty Tribunal
1111 20th Street, N.W.
Washington, DC 20036

General Accounting Office
441 G Street, N.W.
Washington, DC 20548

Government Printing Office
North Capitol and H Streets,
 N.W.
Washington, DC 20401

Library of Congress
101 Independence Ave., S.E.
Washington, DC 20540

Office of Technology
 Assessment
600 Pennsylvania Ave., S.E.
Washington, DC 20003

JUDICIAL BRANCH

Administrative Office of the
 U.S. Courts
Washington, DC 20544

Federal Judicial Center
1520 H Street, N.W.
Washington, DC 20005

Supreme Court of the United
 States
One First Street, N.E.
Washington, DC 20453

U.S. Court of Claims
717 Madison Place, N.W.
Washington, DC 20005

U.S. Court of Customs and
 Patent Appeals
717 Madison Place, N.W.
Washington, DC 20439

U.S. Court of International
 Trade
One Federal Plaza
New York, NY 10007

U.S. Court of Military Appeals
450 E Street, N.W.
Washington, DC 20442

U.S. Tax Court
400 Second Street, N.W.
Washington, DC 20217

INDEPENDENT AGENCIES AND COMMISSIONS

Action
806 Connecticut Ave., N.W.
Washington, DC 20525

American Red Cross
17th and D Streets, N.W.
Washington, DC 20006

Board of Governors of the Federal Reserve System
Federal Reserve Building
Washington, DC 20551

Chamber of Commerce of the
    United States
1615 H Street, N.W.
Washington, DC 20062

Commission on Civil Rights
1121 Vermont Ave. N.W.
Washington, DC 20425

Commission of Fine Arts
708 Jackson Place N.W.
Washington, DC 20006

Commodity Futures Trading
    Commission
2033 K Street, N.W.
Washington, DC 20581

Community Services
    Administration
1200 19th Street, N.W.
Washington, DC 20506

Consumer Product Safety
    Commission
5401 Westbard Ave.
Bethesda, MD 20207

East-West Foreign Trade
    Board
15th Street and Pennsylvania
    Ave., N.W.
Washington, DC 20220

Environmental Protection
    Agency
401 M Street, S.W.
Washington, DC 20460

Equal Employment Opportunity Commission
2401 E Street, N.W.
Washington, DC 20507

Export-Import Bank of the
    United States
811 Vermont Ave., N.W.
Washington, DC 20571

Farm Credit Administration
1501 Farm Credit Drive
McLean, VA 22102

Federal Communications
    Commission
1919 M Street, N.W.
Washington, DC 20554

Federal Council on the Aging
200 Indedpendence Ave., S.W.
Washington, DC 20201

Federal Deposit Insurance
    Corporation
550 17th Street, N.W.
Washington, DC 20429

Federal Election Commission
999 E Street, N.W.
Washington, DC 20463

Federal Home Loan Bank
Board
1700 G Street, N.W.
Washington, DC 20552

Federal Labor Relations
Authority
500 C Street, S.W.
Washington, DC 20424

Federal Maritime Commission
1100 L Street, N.W.
Washington, DC 20573

Federal Mine Safety and
Health Review Commission
1739 K Street, N.W.
Washington, DC 20006

Federal Reserve System
20th Street &
Constitution Ave.
Washington, DC 20551

Federal Trade Commission
Pennsylvania Ave. and Sixth
Street, N.W.
Washington, DC 20580

Federal Trade Commission
Consumer Protection
Bureau
Pennsylvania Ave. and Sixth
Street, N.W.
Washington, DC 20580

General Services
Administration
18th and F Streets, N.W.
Washington, DC 20405

Interstate Commerce
Commission
12th Street and Constitution
Ave., N.W.
Washington, DC 20423

Legal Services Corporation
733 15th Street, N.W.
Washington, DC 20005

National Academy of Sciences
2101 Constitution Ave., N.W.
Washington, DC 20418

National Aeronautics and Space
Administration
600 Independence Ave., S.W.
Washington, DC 20546

National Credit Union
Administration
1776 G Street, N.W.
Washington, DC 20456

National Endowment for the
Arts
2401 E Street N.W.
Washington, DC 20506

National Endowment for the
Humanities
806 15th Street, N.W.
Washington, DC 20506

National Foundation on the
Arts and the Humanities
1100 Pennsylvania Ave., N.W.
Washington, DC 20506

National Labor Relations Board
1717 Pennsylvania Ave., N.W.
Washington, DC 20570

National Mediation Board
1425 K Street, N.W.
Washington, DC 20572

National Park Foundation
1825 K Street, N.W.
Washington, DC 20006

National Railroad Passenger
Corporation
400 North Capitol Street
Washington, DC 20001

National Science Foundation
1880 G Street, N.W.
Washington, DC 20550

National Transportation Safety
Board
800 Independence Ave., S.W.
Washington, DC 20594

Nuclear Regulatory
Commission
1717 H Street, N.W.
Washington, DC 20555

Occupational Safety and Health
Review Commission
1825 K Street, N.W.
Washington, DC 20006

Office of Personnel
Management
1900 E Street, N.W.
Washington, DC 20415

Panama Canal Commission
423 13th Street, N.W.
Washington, DC 20004

Peace Corps
806 Connecticut Ave., N.W.
Washington, DC 20525

Postal Rate Commission
133 H Street, N.W.
Washington, DC 20268

Securities and Exchange
Commission
450 5th Street, N.W.
Washington, DC 20549

Small Business Administration
1441 L Street, N.W.
Washington, DC 20416

Smithsonian Institution
1000 Jefferson Drive, S.W
Washington, DC 20560

Tennessee Valley Authority
412 First Street, S.E.
Washington, DC 20444

Trade Policy Commission
1800 G Street, N.W.
Washington, DC 20506

U.S. Information Agency
301 4th Street, S.W.
Washington, DC 20547

U.S. International Development Corporation Agency
320 21st Street, N.W.
Washington, DC 20523

U.S. International Trade
Commission
701 E Street, N.W.
Washington, DC 20436

U.S. Metric Board
1600 Wilson Boulevard
Arlington, Va 22209

U.S. Parole Commission
320 First Street, N.W.
Washington, DC 20537

U.S. Postal Service
574 L'Enfant Plaza West, S.W.
Washington, DC 20260

U.S. Railroad Retirement
Board
844 Rush Street
Chicago, IL 60611

U.S. Railway Association
955 L'Enfant Plaza North,
  S.W.
Washington, DC 20595

Veterans Administration
810 Vermont Ave., N.W.
Washington, DC 20420

Water Resources Council
2120 L Street, N.W.
Washington, DC 20037

Note: Additional organizations are listed in the *U.S. Government Organization Manual*; *The National Directory of Addresses and Telephone Numbers*; the Washington, D.C., *Telephone Directory*; and popular almanacs such as the *Information Please Almanac*.

CORRECT LETTER SALUTATIONS

Rule	Examples
Abbreviate the personal titles *Mr.*, *Ms.*, *Mrs.*, *Messrs.*, and *Dr.*	Dear *Mr.* Jackson: Dear *Ms.* Samuels; Dear *Messrs.* Prentiss and Rogers; Dear *Dr.* Du Bois
Spell out religious, military, and professional titles such as *Father*, *Major*, and *Professor*.	Dear *Sister* Adele; Dear *Colonel* Frost; Dear *Professor* Wittaker
Capitalize the first word of the salutation and the person's name and title.	Dear Mrs. Watts; Right Reverend Monsignor; Your Excellency; Dear Rabbi Feldman
Use the person's full name when the gender of the addressee is unknown.	Dear L. Z. Baker; Dear Leslie Bell
Use *Sir* and *Madam* when name or name and gender are unknown.	Dear *Sir*; Dear *Madam*; Dear *Madam or Sir*; Dear *Sir or Madam*
In addressing a firm, use *Ladies* or *Mesdames* and *Gentlemen* or *Messrs.* when the firm is composed entirely of men or women. Otherwise refer to both men and women in the salutation.	*Ladies*; *Gentlemen*; *Ladies and Gentlemen*
In letters to more than one woman, use individually preferred titles, if	Dear *Ms.* Wagner, *Miss* Franklin, and *Mrs.* Masterson; Dear *Mrs.* Pillsbury

Rule	Examples
known; otherwise, you may use *Mss.* (or *Mses.*), *Misses*, or *Mesdames*.	and *Mrs.* Benjamin; Dear *Mesdames* Pillsbury and Benjamin; Dear *Ms.* Santos and *Ms.* Elso; Dear *Mss.* Santos and Elso
In letters to more than one man use *Mr.* with each name or *Messrs.* or *Gentlemen*.	Dear *Mr.* Glassman and *Mr.* Bennett; Dear *Messrs.* Merriam and Longman; *Gentlemen*
In addressing men and women, each by name, use *Mr.* and *Ms.* or the woman's preferred title.	Dear *Mr.* Klaus and *Ms.* Zenna; Dear *Mr.* Rowan and *Mrs.* Larkin
In letters to groups of persons, use a collective term.	Dear *Friends*; Dear *Members*; Dear *Classmates*
Use *My dear* and other formal greetings only in official and formal correspondence.	*My dear* Mrs. Reagon: *Right Reverend and dear sir*

Note: For further examples, see *Forms of Address for Honorary and Official Positions* and *Current Forms of Address* in this chapter.

FORMAL AND INFORMAL COMPLIMENTARY CLOSES

Formal Closings	Informal Closings
Respectfully yours	Sincerely
Respectfully	Sincerely yours
Yours very truly	Cordially
Very truly yours	Cordially yours
Yours truly	Best wishes
Very sincerely yours	Best regards
Very cordially yours	Warmest regards.
	Regards

Note: Refer to the various letter formats in this chapter for the correct position of the complimentary close. The trend is toward personal and informal closings; formal closings should be used only in legal, official, and other formal correspondence. Among the informal closings, some such as *warmest regards* are suitable for friends and associates; other, less personal closings such as *sincerely* are suitable for informal, but less personal, letters to firms or unknown individuals. For closings in official correspondence, see *Forms of Address for Honorary and Official Positions* in this chapter.

CORRECT SIGNATURE LINES

Type of Signature	Examples

Firm name: Write a firm name in all capitals (as it appears on the letterhead) two spaces below the complimentary close.

Sincerely yours,

OFFICE SUPPLY COMPANY

Mary Drew

Mary Drew
Purchasing Manager

Man: Write a man's name, without the personal title *Mr.*, exactly as he signs it (*not* J. M. McDavitt if he always signs his names James McDavitt). The only time that one might put *Mr.* in parentheses before the name is in cases where it is not clear if the signer is a man or woman. Place any initials such as academic degrees after the name.

James M. McDavitt

James M. McDavitt, CPA
General Accounting Manager

Leslie Henderson

(Mr.) Leslie Henderson

Single woman: Place the title *Miss* in parentheses before the name only if the signer prefers to include it. Otherwise, use no personal title.

Ann Maxwell

Ann Maxwell
Senior Editor

Ann Maxwell

(Miss) Ann Maxwell
Senior Editor

Married or widowed woman: Place the title *Mrs.* in parentheses before the name only if the signer prefers it. Otherwise, use no personal title. In social

Jeanne Foxworth

Jeanne Foxworth
Personnel Director

Type of Signature	Examples

letters, put the woman's married name in parentheses beneath the written signature.

Jeanne Foxworth

(Mrs.) Jeanne Foxworth
Personnel Director

Jeanne Foxworth

(Mrs. Paul R. Foxworth)

Divorced woman: Do not use a personal title (*Miss* or *Mrs.*) unless the woman prefers it. If she does, use *Mrs.* only if she retains her married name or uses her maiden and married names combined. Use *Miss* if she uses her maiden name. Do not use her former husband's first name in any instance.

Maxine Steinbeck

Maxine Steinbeck
Supervisor

Maxine Steinbeck

(Mrs.) Maxine Steinbeck
Supervisor

Maxine Johnson Steinbeck

(Mrs. Johnson-Steinbeck)

Maxine Johnson

(Miss) Maxine Johnson

Secretary: If the secretary is the signer, follow the above rules for men and women. The title of *Secretary to Mr./ Ms. . . .* should not include the employer's first name or initials unless another person in the firm has the same last name.

John Sutherland

John Sutherland **R.S.**
President

Dean Eckert

Dean Eckert
Secretary to Mrs. Alcott

Note: A personal title in parentheses before a name (*Mrs.*) means that the person wants to be addressed using that title. The initials *M.D.* after a name mean that the person wants to be addressed as *Dr.* A professional title such as *Professor* or a military rank such as *Colonel, USAF* typed beneath a name means that the person wants to be addressed by that title or rank.

PUNCTUATION STYLE FOR LETTERS

Style	Principal Features
Open	Except for sentences in the body of the letter, punctuation is omitted after the city in the inside address and after the salutation and complimentary close.
Mixed (or standard)	A colon is used after the salutation and a comma after the city in the inside address and after the complimentary close.

Note: The various letter formats at the beginning of this chapter use a mixed punctuation style. Although the open style is gaining in popularity, the mixed style remains the most prevalent.

SAMPLE LETTER OPENINGS AND CLOSINGS

Type of Letter	Opening	Closing
Reply	Here's the information you requested about or Model XY-1 copier.	If we can provide more information to help you make a selection, Mr. Billings, please let us know. We appreciate your interest.
Reservations	Please reserve first-class space for Ms. Paula Jones, assistant manager, Richmond & Associates.	We would appreciate immediate confirmation of this reservation. Thank you.
Acknowledgment	Thanks very much for sending the sales report I requested.	I appreciated your quick response, Mr. Burke. I know that the report will be most helpful in my work.

Type of Letter	Opening	Closing
Reminder	I hope you're planning to be at our October 5 departmental meeting at the Holiday Inn.	I'd appreciate it if you could telephone me at 611-4300 or drop me a note to confirm that you will be attending. Thanks very much, Bill. Hope to see you then.
Appointment	Mr. Harris would like to know if you could come to his office at 2 o'clock on Monday, May 12, to discuss the status of the Wilson account.	Please let me know whether this time will be convenient for you, Mrs. Kellner. Thank you very much.
Introduction	It's a pleasure to introduce to you our new manager of planning, Ms. Lee Farnsworth.	I'd appreciate it if you would welcome Lee and brief her on your operations. Thanks very much, Ted.
Apology	You're right—my report was due yesterday, and I'm sorry to say an unexpected interruption prevented me from finishing it.	I hope my suggested revised submission date will be acceptable, Mike. Please accept my apology for any problems my tardiness has caused.
Appreciation	I want you to know how much I appreciated your help at the seminar last week.	Thanks so much for all of your good work, Diane. We wouldn't have made it without you.
Congratulations	News of your promotion just reached my office, Roy. Congratulations and warmest wishes from all of us!	I'm confident you'll enjoy much success in your new position, and it's a genuine pleasure to know that someone with your excellent qualifications will be at the helm in our West Coast office.

Type of Letter	Opening	Closing
Sympathy	It was with deep regret that I learned about the death of your husband today.	It was a pleasure to know Bill, and we will all remember him with much respect, admiration, and fondness.
Collection	Although we have sent you numerous statements and letters about your past-due account of $141.99, we have not yet received a reply from you.	Please put your check in the mail today or contact us immediately. We must hear from you by Friday, March 7, 19__, to avoid taking further action.
Sales Promotion	Most guidebooks take you so far and no farther. Then you're on your own to search for additional information.	Just fill out the enclosed reply form to reserve your copy of the new *Secretary's Guidebook*. Why not do it immediately while you're thinking about it?

Note: See also the various model letters at the end of this chapter.

COMPOSITION GUIDELINES FOR VARIOUS TYPES OF LETTERS

Type of Letter	Composition Guidelines
Inquiry	To make an inquiry, describe your reason for writing, if pertinent; state specifically what information you need; indicate what action, if any, you want the reader to take.
	To respond to an inquiry, give as much information as you can in your first letter; be specific; recommend what additional action or correspondence is needed, if any; thank the writer for his or her interest.

Type of Letter	Composition Guidelines
Request	To make a request, state what you want (possibly why you want it); indicate what action you want the receiver to take; give all pertinent facts (time, place, price, delivery, and so on); express appreciation if a favor or special effort is required of the receiver.
	To respond to a request, state your reply clearly; respond thoughtfully if you must say no; recommend what additional action or correspondence is needed, if any.
Reservation	Be specific and state reservation details clearly; give all pertinent facts (time, place, date, order number, credit card number, and so on); ask for (and give) written confirmation when time permits.
Order	Be specific and state clearly what you want to order or in confirming what has been ordered; double-check all facts (price, quantity, delivery date, and so on); clearly explain any changes that may be necessary; thank the customer for the order.
Acknowledgement	For a simple acknowledgement, answer promptly; state what you received; express appreciation for the information or item you received.
	To acknowledge *and* supply additional information, also answer promptly; state what you received; offer as much information as you can in reply to a request; express appreciation for anything received.
Reminder	State the facts concerning the subject of the reminder; in a case of commitment, repeat the date of the original commitment and how it was made (by letter, telephone, or other means); request confirmation by letter, phone, or wire; avoid any implication that the receiver is careless or forgetful.
Follow-up	State the facts concerning the item or letter being tracked; ask for a prompt reply; avoid any implication that the receiver is careless or forgetful.
Appointment	To make an appointment, indicate why you want the appointment; suggest a time, place, and date; request a confirmation or reply.

Type of Letter	Composition Guidelines
	To respond to a request for an appointment, repeat the pertinent facts (time, place, date, and so on); if necessary, suggest alternatives; request a reply if changes are suggested; be thoughtful if you must say no to a request.
Introduction	State any essential facts about the person being introduced; indicate why the receiver would want to meet the person; give the receiver a chance to say no; in agreeing to meet someone, be appreciative; in refusing to meet someone, be diplomatic; thank the writer or receiver.
Reference and recommendation	State any facts that will help the person requesting or receiving your recommendation; be objective and honest; be considerate when you are unable to recommend someone; if you receive a recommendation in reply to your request for one, express your appreciation for the information.
Employee letter	In motivational letters to employees, avoid lecturing or talking down; be sincere; present any pertinent facts enthusiastically and from a positive viewpoint.
	In letters of rejection to employees, thank the receivers if something was offered (e.g., a suggestion); tell employees tactfully why you must decline what they have offered or requested; if appropriate, encourage them to make future efforts.
Appreciation	Write naturally and sincerely; indicate why you appreciate what was done; offer to reciprocate, if appropriate; encourage receiver to contribute further, if appropriate.
Goodwill	Take advantage of various occasions and events to say something nice to someone; do not ask for a favor in return when you offer something; write naturally and sincerely.
Congratulation	Be sincere and enthusiastic; avoid any hint of envy; confine your comments to the receiver's accomplishment and avoid remarks that might overshadow it.
Social-business	To send an informal invitation, state what the occasion is, indicate any reason for the occasion (e.g., a dinner to honor someone); give all details (time, place, who

Type of Letter	Composition Guidelines
	will be there, and so on); ask for a reply by a special date.
	To reply to an informal invitation, repeat the essential details (time, place, and date); express pleasure if accepting and regret when declining; if appropriate, indicate why you are declining.
	In letters for special occasions (birthdays, holidays, illnesses, and so on), write naturally and sincerely; indicate the reason for your letter; confine your comments to the occasion and avoid remarks that might overshadow it.
Complaint	To make a complaint, give all pertinent details; indicate the adjustment you are seeking; be firm but not unreasonable; be fair in your criticism and request for resolution.
Adjustment	To respond to a complaint or to make an adjustment, be considerate and understanding; apologize if appropriate and try to satisfy the writer's request; avoid explanations that appear to be a refusal to accept responsibility.
Credit	In letters requesting credit, state all information the receiver will need; in letters responding to credit requests, be honest and accurate; show consideration when credit must be refused.
Collection	Develop a series of letters, from a casual reminder to a prelude to legal action; revise the tone in each letter from the initial friendly reminder of an overdue account to the final stern demand for payment before legal action is taken; review the situation thoroughly before developing a single collection letter or a series; select realistic deadlines that give the receiver time to pay.
Sales promotion	In introducing products and services, phrase your comments to arouse interest and encourage action; describe what is being offered and its value to the receiver; indicate if any special offers or incentives are available; leave the door open for further contact.
	In follow-up sales letters, repeat your description of the product or service and its value to the receiver; repeat the special offers or incentives, if any; state any new

Type of Letter	Composition Guidelines

or additional information that may stimulate the receiver to act; keep the door open for further contact.

Note: For examples of many of these letters, see *Model Business Letters*, *Model Social-Business Letters*, and *Model Memos* at the end of this chapter.

FORM-LETTER EFFECTIVENESS CHECKLIST

	Yes	No
Is the form letter designed so that a typist can make typed fill-ins easily?	( )	( )
Has a test been made to see whether a file copy of the letter is actually needed or whether the prescribed number of copies can be reduced?	( )	( )
Is the letter easily understood on the first reading?	( )	( )
Is it free of old-fashioned letter language, such as "reference is made to," "you are advised that," and "examination of our records discloses"?	( )	( )
Has a "usage" test been made to see whether it is practical to carry a printed stock?	( )	( )
Does the letter concern a routine business or informational matter?	( )	( )
Is there a mark to show the typist where to begin the address so that it will show in the window of an envelope?	( )	( )
Will the supply on hand be used up in a few months' time?	( )	( )
Is the letter identified in any way, for example, by a number printed in one of the corners?	( )	( )
If you were the person receiving the form letter, would you consider it effective and attractive?	( )	( )
Has a test been made of typed letters to see whether it is practical to replace any of them with form letters?	( )	( )

	Yes	No
Has provision been made for reviewing all requests for form letters to make sure that unnecessary, poorly written, and poorly designed letters do not slip into print?	( )	( )
Do you have standards that you expect all form letters to meet?	( )	( )
Are form letters put into use by written instructions explaining when they are to be used, enclosures (if any) that should be made, and carbon-copy requirements?	( )	( )
Do you have a systematic way of numbering form letters?	( )	( )
When form letters become obsolete, are immediate instructions issued to discontinue their use and to remove old stock from supply cabinets and desks?	( )	( )

Source: National Archives and Records Service, Records Management Division, General Services Administration, Washington, D.C.

Note: A checkmark in the "no" column indicates the need for corrective action.

MODEL BUSINESS LETTERS

Request

Please send us a copy of your free booklet "IRA Investment Opportunities." We would also appreciate receiving any other complimentary information you have about IRA accounts and investment opportunities.

Thank you very much.

Acknowledgment

Your letter of May 5 arrived shortly after Mr. Benedict had left on a three-week business trip. Since you indicated that it does not require an immediate reply, I'll hold it for prompt attention on his return.

Apology

We're sorry for the unavoidable delay in your order of binders. The factory just notified us that a new supply will be available in three weeks, and we will ship your order immediately upon receipt of this supply.

Please accept our sincere apologies for any inconvenience the delay has caused you. We appreciate your order and hope we can be of help to you in the future.

Appointment

Mr. Attleboro would like to know whether you could meet him in his office on Friday, February 9, at 3:30 P.M. There are a few changes in your outline that he wants to discuss with you.

I'd appreciate it if you would ask your secretary to telephone me at 929-8017, extension 2113, to let me know if this time is convenient.

Thank you very much.

Reminder

I hope you're still planning to attend our December 2 departmental meeting. It's scheduled for 10:30 A.M. in our third-floor conference room.

I'd appreciate it if you would telephone me this week at 432-7765 to let me know if you will be there.

Thanks very much, Elaine. Hope to see you then.

Refusal

I have carefully considered your request for a salary increase of $2,400 to begin January 1, 19__. However, I'm very sorry to let you know that our firm cannot meet your request at this time.

Your job record is good, and we greatly appreciate your desire to make further contributions, but financial constraints prevent us from making any salary increases at this time. I've made a note, though, to review your request again in six months, and you will be notified then if conditions have changed.

In the meantime, we hope you will continue to enjoy your work, and we look forward to a long and mutually rewarding association.

Introduction

It's my pleasure to introduce Janet Schultz to you as a prospective applicant for a position at the Resource Center. She will contact you next week to request an interview.

Ms. Schultz is presently working as a secretary to the general manager of the TV Cable Company. Before that, she was my secretary for six years. During that time, her work was consistently of high quality, and I found her to be completely responsible, very capable, and always enthusiastic.

I'd appreciate any consideration you can extend to her. Thanks very much, Walter.

Appreciation

Thanks so much, Jim, for a wonderful weekend with you and Paula. I truly enjoyed visiting with both of you in your home. You must give me a chance to reciprocate the next time you're in Denver.

Please give my best to Paula.

Complaint

The model 1-AR-559 dictation unit that we purchased last month is not working properly. We have followed the instructions very carefully, and your service representative has examined the machine several times in the past month. But the equipment still does not operate as it should, and we must conclude that it is defective.

Please let us know how soon we can expect a replacement unit. Normally, this equipment is used daily, and its absence will create a considerable backlog for us. So we hope a new unit will be forthcoming immediately.

Thank you for your help. I'll look forward to hearing from you shortly.

Credit

Our seven-year association with Neucomb Hardware has been very satisfactory. They have paid all of our invoices in full within 30 days, with purchases averaging about $1,500 a month. Based on our experience, we are happy to recommend them for a similar line of credit.

Do let me know if you need any further information.

Note: See also *Composition Guidelines for Various Types of Letters* in this chapter.

MODEL SOCIAL-BUSINESS LETTERS

Invitation

Would you be able to have lunch with me on Wednesday, April 17? If you're free, I'd like to have you be my guest at the Club 420.

Two of my associates, Roy Habeston and Julia McCord, will be there too, and we plan to meet in the lobby at noon. They worked with me on the Phoenix project last year and have some new renovation ideas that might interest you.

Hope you can join us, Phil. You can phone me at 761-2000 any day this week to let me know.

Acceptance

I'd be happy to speak at your Business Retailers meeting at the Community Building on Tuesday, January 11, at 7:30 P.M.

The topic "Continuing Education Opportunities for Retailers" is fine with me. As you requested, I'll confine my remarks to local opportunities and will limit my address to 30 minutes.

Your invitation is most welcome, and I'm looking forward to meeting you and your colleagues at the Business Retailers Association.

Birthday

Here's wishing you a wonderful day on September 11 and much happiness throughout the coming year. A very happy birthday to you, Linda!

Sympathy

Mr. Jamison and I were deeply saddened to learn about the death of your husband. We enjoyed and respected his friendship and will miss him very much.

Our heartfelt sympathy goes out to you and your children, Louise. Do let me know how we can help you during this very difficult time.

Thank You

I want to thank you for your help while I was out of town last month. Everything in the department ran smoothly under your watchful eye, and it gave me great peace of mind to know you were there.

Many thanks, Carl. I hope I can be of help to you some day too.

Note: See also *Composition Guidelines for Various Types of Letters* in this chapter.

MODEL MEMOS

Reminder

Just a reminder that the program for our sales seminary is scheduled to go to the printer June 6. I'd appreciate it if you would drop me a note indicating the present status of the project. Thanks, George.

Announcement

The next Finance Committee meeting will be Thursday, July 19, from 10:30 A.M. until 1:30 P.M. at the Howard Johnson Motor Lodge, Route 7, in Salem. Lunch will be provided.

The agenda will be mailed on July 1, so if you have anything to be included, let me know by the end of June.

I'd appreciate hearing from you right away if you're unable to attend. Thanks very much.

Transmittal

Scott, here's a modified blueprint for the Madison project. I'll fill you in on the details when I see you next week.

Request

Would you be able to make a change in the layout for the inside back cover of our new catalog? I just had a call from our New York office, and they would like to include a sketch of the new plant.

It sounds like a good idea, so I hope we can work it in. Would you please let me know right away? Thanks, Jane.

Acknowledgment

Your idea for a summer-doldrums contest is very interesting, Jack. I'll phone you next week when I return from the computer show, and we can talk more about it then.

Note: See also *Composition Guidelines for Various Types of Letters, Model Business Letters,* and *Model Social-Business Letters* in this chapter.

MODEL INVITATIONS

FORMAL INVITATION

Mr. and Mrs. Roger West
request the pleasure of your company
at a reception
in honor of Mr. Donald Pendleton
on Saturday, the sixth of October
at half past six o'clock
at 1640 Denton Boulevard

Black tie
R.S.V.P.

FORMAL REPLY

Miss Edna Gray
accepts with pleasure the
kind invitation of Mr. and Mrs. West
to be present at the reception
in honor of Mr. Donald Pendleton
on Saturday, the sixth of October
at half past six o'clock
at 1640 Denton Boulevard

Note: For information about informal invitations, see *Composition Guidelines for Various Types of Letters*, Social Business, and *Model Social-Business Letters*, Invitation, in this chapter.

CHAPTER 6

Report Preparation
and Production

PRINCIPAL PARTS IN DIFFERENT STYLES OF REPORTS

Type of Report	Principal Parts
Letter or memo report	Traditional letter or memo format (see Chapter 5) that may include subheadings in the body of the letter. Although the report is written like a letter, it should state the person who authorized the report and the date of authorization, the objective of the report, its scope, and your conclusions and recommendations.
Form report	A standard preprinted form with specific blanks to fill in the required data, for example, an expense report form. (See *Travel Expense Report Form* in Chapter 3.)
Short informal report	Principal parts may include some or all of the following, positioned in the order stated: preliminary summary (brief statement of conclusions and recommendations); introduction (brief statement of objectives and limitations of report); body (discussion of topic and analysis); conclusions and recommendations (brief statement of results of study and suggestions for plan of action); and appendix (supplementary material such as graphs and tables). Other parts such as a bibliography are included if appropriate.
Long formal report	Long, formal reports usually include these principal parts in the order shown.
	Front matter: cover; flyleaf (blank page between the cover and title page); title page (see *Report Title Page* in this chapter); letter of transmittal (one-page letter on company letterhead addressed to the person who will receive the report; explains the purpose of the report; may also be sent separately); table of contents (may be simple or detailed; see *Report Table of Contents* in this chapter); summary, synopsis, or abstract (brief—two to six paragraphs—condensed version of the report).
	Body: introduction (statement of the problem); review of research; data analysis; conclusions and recommendations (statement of results of study and suggestions for plan of action).
	Backmatter: appendix (forms, tables, and other supporting material; see *Principal Parts of Tables* and *Table*

Type of Report	Principal Parts

Format in this chapter); bibliography (resources cited and those used in preparing report); index.

Optional parts: Some reports also contain a letter of authorization (after the transmittal letter); a foreword (before the table of contents); list of illustrations (after the table of contents); notes section (all text footnotes collected together after the appendix); a glossary (before the bibliography).

REPORT TITLE PAGE

IMPACT OF THE
TIME-AWARENESS FACTOR
IN TIME MANAGEMENT

Prepared for

David J. Searle, Director
Barnaby Institute
1015 Sixth Street, Omaha, Nebraska 68102

Prepared by

Nancy M. Chalmers, Consultant
Halsted & Warner
426 Terrace Lane, Kansas City, Missouri 64133

Note: Companies differ in the type and amount of information they require on their report title pages.

REPORT TABLES OF CONTENTS

CONTENTS

PRINCIPAL PARTS OF A BOOK AND PROPER SEQUENCE

Frontmatter: Half title page (i)
Series title, list of contributors, or frontispiece (ii)
Title page (iii)
Copyright page (iv)
Dedication or epigraph (v)
Blank (vi)
Table of contents (vii)
List of illustrations (recto page)
List of tables (recto page)
Foreword (recto page)
Preface (recto page)
Acknowledgments (recto page)
Introduction (when not part of body) (recto page)

Body: Half title page (recto page)
Part title page (if any) (recto page)
First text page (recto page)

Backmatter: Appendixes (recto page)
Notes (recto page)
Glossary (recto page)
Bibliography (recto page)
Index (recto page)

Note: Recto = right-hand page.

ESSENTIAL STEPS IN REPORT PREPARATION

Step	Description
Organization	The first step should be a matter of drawing up a blueprint for the project, that is, deciding what to do, how, and when. This includes deciding what your message must accomplish, to whom to direct it, how much information to include (scope), where to find the information you need, what tools to use, how much time you have for each task, and so on. In short, set up a specific plan of steps to take—how, where, when, and why.

Research	Decide what information you need, where to go to find it (libraries, schools, etc.), what tools to use (telephone, camera, tape recorder, etc.), how to record the information (cards, paper, tape, questionnaire, etc.), what costs you will have, and so on. Before beginning state and define your thesis, listing subtopics and sub-subtopics under your main topic in outline fashion (see *Outline Numbering Patterns* in this chapter); these subtopics may become your report subheads. List all possible sources of information. Finally, collect the data you need.
Drafting	Build upon your outline subtopics. First, convert them into sentences and then discuss each item, further developing the sentences into paragraphs (see *Comparison of Topic and Sentence Outlines* in this chapter). In other words, expand each one- or two-word subtopic into a statement and then add more information (more sentences) about each statement. Write the first draft quickly. Later add footnotes, bibliography, tables, and so on.
Revision	Go back over each draft, correcting and polishing it. Check not only spelling, punctuation, capitalization, word division, and other points of style, but look for poor sentence structure, awkward transitions from paragraph to paragraph, and other weaknesses. Consider whether the various ideas in the report are explained clearly and persuasively. Examine the draft for completeness and proper sequence of parts. Use the *Manuscript-Editing Checklist* in this chapter. (See also *Proofreading Symbols* and *Sample Page of Edited Manuscript* in this chapter.)
Manuscript preparation	Prepare the report double spaced with adequate margins and spacing around subheads. (See *Principal Parts in Different Styles of Reports*, *Report Title Page*, and *Report Table of Contents* in this chapter.) Follow the example of other prepared reports in your organization. Arrange for artwork, typesetting, and printing as needed. (See *Copyright Guidelines* in this chapter.)

OUTLINE NUMBERING PATTERNS

Example 1   I. Basic filing systems

    1. Alphabetical filing
       (a) Types of systems
          (1) Name file
          (2) Subject file
          (3) Combined name and subject file
          (4) Subject-duplex file

    2. Numerical filing
       (a) Types of systems
          (1) Consecutive-number file
          (2) Terminal-digit file
          (3) Coded-number file

Example 2   I. Basic filing systems
    1. Alphabetical filing
       A. Types of systems
          1. Name file
          2. Subject file
          3. Combined name and subject file
          4. Subject-duplex file

    2. Numerical filing
       A. Types of systems
          1. Consecutive-number file
          2. Terminal-digit file
          3. Coded-number file

Example 3   I. Basic filing systems
    A. Alphabetical filing
       1. Types of systems
          a. Name file
          b. Subject file
          c. Combined name and subject file
          d. Subject-duplex file

    B. Numerical filing
       1. Types of systems
          a. Consecutive-number file
          b. Terminal-digit file
          c. Coded-number file

Note: Organizations use a variety of number-letter patterns. Use the one preferred in your office. Regardless of which pattern you select, use it consistently throughout the report.

COMPARISON OF TOPIC AND SENTENCE OUTLINES

Topic Outline	Sentence Outline
I. Basic calendar styles	I. The three basic calendar styles are the wall, desk, and pocket calendars.
A. Essential calendars	A. A typical business office requires three calendars.
1. Secretary's calendar	1. The secretary often uses a standard desk calendar or a yearbook.
2. Executive's desk calendar	2. The executive also frequently uses a standard desk calendar or a yearbook
3. Executive's pocket calendar	3. In addition, the executive needs a small pocket memo calendar to carry outside the office.

Note: A topic outline is a useful blueprint for conducting research. Once the data are collected, a practical way to begin writing is to convert each word or phrase in the topic outline into a full sentence. See *Essential Steps in Report Preparation* (Drafting).

MANUSCRIPT-EDITING CHECKLIST

Frontmatter (title page, copyright page, etc.: complete? in proper order? proper layout of each page?)   ( )
Opening (appropriate? well written? leads reader into the body?)   ( )
Sections, subdivisions (logical? in proper order?)   ( )
Heads and subheads (effective? appropriate? consistent in style?)   ( )
Paragraphs (developed properly? smooth and effective transitions from one to another?)   ( )
Sentences (gramatically correct? well written? effective?)   ( )
Ending (appropriate? well written? brings reader to desired conclusion?) ( )
Footnotes, bibliography, other references (consistent and proper style? complete? positioned properly in manuscript?)   ( )
End matter (appendixes, index, etc.: complete? in proper order?)   ( )
Format (appropriate? consistent throughout?)   ( )
Illustrations (necessary to text discussion? proper format? accurate? positioned properly in manuscript?)   ( )

Grammar (correct? consistent?)   ( )
Spelling (correct? consistent?)   ( )
Punctuation (correct? consistent style throughout?)   ( )
Capitalization (correct? consistent style throughout?)   ( )
Word choice (correct? effective?)   ( )
Voice (active-passive; appropriate? effective?)   ( )
Conciseness (nonessential information deleted? wordiness deleted?)   ( )
Clichés (deleted?)   ( )
Irrelevancies (deleted?)   ( )
Clarity (complicated expressions simplified or clarified? points adequately   ( )
    developed and explained?)
Preciseness (vague words and expressions made specific? inclusive   ( )
    thoughts developed to the point?)
Pomposity (deleted?)   ( )
Vogue words (deleted or changed?)   ( )
Jargon (deleted or changed?)   ( )
Gobbledygook (deleted or changed?)   ( )
Euphemisms (deleted or changed?)   ( )
Prefixes, suffixes (correct? consistent style throughout?   ( )
Trite expressions (deleted or changed?)   ( )
Discriminatory expressions (deleted or changed?)   ( )
Other _____

Note: To use this checklist, examine your draft for completeness and correctness, and when you are satisfied that you have given attention to each item, check it off. Add as many items as you wish to your own list.

PROOFREADING SYMBOLS

∧ Make correction indicated in margin.

Stet Retain crossed-out word or letter; let it stand.

Stet Retain words under which dots appear; write "Stet" in margin.

X Appears battered; examine.

= Straighten lines.

✓✓✓ Unevenly spaced; correct spacing.

‖ Line up; i.e., make lines even with other matter.

run in Make no break in the reading; no paragraph.

no ¶ No paragraph; sometimes written "run in."

Out see copy Here is an omission; see copy.

¶ Make a paragraph here.

tr Transpose words or letters as indicated.

d Take out matter indicated; delete.

d Take out character indicated and close up.

ϕ Line drawn through a cap means lower case.

Ꝺ Upside down; reverse.

⊃ Close up; no space.

Insert a space here.

⊥ Push down this space.

□ Indent line one em.

⊏ Move this to the left.

⊐ Move this to the right.

⊓ Raise to proper position.

⊔ Lower to proper position.

/// Hair space letters.

wf. Wrong font; change to proper font.

Qu? Is this right?

lc Set in lower case (small letters).

sc Set in small capitals.

Caps Set in capitals.

c&sc Set in caps and small caps.

rom Change to roman.

ital Change to italic.

≡ Under letter or word means caps.

= Under letter or word means small caps.

— Under letter or word means italic.

∼∼∼ Under letter or word means boldface.

⋀ Insert comma.

⸮ Insert semicolon.

:/ Insert colon.

⊙ Insert period.

/?/ Insert interrogation mark.

/!/ Insert exclamation mark.

-/ Insert hyphen.

ⱽ Insert apostrophe.

˅˅ Insert quotation marks.

◡ Insert superior letter or figure.

∧ Insert inferior letter or figure.

[/] Insert brackets.

(/) Insert parentheses.

-/- One-em dash.

≠ Two-em parallel dash.

Ⓢ Spell out.

Source: From *Private Secretary's Encyclopedic Dictionary*, 3rd ed. rev. by Mary A. DeVries. © 1984 by Prentice-Hall, Inc. Published by Prentice-Hall, Inc., Englewood Cliffs NJ 07632.

SAMPLE PAGE OF UNEDITED MANUSCRIPT

Telephone Service

Though the office manager usually is responsible for looking into what's available in telepohne service at a low cost, the secretary must know how to use telephone service and equipemnt and sometimes how to select it. A communications consultant from your local telephone office is avialable when you call to give free adcvice about services and equpiment.

Telephone Conveneince Aids

Lors of arrangements can be arranged for meeting the particular requirements of the professional or business executive. Lots of available equipment and accessories makes possible a tialor-made service to fit the exact requirements at any location in your office.

Business Services

Many services are offered to subscribers:

1. WATS. Wide-area telephone service is designed for companies that make and receive many long-distsnce calls. Access lines to customers are connected to a nationwide dialing s network that may include intra-state and inter-state service.

2. Switching systems. Private-branch exchange (BBX) and computerized

SAMPLE PAGE OF EDITED MANUSCRIPT

Telephone Service

Though the office manager usually is responsible for ~~looking into what's~~ administering ~~available in~~ telephone service at ~~a low cost~~ minimum, the secretary must know how to use telephone service and equipment, and sometimes ~~how to~~ select it. A communications consultant from your local telephone office ~~is available~~ ~~when you call to~~ will give free advice about services and equipment.

Telephone Convenience Aids

~~Lots of~~ Many telephone arrangements ~~can be arranged~~ are available for meeting the particular requirements of the professional or business executive. ~~Lots~~ The wide assortment of available equipment and accessories makes possible a tailor-made service to fit the exact requirements at any location in your office.

Business Services

Many services are offered to subscribers:

1. WATS. Wide-area telephone service *(WATS)* is designed for companies that make and receive many long-distance calls. Access lines to customers are connected to a nationwide dialing network that may include intrastate and interstate service.

2. Switching systems. Private-branch exchange (PBX) and computerized

Note: See Proofreading Symbols on page 257.

SAMPLE OF CORRECTED PAGE OF PROOF

HOW TO CORRECT PROOF

It does not appear that the earliest printers had any method of correcting errors before the form was on the press. The learned learned correctors of the first two centuries of printing were not proofreaders in our sense, they were rather what we should term office editors. Their labors were chiefly to see that the proof corresponded to the copy, but that the printed page was correct in its latinity, that the words were there, and that the sense was right. They cared but little about orthography, bad letters, or purely printers' errors, and when the text seemed to them wrong they consulted fresh authorities or altered it on their own responsibility. Good proofs, in the modern sense, were impossible until professional readers were employed, men who had first a printer's education, and then spent many years in the correction of proof. The orthography of English, which for the past century has undergone little change, was very fluctuating until after the publication of Johnson's Dictionary, and capitals, which have been used with considerable regularity for the past 80 years, were previously used on the miss or hit plan. The approach to regularity, so far as we have, may be attributed to the growth of a class of professional proofreaders, and it is to them that we owe the correctness of modern printing. More errors have been found in the Bible than in any other one work. For many generations it was frequently the case that Bibles were brought out stealthily, from fear of governmental interference. They were frequently printed from imperfect texts, and were often modified to meet the views of those who publised them. The story is related that a certain woman in Germany, who was the wife of a Printer, and had become disgusted with the continual assertion of the superiority of man over woman which she had heard, hurried into the composing room while her husband was at supper and altered a sentence in the Bible, which he was printing, so that it read Narr instead of Herr, thus making the verse read "And he shall be thy fool" instead of "And he shall be thy lord." The word not was omitted by Barker, the King's printer in England in 1632, in printing the seventh commandment. He was fined £3,000 on this account.

Source: From *Private Secretary's Encyclopedic Dictionary*, 3rd ed., rev. by Mary A. DeVries. © 1984 by Prentice-Hall, Inc. Published by Prentice-Hall, Inc., Englewood Cliffs NJ 07632.

NOTES AND BIBLIOGRAPHY STYLE GUIDE

Footnotes	Bibliography Entries

1. Keith Marchant et al., *Selling Abroad*: *Case Studies* (New York: ABC Publishers, 1984), 602–3, 700–701, 711–14.

2. Mary Jones, "New Marketing Strategies," in *Introduction to Marketing*, ed. Harold Brown (Mountain Home, AR: College Press, 1981), 50–61.

3. Thomas Cole, Leon Berne, and Edna Cooper, *Selling Techniques in the Twentieth Century*, National Marketing Association, Executive Bulletin no. 170 (Washington, D.C., 1979), 12.

4. Editorial, *New York Times*, 16 August 1983.

5. Joanne Eckert, "Advertising and Sales Promotion," *Sales Journal* 5, no. 1 (April 1982): 41.

6. Adam Samuels, "Marketing Trends in Twelve SMSAs" (Ph.D. diss., XYZ University, 1972), 101–2.

7. Ibid.

8. Cole, Berne, and Cooper, *Selling Techniques*, 11.

9. Paul Michaels, ed., *U.S. Regional Markets*, vol. 12 of *Regional Markets in North and South America* (Boston, 1899), 219–441.

10. Samuels, "Marketing Trends," 101–2.

11. Michaels, *Regional Markets* 12:219–20.

Cole, Thomas, Leon Berne, and Edna Cooper. *Selling Techniques in the Twentieth Century*. National Marketing Association. Executive Bulletin no. 170. Washington, D.C., 1979.

Eckert, Joanne. "Advertising and Sales Promotion." *Sales Journal* 5, no. 1 (April 1982).

Editorial. *New York Times*. 16 August 1983.

Jones, Mary. "New Marketing Strategies." In *Introduction to Marketing*, edited by Harold Brown, Mountain Home, Ark.: College Press, 1981.

Marchant, Keith et al. *Selling Abroad*: *Case Studies*. New York: ABC Publishers, 1984.

Michaels, Paul, ed. *U.S. Regional Matters*. Vol. 12 of *Regional Markets in North and South America*. Boston, 1898.

Samuels, Adam. "Marketing Trends in Twelve SMSAs." Ph.D. diss., XYZ University, 1972.

Stokes, Lee, ed. and comp. *Coast-to-Coast Selling*. 4 vols. 1916. Reprint. San Francisco: Sales Publications, 1980.

Footnotes	Bibliography Entries

12. Lee Stokes, ed. and comp.,
Coast-to-Coast Selling (1916; reprint,
San Francisco: Sales Publications,
1980), 1:194–95.

Note: The examples shown here are suitable for nonscientific writing in which the footnotes are placed at the bottom of each page where cited in the text or collected after the text in a single section entitled "Notes." In all examples, *Inc.* and *Ltd.* are omitted from the publisher's names. In note 3, the association is the publisher, so the publisher's name is not repeated after the city. In note 1, New York City is so well known that the state abbreviation *N.Y.* is omitted. In note, 2, however, *Ark.* is added since Mountain Home is not well known, and in note 3, *D.C.* is added to avoid confusion with Washington State. In note 9, the work is so old that the publisher either is no longer known or reference is unnecessary. Data in the bibliography are similar, although the style differs. Bibliography entries are alphabetized at the end of the report or book, before the index. Facts in footnotes must always be consistent with facts in the bibliography.

PRINCIPAL PARTS OF TABLES

Part	Function
Table number	The table number is usually positioned above the table title, but it may precede the title on the same line. Each table should be numbered consecutively from beginning to end or, alternatively, may be numbered consecutively within each chapter in a large work, particularly if it is a multiauthor work (Table 1, Table 2, Table 3; Table 1.1, Table 1.2, Table 2.1, Table 2.2); appendix tables are usually numbered separately (A-1, A-2, and so on). Use either periods or hyphens when double numbers are used; the first number is the chapter and the second is the table number (7.6 is the sixth table in Chapter 7). Refer to *each* table in the text of the report (e.g., see Table 3.9).
Table title	The table title, immediately below the table number, is set above the body of the table. Keep the title as brief as possible and put comments and explanations in footnotes, not in the title. The title should serve only to identify the table. Subheads such as "In Thousands of

Part	Function
	Dollars'' should be placed in parentheses on a separate line immediately beneath the main title. Capitalize each main word in the title (*Fallow Land in the Midwest, 1980–84*).
Column heads	Heads are placed above the columns with main words capitalized (*Percentage of Workers*). The heading above the first column (see Stub, below) is usually singular; the other column heads may be plural. Column heads should be brief; subheads such as ''Millions'' and ''%'' are placed in parentheses at the end of the column head or on the first line below the column head. When more than one level of head is needed, the heads are called decked heads. (See *Table Format* in this chapter.)
Stub	The stub is the left-hand column in a table, the vertical list of items. Subheads under each item in the stub are usually indented two spaces. The word *Total* is usually indented two spaces more than the item above. Capitalize only the first word in each stub item (*Tool and die industry*).
Body	The table body consists of the columns (two or more) of information, which may be numbers or information expressed in words. Center short items; place long items flush left. Figures must be aligned at the decimal point. When the figures are the same type (e.g., all percentages), place the symbol (%) after only the top figure in each column.
Source note	The source note immediately follows the body of the table. It identifies the source of the data used in the table and gives proper copyright credit and permissions information in the case of copyrighted material.
Footnotes	Footnotes, which are placed below the source note, may be general and begin with the word *Note* or may refer to items in the body and use numbers, letters, or symbols (1, 2, 3; a, b, c; *, **, ***; and so on). Avoid using a footnote number, letter, or symbol with the table title. Use a general *Note* if you have a comment to make in regard to the title or the overall table.

Note: For the position of each item discussed here, refer to *Table Format* in this chapter.

TABLE FORMAT

Table 5.11

Freshman Enrollment in Four Courses,
Career Business School, 1981–84

Class	Enrollment (% of Total Class)			
	1981	1982	1983	1984
Typing	95%	96%	92%	98%
Shorthand	97	94	88	89
Secretarial Accounting	12[a]	35	54	60
Communications[b]	46	62	87	90

Source: Career Business School, *Teacher's Bulletin* 1 (December 1984): 6.

Note: The four business courses selected for comparison are required courses at the Career Business School in Dallas, Texas.

a. Only 12 percent of the freshman class enrolled in accounting in 1981 because previously this was a sophomore-level course, and a late offering to freshmen failed to capture the attention of many enrollees.

b. The significant increase in communications enrollment between 1981 and 1984 reflects the growing importance of communications in the business world.

STANDARD SIZES OF COMMON PRINTED MATERIAL

Item	Standard Sizes (Inches)
Books	5½ × 8½, 6⅛ × 9¼, 5 × 7⅜, 5⅜ × 8, 5½ × 8¼, 5⅝ × 8⅜
Broadsides	17 × 22, 19 × 25, 20 × 26, 23 × 35
Folders	3½ × 6¼, 4 × 9, 5½ × 8½, 6 × 9, 8½ × 11, 9 × 12
Forms	7 × 8½, 8½ × 11, 8½ × 14
Catalog sheets	8½ × 11, 11 × 17
Statements	5½ × 8½, 7 × 8½
Invoices	7 × 8½, 8½ × 11

Item	Standard Sizes (Inches)
Letterheads	$8\frac{1}{2} \times 11$, $7\frac{1}{4} \times 10\frac{1}{2}$, 6×9, $5\frac{1}{2} \times 8\frac{1}{2}$
Business cards	$2 \times 3\frac{1}{2}$, $3\frac{1}{2} \times 4$ (folder style)
Envelopes	Stationery: $4\frac{1}{8} \times 9\frac{1}{2}$ (no. 10), $3\frac{7}{8} \times 8\frac{7}{8}$ (no. 9), $3\frac{7}{8} \times 7\frac{1}{2}$ (no. 8), $3\frac{5}{8} \times 6\frac{1}{2}$ (no. $6\frac{3}{4}$), $3\frac{1}{2} \times 6$ (no. $6\frac{1}{4}$), $4\frac{5}{8} \times 5\frac{5}{16}$ (no. 5); catalog and booklet: 6×9, 7×10, $8\frac{3}{4} \times 11\frac{1}{4}$, 9×12, $9\frac{1}{2} \times 12\frac{1}{2}$, 10×13
Mailing address labels	3×5, 4×5

Note: Consult your printer for other sizes that may be available through local suppliers. See also *Stationery and Envelope Sizes and Applications* in Chapter 1.

ECONOMIES IN PRINTING

Item	Economies
Copy preparation	Prepare your manuscript clearly and neatly, double spaced, with adequate margins to facilitate type marking and measuring. If possible, avoid a complicated format that will require additional time and work in typesetting and printing; if such a format is necessary, be certain that it is clearly marked for typesetting and submit a layout with the manuscript copy (see Layout on page 266).
Editing	Make all possible editorial corrections and changes *before* submitting your manuscript to the typesetter or printer. If corrections and changes make the copy difficult to follow, retype the manuscript; otherwise, make all corrections neatly between the lines of type. Use the margins to write instructions (circle instructions and anything that is *not* to be typeset). (See *Sample Page of Edited Manuscript*, *Proofreading Symbols*, and *Manuscript Editing Checklist* in this chapter.)
Illustrations	Use illustrations that fit your budget. Most line art, for example, is less expensive than other art. In all cases, submit properly prepared artwork and photographs that

Item	Economies
	do not require unnecessary additional time and work by the printer's staff. For example, submit photographs already cropped (area you want to use marked off) and scaled (measured to be reduced or enlarged precisely to fit the allowable space in the final printed document). Camera-ready artwork is prepared for photographing without numerous additional steps at the printing establishment. Usually, it is less expensive to have an artist prepare camera-ready material than it is to have the various steps handled at the printing firm.
Layout	Provide a layout (an artist's concept of how the printed piece will look—that is, size, position, and so on of copy and illustrations; if you do not have an artist to do this for you, prepare your own rough drawing). Submit the layout with your manuscript and discuss it with the printer to be certain the design is easily achieved and within your budget.
Type specifications	With the help of your typesetter or printer, select readily available typefaces, including headlines, for the process the printer will be using (e.g., photocomposition). Consult a book of sample typefaces and sizes used by your printer and typemark your manuscript clearly before submitting it (write the proper typeface and size next to each headline and block of copy· 10/12 Times Roman, for example, refers to a particular style typeface in a 10-point size with a 2-point leading, or space between lines). Secure quotes on typesetting costs from two or three printers (or typesetters).
Proofs	Ask your printer for proofs of typeset material (*galley proofs* for material not yet divided into pages and *page proofs* for material set into pages) and printed material (depending on your printer, variously called press proofs, negative proofs, brownlines, and bluelines or blueprints; color-key proofs show color). Examine proofs carefully for correctness and completeness and mark any late corrections on the proof *before* the final documents are printed. (See *Sample Page of Corrected Proof* in this chapter.)
Paper	Ask your printer to help you select paper that comes in an appropriate (and standard) size, weight, and finish

Item	Economies
	for your job. Costs of different papers vary widely depending on the paper specifications (size, weight, and so on), characteristics (coated, pebble finish, and so on), the quantity needed, local-supplier availability, and other factors. For additional information, call a paper manufacturer and ask for samples of standard papers and economical papers, along with available sizes, weights, finishes, and so on.
Printing	Secure two or three free quotes on the printing project and discuss the appropriateness of each printer's press and capabilities for your project needs. Some presses may be too small for your job; some may not be suitable for the quality of reproduction you want. Explain your project in detail so that you will receive a fairly accurate quote from each firm.
Binding	Plan your binding needs in advance and explore the options: glue binding, side stitching, saddle stitching, perfect binding, plastic binding, and spiral binding. Ask your printer to explain the advantages and disadvantages as well as the costs for each type of binding. Large books and some magazines, for example, commonly use perfect binding. Smaller booklets are more often saddle stitched with staples on the back fold. Some books are side-stitched with staples before a cover is wrapped around the outside. Manuals are sometimes bound with a plastic or wire spiral at the side.
Mailing	The high cost of postage in large mailings makes it imperative that you consult your post office concerning the class of mailing (e.g., first, second, third, fourth class; book rate; bulk rate; and so on) and procedures for preparing the mail. (See the various tables pertaining to mailings and postal regulations in Chapter 2.) Also, discuss the cost of mailing envelopes and boxes with your printer (or an addressing and mailing firm) as well as the cost of mailing address labels. Ask for possible economies in using self-covers (label and postage applied directly on the cover) and inexpensive mailing wraps.

Note: An important key to overall economy is to plan your entire project in advance, meeting deadlines for all aspects of the work, and exploring with typesetters, printers, mailers, and others all possible shortcuts and economies that will not sacrifice the quality you desire.

COPYRIGHT GUIDELINES

Item	Guidelines
New law	A new copyright statute (Title 17 of the United States Code) became effective on January 1, 1978. All published and unpublished copyrightable works are now subject to a single system of statutory protection. The copyright owner has the exclusive right to reproduce an original work and to prepare derivative works. Registration of a work in the Library of Congress Copyright Office is not necessary for copyright protection, but it is necessary for bringing a court action in regard to infringement.
Early copyrights	The maximum total term of copyright protection for works already protected by federal statute is 75 years: a first term of 28 years plus a renewal term of 47 years. (Ask the Copyright Office for Circular R15 and renewal Form RE.)
Copyrights effective January 1, 1978, and after	The new law established a single copyright term with no renewal requirements. For works created on or after January 1, 1978, a basic life-plus-50 system (in effect in most other countries) applies. That is, protection applies for the life of the author(s) plus 50 years after death of the last surviving author. For works made for hire and anonymous or pseudonymous works, the protection applies for 75 years from publication or 100 years from creation, whichever is shorter.
Year-end expiration	All copyright terms will run through the end (December 31) of the calendar year in which they would otherwise expire. For works originally copyrighted between 1950 and 1977, the renewal period will run from December 31 of the twenty-seventh year of the copyright until December 31 of the following year.
Public domain	Works in the public domain are not protected under the new law. Also, copyright that has been lost on a work cannot be restored.
Copyright notice	A notice of copyright published in a printed work includes the letter *c* in a circle, the word *copyright* or the abbreviation *copr.*, the year of first publication of a work, and the name of the copyright owner: *Copyright © 1984 by Prentice-Hall, Inc.* A U.S. citizen whose work carries the proper notice also receives protection in other coun-

Item	Guidelines
	tries that are members of the Universal Copyright Convention.
Information and forms	Write to the Copyright Office, Library of Congress, Washington, D.C. 20559, for free forms (different forms are used for different types of works) and instructions on proper procedure for registering a work and the applicable fee to submit.

LIBRARY CLASSIFICATION SYSTEMS

Dewey Decimal System		Library of Congress System

	Dewey Decimal System	Library of Congress System
000.	General works	A. General works and polygraphy
100.	Philosophy	B. Philosophy and religion
200.	Religion	C. History and auxiliary sciences
300.	Sociology	D. History and topography outside the U.S.
400.	Philology	E. and F. American history and topography
500.	Natural science	
600.	Useful arts	G. Geography and anthropology
700.	Fine arts	H. Social sciences
800.	Literature	J. Political sciences
900.	History	K. Law
		L. Education
		M. Music
		N. Fine arts
		P. Language and literature
		Q. Science
		R. Medicine
		S. Agriculture and plant and animal husbandry
		T. Technology
		U. Military science
		V. Naval science
		Z. Library science and bibliography

Note: The ten Dewey Decimal categories are subdivided as needed (200, 210, 220; 220.1, 220.2, 220.3; and so on). The 20 Library of Congress categories are combined as needed (CB; LK; and so on), adding additional numbers and letters to indicate further subdivision of categories.

BASIC REFERENCE SOURCES

Category	Basic Sources
Directories and biographies	*American Medical Directory* (American Medical Association); *Congressional Record* (U.S. Government Printing Office); *Current Biography* (H. W. Wilson); *Directory of Corporations, Directors, and Executives* (Standard and Poor's Corp., McGraw-Hill); *The Federal Register* (U.S. Government Printing Office); *Gale's Encyclopedia of Associations*; *Hotel and Motel Red Book* (American Hotel Association Directory Corp.); *Martindale-Hubbell Law Directory*; *Million Dollar Directory* (Dun and Bradstreet); *N. W. Ayer & Son's Directory of Newspapers and Periodicals*; *National Directory of Addresses and Telephone Numbers* (Concord Reference Books); *Official Airline Guide*; *Official Guide of the Railways* (National Railway Publications Co.); *Patterson's American Education* (Educational Directories); *Poor's Register of Corporations, Directories, and Executives of the United States and Canada*; *Thomas' Register of American Manufacturers*; *Ulrich's International Periodicals Directory* (R. R. Bowker); *U. S. Government Manual* (U.S. Government Printing Office); *Webster's Biographical Dictionary*; various *Who's Who* (Marquis).
Encyclopedias and fact books	*Encyclopaedia Britannica*; *Encyclopedia Americana*; *New Columbia Encyclopedia*; *Van Nostrand's Scientific Encyclopedia*; *McGraw-Hill Encyclopedia of Science and Technology*; *Columbia Lippincott Gazetteer of the World*; *Information Please Almanac Atlas and Yearbook* (A & W Publishers); *Economic Almanac* (Conference Board); *Statistical Yearbook* (United Nations); *Statistical Abstract of the United States* (U.S. Government Printing Office); *Facts on File*.
Atlases	*Goode's World Atlas* (Rand McNally); *Ambassador World Atlas* (Hammond); *International World Atlas* (Hammond); *Rand McNally Road Atlas*; *North American Road Atlas* (American Automobile Association).
Dictionaries, word books. and quotation sources	*Webster's Third New International Dictionary*; *Webster's Ninth New Collegiate Dictionary*; *Roget's Thesaurus of Synonyms and Antonyms* (Putnam's); *Funk and Wag-*

Category	Basic Sources
	nall's Modern Guide to Synonyms and Related Words; *Webster's New World Thesaurus*; *Barlettt's Familiar Quotations* (Little, Brown).
Indexes	*Applied Science and Technology Index* (H. W. Wilson); *Biography Index* (H.W. Wilson); *Books in Print* (R. R. Bowker); *Business Books and Serials in Print* (R. R. Bowker); *Paperback Books in Print* (R. R. Bowker); *Business Periodicals Index* (H. W. Wilson); *Cumulative Book Index* (H. W. Wilson); *Monthly Catalog of U.S. Government Publications* (U.S. Government Printing Office); *New York Times Index*; Public Affairs Information Service; *Reader's Guide to Periodical Literature* (H. W. Wilson); *Wall Street Journal Index* (Dow Jones and Co.).
Business and financial publications	*Barron's, National Business and Financial Weekly*; *Business Week* (weekly); *Commercial and Financial Chronicle* (semiweekly); *The Conference Board Business Record* (monthly); *Consumer Reports* (monthly); *Current Industrial Reports* (quarterly or throughout the year); *Dun & Bradstreet Reference Book* (bimonthly); *Dun's Review and Modern Industry* (monthly); *Economic Indicators* (monthly); *Federal Reserve Bulletin* (monthly); *Fortune* (monthly); *Harvard Business Review* (monthly); *Monthly Labor Review*; Moody's Investor Service (e.g., *Bond Record, Manual of Investments, Industrial Manual, Handbook of Common Stocks*); *Nation's Business* (monthly); *The New York Times* (daily); *Prentice-Hall Federal Tax Guide* (annual); Standard and Poor's Corporation (e.g., *Standard Corporation Records, Standard and Poor's Trade and Securities Service*, and *Standard and Poor's Bond Guide*); *Survey of Current Business* (monthly); *Value Line* (loose-leaf service); *Wall Street Journal* (daily).

Note: The name of the publisher is given in parentheses when a work is not necessarily well known or when the name of the publisher is not evident in the title of the work. Always consult the latest edition of a work; many of the above works are available in a well-stocked public, academic, or specialized library reference room.

CHAPTER 7

Data Processing
and Finance

STANDARD SIGNS AND SYMBOLS

ARROWS

→ direction
↖ direction
↦ direction
↷ direction
↶ direction
← bold arrow
↻ open arrow
⇌ reversible reaction

BULLETS

● solid circle; bullet
● bold center dot
• movable accent

CIRCLED SYMBOLS

◐ angle in circle
⦵ circle with parallel rule
△ triangle in circle
⊙ dot in circle
⦶ dot in triangle in circle
⊕ cross in circle
® registered mark
© copyright
① Ceres
② Pallas
③ Juno
④ Vesta

COMPASS

° degree
⦂ degree with period
′ minute
⦁ minute with period
″ second
⦂ second with period
⦂ canceled second

SEX

♂ or ♂ male
□ male, in charts
♀ female
○ female, in charts
☿ hermaphrodite

SHAPES

◆ solid diamond
◇ open diamond
○ circle
▲ solid triangle
△ triangle
□ square
■ solid square
▱ parallelogram
▭ rectangle
▣ double rectangle
★ solid star
☆ open star
└ right angle
∠ angle
√ check
✔ check

MEASURE

℔ pound
ℨ dram
ƒℨ fluid dram
℥ ounce
ƒ℥ fluid ounce
O pint
£ pound sterling
$ dollar
¢ cents
& ampersand

MISCELLANEOUS

§ section
† dagger
‡ double dagger
℀ account of
℅ care of
⑭ score
¶ paragraph
þ Anglo-Saxon
℄ center line
♂ conjunction
⊥ perpendicular to
″ ditto
∝ variation
℞ recipe
⊐ move right
⊏ move left
○ or ⊙ or ① annual
⊙⊙ or ② biennial
∈ element of
℈ scruple
ƒ function
! exclamation mark
⊞ plus in square
♃ perennial
φ diameter
☍ opposition
ℇ mean value of c
U mathmodifier
⊂ mathmodifier
⊡ dot in square
△ dot in triangle
⊠ station mark
@ at

Source: *United States Government Printing Office Style Manual* (Washington, DC: U.S. Government Printing Office, 1984).

Note: See also *Diacritical Marks* and *Principal Marks of Punctuation* in Chapter 4.

MATHEMATICAL SIGNS AND SYMBOLS

— vinculum (above letters)
‡ geometrical proportion
−: difference, excess
‖ parallel
‖s parallels
≠ not parallels
| | absolute value
· multiplied by
: is to; ratio
÷ divided by
∴ therefore; hence
∵ because
:: proportion; as
≪ is dominated by
> greater than
⊏ greater than
≧ greater than or equal to
≧ greater than or equal to
≷ greater than or less than
≯ is not greater than
< less than
⊃ less than
≶ less than or greater than
≮ is not less than
< smaller than
≦ less than or equal to
≦ less than or equal to
≧ or ≥ greater than or equal to
≲ equal to or less than
≦ equal to or less than
≯ is not greater than equal to or less than

≷ equal to or greater than
≶ is not less than equal to or greater than
⊥ equilateral
⊥ perpendicular to
⊢ assertion sign
≜ approaches
≜ approaches a limit
≚ equal angles
≠ not equal to
≡ identical with
≢ not identical with
⑭⑭ score
≈ or ≑ nearly equal to
═ equal to
~ difference
≃ perspective to
≅ congruent to approximately equal
≏ difference between
♢ equivalent to
(included in
) excluded from
⊂ is contained in
∪ logical sum or union
∩ logical product or intersection
√ radical
√ root
∛ square root
∛ cube root
∜ fourth root
/ virgule; solidus; separatrix; shilling
± plus or minus
∓ minus or plus

∜ fifth root
∜ sixth root
π pi
e base (2.718) of natural system of logarithms; epsilon
ε is a member of; dielectric constant; mean error; epsilon
+ plus
+ bold plus
− minus
− bold minus
× multiplied by
≡ bold equal
number
℔ per
% percent
∫ integral
| single bond
\ single bond
/ single bond
‖ double bond
\\ double bond
⫽ double bond
⬡ benzene ring
∂ or δ differential; variation
∂ Italian differential
→ approaches limit of
~ cycle sine
⌐ horizontal integral
∮ contour integral
∝ variation; varies as
Π product
Σ summation of; sum; sigma
! or ⌐ factorial product

Source: *United States Government Printing Office Style Manual* (Washington, DC: U.S. Government Printing Office, 1984).

Note: See also *Diacritical Marks* and *Principal Marks of Punctuation* in Chapter 4. See also other tables and lists in this chapter.

PROGRAM FLOWCHARTING SYMBOLS

Processing. Group of program instructions that perform a processing function within a program

Input/output. Any function of an input/output device that makes information available for processing, recording, processing information, tape positioning, and so on

Decision. Used to document points in a program where a branch to alternate paths is possible based on variable conditions

Program modification. Instruction(s) that change the sequence of a program

Predefined process. Process, or groups of operations, not specified elsewhere

Terminal. Beginning, end, or point of interruption in a program

Connector. Entry from or exit to another part of the program flowchart

Off-page connector. Used to designate entry to or exit from a page

Flow direction. Direction of processing or data flow

Annotation. Addition of descriptive comments or explanatory notes.

Note: A *program flowchart* is a diagram that describes a computer program in a series of steps.

SYSTEM FLOWCHARTING SYMBOLS

Punched card. Punched cards including stubs

Perforated (punched) tape. Paper or plastic, chad or chadless

Document. Paper documents and reports

Magnetic tape.

Transmittal tape. Proof or adding machine tape or other batch-control information

Off-line storage. Of either paper, cards, or magnetic or punched tape

On-line storage. For example, drum or disk storage

Display. Information displayed by plotter or video

Manual input. Information supplied to or by a computer using an on-line device, for example, a keyboard

Sorting and collating. Operation using sorting or collating equipment

Clerical or manual operation. Off-line operation not requiring mechanical assistance

Auxiliary operation. Machine operation supplementing main processing function

Keying operation. Operation using a key-driven device

Communication link. Automatic transmission of information from one location to another via communications lines

Note: A *system flowchart* is a diagram that shows the relationships among events in a data-processing system and describes the flow of data through the system.

EDP OPERATIONS DIAGRAM

EDP OPERATIONS DIAGRAM

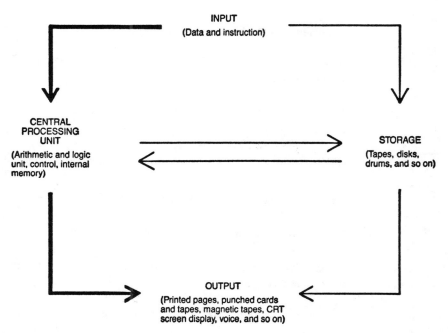

Note: EDP = Electronic data processing.

BINARY-CODED DECIMAL SYSTEM

Decimal Code	Binary Code
0	0000
1	0001
2	0010
3	0011

Decimal Code	Binary Code
4	0100
5	0101
6	0110
7	0111
8	1000
9	1001
10	0001 0000

Note: A *binary code*, or *binary notation*, is a system for representing all information by binary digits. A *binary digit* (the form of information used by digital computers) is either 1 or 0. In a *binary-coded decimal system*, each decimal digit (see 0 to 10, above) is represented by the corresponding binary digits. For example, the year 1985 (numbers 1, 9, 8, and 5 on the decimal scale) written in binary code would be 0001 1001 1000 0101.

COMMON COMPUTER LANGUAGES

ADA	A high-level programming language adopted by the U.S. government as a common language for all computers but also used for nongovernmental systems.
ALGOL	Algorithmic Oriented Language. A high-level programming language used primarily for mathematical and scientific applications.
APL	A Programming Language. A high-level programming language designed for use on computers with large memory banks and suitable for use at remote conversational terminals, often used in solving statistical problems.
APT	Automatically Programmed Tools. A programming language designed for use on numerically controlled machine tools.
BASIC	Beginner's All-purpose Symbolic Instruction Code. A high-level programming language noted for being easy to use and learn, often used on microcomputers.
COBOL	Common Business Oriented Language. A high-level programming language used primarily in business data processing.

FORTRAN	Formula Translator. A high-level language designed primarily for scientific, mathematical, and engineering applications.
INFRAL	Information Retrieval Automatic Language. A computer language designed to prepare bibliographies from indexed data.
PASCAL	A high-level computer language based on ALGOL, used primarily in systems programming.
PL/1	Programming Language/1. A high-level programming language used in business and scientific applications.
QUICKTRAN	Quick FORTRAN. A high-level programming language used in the conversational mode on time-sharing systems.
RECOL	Retrieval Command Language. A computer language used to search databases.

Note: *High-level languages* are those that use instructions closely resembling familiar language, rather than machine code.

BASIC DATA-PROCESSING PROCEDURES

Stage	Process
Data origin	Business information to be processed comes from a variety of sources—cards, forms, and so on—where it is initially recorded.
Classification	Recorded information must be classified according to some logical method—alphabetical, numerical, alphanumerical—that enables one to group data by category.
Sorting	Once information is classified, it can be organized in categories according to one or more identifiable characteristics such as sales volume, credit rating, and geographic location.
Input	Information to be processed electronically must be converted to a form that the machine can accept and act upon. Most data are input into business computers by keyboard or by punched cards and tapes or magnetic tape. Information to be processed manually may need to be transferred to some record book or log such as a payroll journal.

Processing	Data that have been fed into a computer or recorded manually in some log is processed by performing calculations (adding, subtracting, dividing, multiplying) or by further classifying and summarizing it. The steps of calculating, further classifying, summarizing, and so on may be performed electronically or manually, with the assistance of various office machines such as a calculator.
Storage	Information that is not required immediately may be stored in the memory of a computer or, manually, in a log or file.
Output	Processed information, which has been arranged in the required manner, may be output electronically on a display screen, printed page, or punched card or tape (which requires a further step for final, readable copy). Processed data may be prepared manually by typewriter or some other manual process.

Note: Data to be useful must be processed (i.e., handled or converted into a more meaningful form). A letter, for example, may be opened, read, answered, and mailed, using various office machines and devices with substantial human involvement in each step. A payroll, on the other hand, may be processed almost totally by computer, with minimal human involvement in many of the steps. Either way, the basic data-processing stages listed above must be followed.

COMMON TERMS FOR MATHEMATICAL SYMBOLS

Symbol	Technical Term	Common Term
/	rising diagonal	slash; slant line
\	falling diagonal	back slash
//	parallel rising diagonal	double slash; double slant line
\\	parallel falling diagonal	double back slash
|	single bond	bar
||	parallel; double bond	double bar
·	multiplied by	centered dot
<	less than	less

Symbol	Technical Term	Common Term
>	greater than	greater
≦	less than or equal to	less equal
≧	greater than or equal to	greater equal
~	difference	wiggle
≈	nearly equal to	double wiggle
U	union sign	cup
∩	intersection sign	hat
Σ	summation of	sum
ε	is an element of	member
[	bracket	brack
]	end (or close) bracket	end (or close) bracket
{	brace	brace
}	end (or close) brace	end (or close) brace

MULTIPLICATION SHORTCUTS

To Multiply by	Add	And Divide by
1¼	0	8
1⅔	0	6
2½	0	4
3⅓	0	3
5	0	2
6¼	00	16
6⅔	00	15
8⅓	00	12
12½	00	8
14²⁄₇	00	7
16⅔	00	6
25	00	4

To Multiply by	Add	And Divide by
31¼	000	32
33⅓	00	3
50	00	2
66⅔	000	15
83⅓	000	12
125	000	8
166⅔	000	6
250	000	4
333⅓	000	3

Source: From *Private Secretary's Encyclopedic Dictionary*, 3rd ed., rev. by Mary A. De Vries. © 1984 by Prentice-Hall, Inc. Published by Prentice-Hall, Inc., Englewood Cliffs NJ 07632.

Note: This table can be used to shorten the multiplication process in certain cases. For example, to multiply 17 by 8⅓, add 00 to 17 (1700) and divide 1700 by 12: 1700 ÷ 12 = 141.67.

DIVISION SHORTCUTS

To Divide by	Multiply by	And Divide by
1¼	8	10
1⅔	6	10
2½	4	10
3⅓	3	10
3¾	8	30
6¼	16	100
7½	4	30
8⅓	12	100
9¹⁄₁₁	11	100
11⅑	9	100
12½	8	100
14²⁄₇	7	100
16⅔	6	100
25	4	100
31¼	16	500
33⅓	3	100
75	4	300

To Divide by	Multiply by	And Divide by
125	8	1,000
175	4	700
275	4	1,100
375	8	3,000
625	8	5,000
875	8	7,000

Source: From *Private Secretary's Encyclopedic Dictionary*, 3rd ed., rev. by Mary A. De Vries. © 1984 by Prentice-Hall, Inc. Published by Prentice-Hall, Inc., Englewood Cliffs NJ 07632.

Note: This table can be used to shorten the division process in certain cases. For example, to divide 12 by 3¾, multiply 12 by 8 (96) and divide 96 by 30 = 3.2. Hence 12 ÷ 3¾ = 3.2.

ARABIC AND ROMAN NUMERALS

I	1	XV	15	CC	200
II	2	XVI	16	CCC	300
III	3	XVII	17	CD	400
IV	4	XVIII	18	D	500
V	5	XIX	19	DC	600
VI	6	XX	20	DCC	700
VII	7	XXX	30	DCCC	800
VIII	8	XL	40	CM	900
IX	9	L	50	M	1,000
X	10	LX	60	MM	2,000
XI	11	LXX	70	MMM	3,000
XII	12	LXXX	80	M$\overline{\text{V}}$	4,000
XIII	13	XC	90	$\overline{\text{V}}$	5,000
XIV	14	C	100		

GENERAL RULES

1. Repeating a letter repeats its value: CC = 200; CCC = 300.
2. A letter placed after one of greater value adds thereto: XI = 11; DC = 600.

3. A letter placed before one of greater value subtracts therefrom: IX = 9; CM = 900.
4. A dash line over a numeral multiplies the value by 1,000: $\overline{X}$ = 10,000; $\overline{L}$ = 50,000; $\overline{C}$ = 100,000; $\overline{D}$ = 500,000; $\overline{M}$ = 1,000,000.

DECIMAL EQUIVALENTS OF FRACTIONS

Fraction	Decimal Equivalent	Fraction	Decimal Equivalent	Fraction	Decimal Equivalent	Fraction	Decimal Equivalent
1/2	0.5000	1/9	0.1111	1/16	0.0625	1/50	0.0200
1/3	0.3333	1/10	0.1000	1/17	0.0588	1/60	0.0167
1/4	0.2500	1/11	0.0909	1/18	0.0556	1/70	0.0143
1/5	0.2000	1/12	0.0833	1/19	0.0526	1/80	0.0125
1/6	0.1667	1/13	0.0769	1/20	0.0500	1/90	0.0111
1/7	0.1429	1/14	0.0714	1/30	0.0333	1/100	0.0100
1/8	0.1250	1/15	0.0667	1/40	0.0250		

TABLE OF LARGE NUMBERS

Denomination	Number of Zeros
Million	6
Billion	9
Trillion	12
Quadrillion	15
Quintillion	18
Sextillion	21
Septillion	24
Octillion	27
Nonillion	30
Decillion	33

Note: In general writing, the zeros are not written for very large numbers. For example, 4,000,000,000,000 would be written as 4 trillion.

SIMPLE INTEREST TABLE

INTEREST ON $100 AT VARIOUS RATES FOR VARIOUS PERIODS

Days	5%	6%	7%	8%	9%	10%	11%	12%
1	0.0139	0.0167	0.0194	0.0222	0.0250	0.0278	0.0306	0.0333
2	.0278	.0333	.0389	.0444	.0500	.0556	.0611	.0667
3	.0417	.0500	.0583	.0667	.0750	.0833	.0917	.1000
4	.0556	.0667	.0778	.0889	.1000	.1111	.1222	.1333
5	.0694	.0833	.0972	.1111	.1250	.1389	.1528	.1667
6	.0833	.1000	.1167	.1333	.1500	.1667	.1833	.2000
7	.0972	.1167	.1361	.1556	.1750	.1945	.2139	.2333
8	.1111	.1333	.1556	.1778	.2000	.2222	.2445	.2667
9	.1250	.1500	.1750	.2000	.2250	.2500	.2750	.3000
10	.1389	.1667	.1944	.2222	.2500	.2778	.3056	.3333
20	.2778	.3333	.3889	.4444	.5000	.5556	.6111	.6667
30	.4167	.5000	.5833	.6667	.7500	.8333	.9167	1.0000
40	.5556	.6667	.7778	.8889	1.0000	1.1111	1.2222	1.3333
50	.6945	.8334	.9722	1.1111	1.2500	1.3889	1.5278	1.6667
60	.8333	1.0000	1.1667	1.3333	1.5000	1.6667	1.8334	2.0000
70	.9722	1.1667	1.3611	1.5555	1.7500	1.9445	2.1389	2.3333
80	1.1111	1.3334	1.5555	1.7778	2.0000	2.2222	2.4445	2.6666
90	1.2500	1.5000	1.7500	2.0000	2.2500	2.5000	2.7500	3.0000
100	1.3889	1.6667	1.9444	2.2222	2.5000	2.7778	3.0556	3.3333

Days	13%	14%	15%	16%	17%	18%	19%	20%
1	0.0361	0.0388	0.0417	0.0444	0.0472	0.0501	0.0528	0.0556
2	.0722	.0778	.0834	.0888	.0944	.0999	.1056	.1112
3	.1083	.1166	.1251	.1332	.1417	.1500	.1583	.1668
4	.1445	.1556	.1668	.1776	.1889	.2001	.2111	.2224
5	.1805	.1944	.2082	.2224	.2361	.2499	.2639	.2776
6	.2167	.2334	.2499	.2668	.2833	.3000	.3167	.3332
7	.2528	.2722	.2916	.3112	.3306	.3501	.3695	.3888
8	.2889	.3112	.3333	.3556	.3778	.3999	.4222	.4444
9	.3250	.3500	.3750	.4000	.4250	.4500	.4750	.5000
10	.3611	.3888	.4167	.4444	.4722	.5001	.5278	.5556
20	.7222	.7778	.8334	.8888	.9444	.9999	1.0658	1.1112
30	1.0833	1.1666	1.2501	1.3334	1.4167	1.5000	1.5833	1.6668
40	1.4445	1.5556	1.6668	1.7778	1.8889	2.0001	2.1111	2.2224
50	1.8056	1.9444	2.0835	2.2222	2.3611	2.5002	2.6389	2.7780
60	2.1667	2.3334	2.4999	2.6666	2.8333	3.0000	3.1667	3.3332
70	2.5278	2.7222	2.9166	3.1110	3.3055	3.5001	3.6945	3.8888
80	2.8889	3.1110	3.3333	3.5556	3.7778	4.0002	4.2222	4.4444
90	3.2500	3.5000	3.7500	4.0000	4.2500	4.5000	4.7500	5.0000
100	3.6111	3.8888	4.1667	4.4444	4.7222	5.0001	5.2778	5.5556

EXACT NUMBER OF DAYS BETWEEN DATES

From Any Day
of   To the Same Day of the Next

	Jan.	Feb.	Mar.	Apr.	May	June	July	Aug.	Sept.	Oct.	Nov.	Dec.
January	365	31	59	90	120	151	181	212	243	273	304	334
February	334	365	28	59	89	120	150	181	212	242	273	303
March	306	337	365	31	61	92	122	153	184	214	245	275
April	275	306	334	365	30	61	91	122	153	183	214	244
May	245	276	304	335	365	31	61	92	123	153	184	214
June	214	245	273	304	334	365	30	61	92	122	153	183
July	184	215	243	274	304	335	365	31	62	92	123	153
August	153	184	212	243	273	304	334	365	31	61	92	122
September . . .	122	153	181	212	242	273	303	334	365	30	61	91
October	92	123	151	182	212	243	273	304	335	365	31	61
November . . .	61	92	120	151	181	212	243	273	304	334	365	30
December . . .	31	62	90	121	151	182	212	243	274	304	335	365

6 PERCENT/60-DAY INTEREST COMPUTATION

Interest on $1.00

360 days = $0.06
  60 days = $0.01 (1/6 of $0.06)
    6 days = $0.001 (1/10 of $0.01)

Procedure

6 days: for any principal (e.g., $1,460.00) at 6 percent, move the decimal point three places to the left ($1.46 interest).

60 days: move the decimal point two places to the left ($14.60 interest).

600 days: move the decimal point one place to the left ($146.00 interest).

6,000 days: interest = principal.

Examples

To compute ordinary interest on $1,460.00 for 20 days at 6 percent (20 days is one-third of 60 days):

Interest for 60 days = $14.60
Interest for 20 days = $14.60 ÷ 3 = $4.87

To compute ordinary interest on $1,460.00 for 140 days at 6 percent (140 days is 60 + 60 + 20 days):

Interest for 120 days = $14.60 × 2 = $29.20
Interest for   20 days = $14.60 ÷ 3 =   4.87
                                      $34.07

To compute ordinary interest on $1,460.00 for 60 days at 10 percent (10 percent is 6 percent + ⅔ of 6 percent):

Interest for 60 days at 6 percent = $14.60
Interest for 60 days at 4 percent
(or 2/3 of 6 percent)   = $ 9.73
                                     $24.33

Note: The 6 percent/60-day method of computation can be used for various periods simply by using a combination of days as shown in the above example for 140 days. The method can also be used for other percentage rates by using a combination of rates as shown in the above example for 10 percent interest.

DISCOUNT TABLE

Common Trade Discounts	Net Dollar Cost ($1.00)
2½%	$0.98
10	0.90
10/2½	0.88
10/5	0.86
10/5/2½	0.83
15	0.85
20	0.80
20/10	0.72

Common Trade Discounts	Net Dollar Cost ($1.00)
20/10/5	0.68
33⅓	0.67

Note: This table shows the net cost of $1.00 after deducting the trade discount. To determine the net cost of an amount other than $1.00, simply multiply the net cost shown in this table by the actual amount. For example, if you want to know the net cost of a $50 item discounted 20 percent, multiply $0.80 by 50 (50 × 0.80 = $40.00).

The successive numbers in the first column (20/10/5) refer to a series of two or more discounts. For example, 20/10/5 means that 20 percent is first deducted from the list price, then 10 percent from the remainder, and finally, 5 percent from the second remainder.

PRINCIPAL BANKING SERVICES

Service	Features
Savings plans	*Passbook savings* usually can be opened for as little money as one chooses, and funds may be withdrawn at any time. Savings are compounded at various periods, depending on bank policy, for example, daily or quarterly. Interest on a passbook account is usually less than it is on other forms of savings such as certificates of deposit. With this type of account customers receive a small booklet in which deposits and withdrawals and interest are recorded. A *statement account* is essentially the same thing, except that deposits, withdrawals, and interest are reported on a monthly statement instead of in a passbook.
	Certificates of deposit, or *CDs*, are purchased for various periods and in various amounts, for example, $100 or more redeemable in 30 months and $1,000 or more redeemable in 96 months. A penalty is imposed when a CD is cashed in early. Interest rates are typically highest on the CDs held for the longest periods.

Service	Features

Money-market certificates are designed to give short-term investors higher rates of interest competitive with rates in the open market. They are issued in various amounts, often multiples of $1,000, for various periods, for example, $10,000 redeemable in 26 weeks.

Savings bonds in various denominations, issued by corporations and governments, may be purchased from banks. These bonds promise to pay a specified sum on a specific future date at a fixed rate of interest. This interest may be paid periodically or may accumulate until redemption of the bond.

Christmas club and vacation club savings refer to an account one may establish to hold deposits throughout the year or for a certain period for use later in Christmas shopping or in traveling. Some banks will transfer funds automatically from another account to one of the various savings clubs.

Individual retirement account, or *IRA*, refers to a type of savings for retirement. These accounts may be opened by anyone with a minimum deposit, and annual deposits may be made up to $2,000 a year ($2,250 if a spouse without earned income is included). Earnings on deposits are nontaxable until the money is withdrawn. Also, taxes are not paid on any money deposited in an IRA until that money is withdrawn. IRA funds may not be withdrawn early without penalty, and they may not be used as collateral in securing a loan. See also *Checking accounts*, Interest checking.

Checking accounts

Regular checking refers to a bank's standard checking account, with or without a minimum-balance requirement and with or without a service charge. Customers receive personalized checks containing their account numbers and a monthly statement reporting deposits, withdrawals, charges, and so on.

Pay-as-you-go accounts, for customers who write very few checks, impose a charge for each check written. Customers receive a monthly statement reporting deposits, withdrawals, and so on, the same as regular-checking customers.

Service	Features
	Commercial checking refers to the account established for a business. Some banks handle payrolls and other matters by computer for business customers in conjunction with their checking accounts. Customers receive the traditional monthly statement as do users of other accounts.
	Interest checking refers to a checking account that pays interest on funds left in the account. In almost every other respect it resembles a regular checking account. Some of these accounts are called *NOW accounts* (negotiable order of withdrawal). Customers receive a monthly statement as do users of other accounts.
	See also *Loans*, Instant loan service.
Loans	*Secured loans* are granted when a customer can provide collateral in the form of property of value to cover the amount of the loan. A car loan, for example, is secured by the car itself, which could be repossessed. A mortgage is secured by the property for which the loan was obtained.
	Unsecured loans may be granted if a borrower's credit rating is good and the bank is willing to risk its money on a customer's signature, without collateral to claim should the customer default.
	Instant loan service usually refers to a line of credit provided by a bank in conjunction with a customer's checking account. Borrowers may write checks above the amount in their accounts up to an established credit limit. Such loans are typically repaid monthly, often at a high rate of interest, much the same as with a revolving charge account.
Automatic deposit, transfer, and deduction	Banks permit individuals and businesses to deposit, transfer, and deduct funds automatically from a customer's checking account. For instance, federal payments such as Social Security checks may be deposited automatically to a customer's account; a specified amount may be transferred each month from a checking account to a savings account; and an insurance company's medical-insurance payment may be deducted automatically from a customer's account. Such transfers and deductions may be reported

Service	Features
	to the customer by a separate statement or on the regular monthly bank statement.
Night depository	Banks usually have a safeguarded depository on the outside of the building where deposits can be left at nonbanking hours. Such deposits are credited to the customer's account and appear on the regular monthly bank statement.
Driveup banking	Both main offices and branches of banks frequently have one or several windows or machines where motorists may stop in their cars and conduct transactions without entering the facility itself.
Bank by mail	Most banks provide mailers (an envelope and form) for customers to use in mailing deposits to the bank. The customer then receives a deposit slip by return mail, and the deposit is recorded in the usual manner at the bank.
24-hour banking	By use of automatic banking machines on the outside of the bank, customers can make deposits, cash checks, make transfers, and so on 24 hours a day. Usually, a plastic card with a personal code is issued for insertion in the machine to activate it. Transactions are automatically recorded and appear on the customer's monthly bank statement.
Safe deposit boxes	Main offices and some branches provide maximum-security safe deposit boxes and vaults for customers at an annual rental charge. Customers may open their box during banking hours. Since the box may not leave the premises, the bank provides private vault anterooms and customer conference rooms for customers to use in reviewing their box contents.
Branch offices	Many banks have one or more branches in convenient locations to broaden their geographic coverage. Customers may then conduct transactions at the main facility or at any of its branches.
Computer services	Large banks and some smaller ones have modern electronic data-processing systems to provide a variety of record-keeping and bookkeeping services for customers: payroll processing, inventory control, and so on. The service may include numerous related features such as microfilm storage of customer documents and data-research activities.

Service	Features
Traveler's checks	Available in various denominations such as $10, $20, $50, and $100, traveler's checks are as good as cash worldwide but are insured against theft, mutilation, loss, and forgery. Customers may purchase as many checks as they wish for a small charge.
Cashier's checks and money orders	*Cashier's check* refers to a check drawn by a bank against itself and issued to borrowers instead of actual cash (currency) or instead of crediting the borrower's account. Customers sometimes purchase cashier's checks to make payments when a creditor will not accept the customer's personal check.
	Bank money order also refers to an order drawn by a bank against itself. Money orders may be purchased by customers the same as cashier's checks to make payments when they do not want to use, or may not use, their own personal checks.
Charge cards	Major card companies such as Mastercard, Visa, and American Express provide accounts through participating banks. Applications may be made through the bank, and monthly bills and statements are issued through the bank.
Car, hotel, and entertainment reservations and rentals	Many banks, particularly large facilities, provide a reservation and rental service for businesses and individuals. Some banks offer a discount service for customers who use a particular car-rental agency or hotel. Tickets to certain sports and civic events can also be purchased through many banks.
Insurance	In cooperation with a designated insurance company, banks may offer accidental death and other types of insurance coverage. Insurance covering accounts such as a loan account may be arranged through many banks.
Notary public	Main bank offices and some branches commonly offer customers free use of a notary public for any type of document that must be notarized.

FOREIGN-MONEY TABLE

Country or area	Basic monetary unit		Principal fractional unit	
	Name	Symbol	Name	Abbreviation or symbol
Afghanistan	Afghani	Af	Pul	
Albania	Lek	L	Quintar	
Algeria	Dinar	DA	Centime	
Andorra	French franc	Fr. F	French centime	
	Spanish peseta	Sp. Ptas.[1]	Spanish centimo	
Angola	Kwanza	Kz	Lwei	
Antigua and Barbuda	Dollar	EC$	Cent	
Argentina	Peso	M$N	Centavo	Ctvo.
Australia	Dollar	A$	Cent	
Austria	Schilling	S	Groschen	
Bahamas, The	Dollar	B$	Cent	
Bahrain	Dinar	BD	Fil	
Bangladesh	Taka	Tk	Paise	
Barbadoes	Dollar	Bds$	Cent	
Belgium	Franc	BF	Centime	
Belize	Dollar	$B	Cent	
Benin	Franc	CFAF	Centime	
Bermuda	Dollar	$B	Cent	
Bhutan	Ngultruns	N	Tikchung	
Bolivia	Peso Boliviana	$b	Centavo	Ctvo.
Botswana	Pula	P	Thebe	
Brazil	New cruzeiro	NCr$	Centavo	Ctvo.
Brunei	Dollar	B$	Cent	
Bulgaria	Lev	L	Stotinka	
Burma	Kyat	K	Pya	
Burundi	Franc	FBu	Centime	
Cameroon	Franc	CFAF	....do	
Canada	Dollar	$ or Can$	Cent	C, ct.
Cape Verde	Escudo	C.V. Esc	Centavo	
Central African Republic	Franc	CFAF	Centime	
Chad	Franc	CFAF	....do	
Chile	Peso	Ch$	Centavo	
China	Yuan	¥	Fen	
Colombia	Peso	Col$	Centavo	Ctvo.
Comoros	Franc	CFAF	Centime	
Congo	....do	CFAF	....do	
Cook Islands	New Zealand dollar	NZ$	Cent	
Costa Rica	Colon	¢	Centimo	Ctmo.
Cuba	Peso	$	Centavo	Ctvo.
Cyprus	Pound	£ or £C	Mil	
Czechoslovakia	Koruna	Kcs	Haler	
Dahomey	Franc	CFAF	Centime	
Denmark	Krone	DKr	Øre	
Djibouti	Franc	DF	Centime	
Dominica	Dollar	EC$	Cent	
Dominican Republic	Peso	RD$	Centavo	Ctvo.
Ecuador	Sucre	S/	....do	Ctvo.
Egypt	Pound	£E	Piaster	
El Salvador	Colon	¢	Centavo	Ctvo.
Equatorial Guinea	Ekuele	EK	Centimo	
Estonia	Ruble	—	Kopek	
Ethiopia	Birr	EB	Cent	
Falkland Islands	Pound	£	Shilling	
Faroe Islands	Danish krone	DKr	Øre	
Fiji	Dollar	$F	Cent	
Finland	Finnmark	Fimr	Penni	Pia.
France	Franc	F	Centime	
French Guiana	....do	F	....do	
French Polynesia	....do	CFPF	....do	
Gabon	....do	CFAF	....do	

Country or area	Basic monetary unit		Principal fractional unit	
	Name	Symbol	Name	Abbreviation or symbol
Gambia, The	Dalasi	DD	Butut	
German Democratic Republic.	Mark	DME	Pfennig	Pf.
Ghana	Cedi	₵	Pesewa	P.
Gibraltar	Pound	£	Shilling	
Greece	Drachma	Dr.	Lepton	
Greenland	Danish krone	DKr	Øre	
Grenada	Dollar	EC$	Cent	
Guadeloupe	Franc	F	Centime	
Guatamala	Quetzal	Q	Centavo	Ctvo.
Guinea	Syli	GS	Cauri	
Guyana	Dollar	G$	Cent	
Haiti	Gourde	G	Centime	
Honduras	Lempira	L	Centavo	Ctvo.
Hong Kong	Dollar	HK$	Cent	
Hungary	Forint	Ft	Filler	
Iceland	Krona	IKr	Eyrir	
Indonesia	Rupiah	Rp	Sen	
Iran	Rial	Rls²	Dinar	
Iraq	Dinar	ID	Fil	
Ireland	Pound	£ or £Ir	Shilling	S., d.,
Israel	Shekel	I£	Agrirot	
Italy	Lira	Lit	Centesimo	Ctmo.
Ivory Coast	Franc	CFAF	Centime	
Jamaica	Dollar	J$	Cent	
Japan	Yen:e1	¥	Sen	
Jordan	Dinar	JD	Fil	
Kampuchea	Riel	KR	————	
Kenya	Shilling	K Sh	Cent	
Kiribati	Australian dollar	A$	...do	
Korea	Chon	W	Chun	
Kuwait	Dinar	KD	Fil	
Laos	Kip	K	At	
Latvia	Ruble	R	Kopek	
Lebanon	Pound	LL	Piaster	
Lesotho	Rand	R	Cent	
Liberia	Dollar	$	...do	
Libya	Dinar	LD	Milleme	
Liechtenstein	Swiss franc	Sw F	Centime	
Lithuania	Ruble	R	Kopek	
Luxembourg	Franc	Lux F	Centime	
Macao	Pataca	P	Avo	
Madagascar	Franc	FMG	Centime	
Malawi	Kwacha	K	Tambal	
Malaysia	Ringgits	M$	Sen	
Maldives	Rupee	Mal Re	Lari	
Mali	Franc	MF	————	
Malta	Pound	£M	Cent	
Martinique	Franc	F	Centime	
Mauritania	Ouguiya	UM	Khoum	
Mauritius	Rupee	Mau Rs³	Cent	
Mexico	Peso	Mex$	Centavo	Ctvo.
Monaco	French franc	Fr	Centime	
Mongolia	Tugrik	Tug	Möngö	
Montserrat	Dollar	EC$	Cent	
Morocco	Dirham	DH	Centime	
Mozambique	Escudo	M. Esc.	Centavo	
Nauru	Australian dollar	$A	Cent	
Nepal	Rupee	NRs¹	Pice	
Netherlands	Guilder	f.	Cent	
Netherlands Antilles	...do	NAE	...do	
New Caledonia	Franc	CFPF	Centime	
New Zealand	Dollar	$NZ	Cent	
Nicaragua	Cordoba	C$	Centavo	Ctvo.
Niger	Franc	CFAF	Centime	
Nigeria	Naira	₦	Kobo	k.
Norway	Krone	NKr	Øre	
Oman	Riyal	ORls	Baiza	
Pakistan	Rupee	PRs	Paisa	

Country or area	Basic monetary unit		Principal fractional unit	
	Name	Symbol	Name	Abbreviation or symbol
Panama	Balboa	B	Centesimo	Ctmo.
Paraguay	Guarani	G	Centimo	Ctmo.
Papua New Guinea ..	Kina	K	Toea	
Peru	Sol	S/	Centavo	Ctvo.
Philippines	Peso	₱	....do	Ctvo.
Poland	Zloty	Zl	Grosz	
Portugal	Escudo	Esc	Centavo	
Qatar	Riyal	QRls	Dirham	
Reunion	French franc	F	Centime	
Romania	Leu	L	Ban	
Rwanda	Franc	RF	Centime	
St. Christopher-Nevis .	Dollar	EC$	Cent	
St Lucia	....do	EC$	....do	
St. Pierre and Miquelon	Franc	CFAF	Centime	
St. Vincent and the Grenadines	Dollar	EC$	Cent	
San Marino	Italian lira	Lit	Centesimo	
Sao Tome e Principe .	Dobra	Db	Centavo	
Saudi Arabia	Riyal	SRls[2]	Halala	
Senegal	Franc	CFAF	Centime	
Seychelles	Rupee	Sey Rs[3]	Cent	
Sierra Leone	Leone	Le	....do	
Singapore	Dollar	S$	....do	
Solomon Islands	Dollar	SI$	....do	
Somalia	Shilling	So. Sh.	....do	
South Africa	Rand	R	Cent	
Spain	Peseta	Ptas[1]	Centimo	
Sri Lanka	Rupee	Cey Rs[3]	Cent	
Sudan	Pound	£S	Piaster	
Surinam	Guilder	Sur. f.	Cent	
Swaziland	Lilangeni (emalengeni, plural)	E	....do	
Sweden	Krona	SKr	Öre	
Switzerland	Franc	SwF	Centime	
Syria	Pound	£Syr	Piaster	
Tanzania	Shilling	T Sh	Cent	
Thailand	Baht	B	Satang	
Taiwan	New Taiwan dollar ..	NT$	Cent	
Togo	Franc	CFAF	Centime	
Tonga	Pa'anga	T$	Seniti	
Trinidad and Tobago .	Dollar	TT$	Cent	
Tunisia	Dinar	D	Millime	
Turkey	Lira	TL	Kurus	
Tuvalu	Australian dollar	A$	Cent	
Uganda	Shilling	U Sh	....do	
U.S.S.R.	Ruble	R	Kopek	
United Arab Emirates .	Dirham	UD	Fil	
United Kingdom	Pound	£ or £ stg.	Shilling	S.,d.
United States	Dollar	$ or US$	Cent	
Upper Volta	Franc	CFAF	Centime	
Uruguay	Peso	N$	Centesimo	
Vanatu	Franc	FNH	Centime	
Vatican City	Italian lira	Lit	Centesimo Ctmo.	
Venezuela	Bolivar	Bs	Centimo	
Vietnam	Dòng	VND	Hao	
Wallis and Futuna	Franc	CFPF	Centime	
Western Samoa	Tala	WS$	Cent	
Yemen (Aden)	Dinar	SYD	Fil	
Yemen (Sanaa)	Rial	Y Rls[2]	....do	
Yugoslavia	Dinar	Din	Para	
Zaire	Zaire	Z	Likuta	
Zambia	Kwacha	K	Ngwee	S., d.
Zimbabwe	Dollar	Z$	Cent	

[1] Singular: Pta.
[2] Singular: Rl.
[3] Singular: Re.

Source: United States Government Printing Office Style Manual (Washington, D.C.: U.S. Government Printing Office, 1984). Based on a list of currency units and abbreviations provided by the International Monetary Fund and the Department of State.

TABLE OF DEBIT AND CREDIT ENTRIES

Account	Rules of Debit and Credit

PERMANENT ACCOUNTS

Asset accounts (money, accounts receivable, notes receivable, furniture, buildings, and so on)	*Increases* are recorded by *debit* entries. *Decreases* are recorded by *credit entries.*
Liability accounts (accounts payable, notes payable, and so on) and *owner's equity accounts* (business assets minus liabilities equals owner's equity)	*Increases* are recorded by credit entries. *Decreases* are recorded by *debit* entries.

TEMPORARY ACCOUNTS

Income accounts (sale of goods and services)	*Increases* in owner's equity are recorded by *credit* entries. *Decreases* in owner's equity are recorded by *debit* entries.
Expense accounts (rent, salaries, and so on)	*Increases* in owner's equity are recorded by *credit* entries. *Decreases* in owner's equity are recorded by *debit* entries.

Note: An amount recorded on the left, or debit, side of an account is called a *debit* or *debit entry*. An amount on the right, or credit, side of an account is called a *credit* or *credit entry*. The relationship among the three principal permanent accounts is expressed as: Assets = Liabilities + Owner's Equity.

INCOME STATEMENT

Creative Industries

Income Statement

For the Year Ended December 31, 19___

Gross sales			$419,765
Less: Sales returns and			
allowances		$ 4,620	
Sales discounts		5,040	9,660
Net sales			$410,105
Cost of goods sold:			
Inventory, Jan. 1, 19___		$ 41,700	
Purchases	$196,811		
Transportation-in	9,122		
Delivered cost of purchases	$205,933		
Less: Purchases returns			
and allowances	$1,599		
Purchase discount	4,313	5,912	
Net purchases		200,021	
Cost of goods available for			
sale		$241,721	
Less: Inventory, Dec. 31,			
19___		29,100	
Cost of goods sold			212,621
			$197,484
Gross profit on sales			
Operating expenses:			
Selling expenses:			
Sales salaries		$ 40,600	
Advertising		20,616	
Depreciation: building		219	
Depreciation: store equip-			
ment		641	
Depreciation: delivery			
equipment		309	
Insurance		2,845	
Miscellaneous		104	
Total selling expenses		$ 65,334	

General and administrative expenses:

Office salaries	$ 34,780		
Uncollectible accounts expense	390		
Depreciation: building	100		
Insurance expense	300		
Miscellaneous	245		
Total general and administrative expense		35,815	
Total operating expense			101,149
Income from operations			$ 96,335
Interest earned on investments			700
Net income			$ 97,035

Note: The income statement is also known as the profit and loss statement, the income and expense statement, the operating statement, the revenue and expense statement, and the report of earnings. Since the type and amount of information reported varies depending on the business, follow examples of previous income statements in your company in determining format and matters of style.

BALANCE SHEET

McKindley Office Suppliers
Balance Sheet
December 31, 19___

Assets

Current assets:			
Cash		$ 7,622.99	
Notes receivable			$14,707.21
Accrued interest receivable		24.65	
Accounts receivable		9,800.75	
Total receivables		$17,448.39	
Less allowances for bad debts		2,037.66	15,410.73
Merchandise inventory			72,944.85
Prepaid insurance			833.33
Stationery and supplies			94.00
Total current assets			$103,990.12
Long-lived assets:			
Store equipment		$ 8,163.77	
Less accumulated depreciation		6,020.00	$ 2,143.77
Delivery equipment		$ 4,802.80	
Less accumulated depreciation		2,551.07	2,251.73
Total long-lived assets			4,395.50
Total assets			$108,385.62

Liabilities

Current liabilities:		
Notes payable		$14,600.90
Accrued interest payable		154.22
Accounts payable		10,850.98
Sales tax payable		1,144.23
FICA tax payable		188.67
Employees income tax payable		671.11
FUTA tax payable		99.03
State unemployment tax payable		62.47
Total current liabilities		$27,771.61

Owner's Equity

Joseph McKindley, capital:		
Capital, January 1		$68,410.66
Net income	$42,211.98	
Less withdrawals	30,008.63	12,203.35
Capital, December 31		80,614.01
Total liabilities and owner's equity		$108,385.62

Note: The balance sheet is also known as the statement of financial position, the statement of assets and liabilities, and the statement of condition. The form shown here is called the *account form*, in which assets are listed on the left side and liabilities and the owner's equity at the right. Note that the Total assets = Total liabilities and owner's equity.

FEDERAL TAX CALENDAR

Tax	Type of Business	Form	Due Date
Income tax	Sole proprietor	Schedule C, Form 1040	Same day as Form 1040
	Individual who is a partner or Subchapter S corporation shareholder	1040	Fifteenth day of fourth month after end of tax year
	Corporation	1120	Fifteenth day of third month after end of tax year
	Subchapter S corporation	1120S	Fifteenth day of third month after end of tax year
Self-employment tax	Sole proprietor or individual who is a partner	Schedule SE, Form 1040	Same day as Form 1040
Estimated tax	Sole proprietor or individual who is a partner or Subchapter S corporation shareholder	1040ES	Fifteenth day of fourth, sixth, and ninth months of tax year and fifteenth day of first month after end of tax year
	Corporation	1120W	Fifteenth day of fourth, sixth, ninth, twelfth months of tax year
Annual return of income	Partnership	1065	Fifteenth day of fourth month after end of tax year
FICA tax and the withholding of income tax	Sole proprietor, corporation, Subchapter S cor-	941	April 30, July 31, October 31, and January 31

Tax	Type of Business	Form	Due Date
	poration, or partnership	501, to make deposits	(Refer to IRS instructions for substituting 501 when you use 941 to report social security and withheld income tax.)
Providing information on FICA tax and the withholding of income tax	Sole proprietor, corporation, Subchapter S corporation, or partnership	W-2, to employee W-3, to the Social Security Administration	January 31 Last day of February
FUTA tax	Sole proprietor, corporation, Subchapter S corporation, or partnership	904 508, to make deposits	January 31 April 30, July 31, October 31, and January 31 but only if the liability for unpaid tax is more than $100
Annual information returns	Sole proprietor, corporation, Subchapter S corporation, or partnership	See Publication 15, *Employer's Tax Guide.*	See Publication 15, *Employer's Tax Guide.*
Excise taxes	Sole proprietor, corporation, Subchapter S corporation, or partnership	See Publication 510, *Excise Taxes*	See Publication 510, *Excise Taxes.*

Note: This calendar lists some of the important tax due dates for a proprietor, corporation, or partnership. If a due date falls on a Saturday, or legal holiday, the deadline is extended to the next day that is not a Saturday, Sunday, or legal holiday. For more information, write to IRS for a free copy of Publication 509, *Tax Calendars*.

IRS TAX PUBLICATIONS AND FORMS

TAX PUBLICATIONS

General Guides

17	Your Federal Income Tax
225	Farmer's Tax Guide
509	Tax Calendars for 19__
553	Highlights of 19__ Tax Changes
595	Tax Guide for Commercial Fishermen
910	Taxpayer's Guide to IRS Information and Assistance

Employer's Guides

15	Employer's Tax Guide (Circular E)
51	Agricultural Employer's Tax Guide (Circular A)
80	Federal Tax Guide for Employers in the Virgin Islands, Guam, and American Samoa (Circular SS)

Specialized Publications

349	Federal Highway Use Tax on Trucks, Truck Tractors, and Buses
378	Fuel Tax Credits
463	Travel, Entertainment, and Gift Expenses
505	Tax Withholding and Estimated Tax
510	Excise Taxes for 19__
517	Social Security for Members of the Clergy and Religious Workers
521	Moving Expenses
523	Tax Information on Selling Your Home
525	Taxable and Nontaxable Income
526	Charitable Contributions
527	Rental Property
529	Miscellaneous Deductions
531	Reporting Income from Tips
533	Self-Employment Tax
534	Depreciation
535	Business Expenses
536	Net Operating Losses and the At-Risk Limits
537	Installment Sales
538	Accounting Periods and Methods

Specialized
Publications
_____

539	Employment Taxes—Income Tax Withholding, FICA and FUTA, Advance Payments of EIC, Withholding on Gambling Winnings
541	Tax Information on Partnerships
542	Tax Information on Corporations
544	Sales and Other Dispositions of Assets
545	Interest Expense
547	Tax Information on Disasters, Casualties, and Thefts
548	Deduction for Bad Debts
549	Condemnations of Private Property for Public Use
550	Investment Income and Expenses
551	Basis of Assets
556	Examination of Returns, Appeal Rights, and Claims for Refund
560	Tax Information on Self-Employed Retirement Plans
561	Determining the Value of Donated Property
572	General Business Credit
575	Pension and Annuity Income
583	Information for Business Taxpayers—Business Taxes, Identification Numbers, Recordkeeping
584	Disaster and Casualty Loss Workbook
586A	The Collection Process (Income Tax Accounts)
587	Business Use of Your Home
589	Tax Information on Subchapter S Corporations
590	Tax Information on Individual Retirement Arrangements
597	Information on the United States-Canada Income Tax Treaty
598	Tax on Unrelated Business Income of Exempt Organizations
908	Bankruptcy
909	Minimum Tax and Alternative Minimum Tax
911	Tax Information for Direct Sellers
1045	Information and Order Blanks for Preparers of Federal Income Tax Returns
1048	Filing Requirements for Employee Benefit Plans

TAX FORMS

SS-4	Application for Employer Identification Number
720	Quarterly Federal Excise Tax Return
940	Employer's Annual Federal Unemployment Tax Return
941	Employer's Quarterly Federal Tax Return
942	Employer's Quarterly Tax Return for Household Employees

Specialized Publications

943	Employer's Annual Tax Return for Agricultural Employees
1040	U.S. Individual Income Tax Return
Schedules A & B	Itemized Deductions & Interest and Dividend Income
Schedule C	Profit or Loss from Business or Profession
Schedule D	Capital Gains and Losses
Schedule E	Supplemental Income Schedule
Schedule F	Farm Income and Expenses
Schedules R & RP	Credit for the Elderly
Schedule SE	Computation of Social Security Self-Employment Tax
Schedule W	Deduction for a Married Couple When Both Work
1040-ES	Estimated Tax for Individuals
1040 X	Amended U.S. Individual Income Tax Return
1045	Application for Tentative Refund
1065	U.S. Partnership Return of Income
Schedule K-1	Partner's Share of Income, Credits, Deductions, etc.
1118	Computation of Foreign Tax Credit—Corporation
1120	U.S. Corporation Income Tax Return
Schedule D	Capital Gains and Losses
Schedule PH	Computation of U.S. Personal Holding Company Tax
1120S	U.S. Small Business Corporation Income Tax Return
Schedule D	Capital Gains and Losses
Schedule K-1	Shareholder's Share of Undistributed Taxable Income, etc.
1120-W	Corporation Estimated Tax (Worksheet)
1120X	Amended U.S. Corporation Income Tax Return
1128	Application for Change in Accounting Period
1138	Extension of Time for Payments of Taxes by a Corporation Expecting a Net Operating Loss Carryback
1139	Corporation Application for Tentative Refund
2210	Underpayment of Estimated Tax by Individuals
2220	Underpayment of Estimated Tax by Corporations
2290	Federal Use Tax Return on Highway Motor Vehicles
2553	Election by a Small Business Corporation
2688	Application for Extension of Time to File U.S. Individual Income Tax Return
3115	Application for Change in Accounting Method
3468	Computation of Investment Credit
4070	Employee's Report of Tips to Employer
4136	Computation of Credit for Federal Tax on Gasoline, Special Fuels, and Lubricating Oil

Specialized
Publications

4255	Recapture of Investment Credit
4466	Corporation Application for Quick Refund of Overpayment of Estimated Tax
4562	Depreciation and Amortization
4625	Computation of Minimum Tax—Individuals
4626	Computation of Minimum Tax—Corporations and Fiduciaries
4684	Casualties and Thefts
4797	Supplemental Schedule of Gains and Losses
4835	Farm Rental Income and Expenses and Summary of Gross Income from Farming or Fishing
4868	Application for Automatic Extension of Time to File U.S. Individual Income Tax Return
5884	Jobs Credit
5695	Residential Energy Credit
6251	Alternative Minimum Tax Computation
6252	Computation of Installment Sale Income
6478	Credit for Alcohol Used as Fuel
6765	Credit for Increasing Research Activities
7004	Application for Automatic Extension of Time to File Corporation Income Tax Return
7005	Application for Additional Extension of Time to File Corporation Income Tax Return
8007	Credit for Employee Stock Ownership Plan

Note: Contact the nearest IRS center for free publications and forms. A full list of currently available printed material and Tele-Tax tapes is described in Publication 910, *Taxpayer's Guide to IRS Information and Assistance*.

CHAPTER 8

Weights, Measures, and Values

TABLES OF WEIGHTS, MEASURES, AND VALUES

LONG MEASURE

12 inches = 1 foot
3 feet = 1 yard
5½ yards or 16½ feet = 1 rod
320 rods or 5,280 feet = 1 mile
1,760 yards = 1 mile
40 rods = 1 furlong
8 furlongs = 1 statute mile
3 miles = 1 league

Common Metric Equivalents

1 inch = 2.540 centimeters
1 foot = 30.480 centimeters
1 yard = 0.914 meters
1 rod = 5.029 meters
1 mile = 1.609 kilometers

SQUARE MEASURE

144 square inches = 1 square foot
9 square feet = 1 square yard
30¼ square yards = 1 square rod
272¼ square feet = 1 square rod
40 square rods = 1 British rood
4 roods = 1 acre
160 square rods = 1 acre
640 acres = 1 square mile
43,560 square feet = 1 acre
4,840 square yards = 1 acre

Common Metric Equivalents

1 square inch = 6.451 square centimeters
1 square foot = 0.093 square meters
1 square yard = 0.836 square meters
1 square rod = 25.293 square meters
1 square mile = 2.590 square kilometers

SOLID OR CUBIC MEASURE (VOLUME)

1,728 cubic inches = 1 cubic foot
27 cubic feet = 1 cubic yard
128 cubic feet = 1 cord of wood
24.75 cubic feet = 1 perch of stone
2,150.42 cubic inces = 1 standard bushel
231 cubic inches = 1 standard gallon
40 cubic feet = 1 ton (shipping)

Common Metric Equivalents

1 cubic inch = 16.387 cubic centimeters
1 cubic foot = 0.028 cubic meters
1 cubic yard = 0.765 cubic meters

SURVEYORS' LONG MEASURE

7.92 inches = 1 link
25 links = 1 rod
4 rods or 100 links = 1 chain
80 chains = 1 mile

SURVEYORS' SQUARE MEASURE

625 square links = 1 square rod
16 square rods = 1 square chain
10 square chains = 1 acre
640 acres = 1 square mile
36 square miles = 1 township

CIRCULAR OR ANGULAR MEASURE

60 seconds (60″) = 1 minute (′)
60 minutes (60′) = 1 degree (1°)
30 degrees = 1 sign
90 degrees = 1 right angle or quadrant
360 degrees = 1 circumference

Note: 1 degree at the equator = about 60 nautical miles.

DRY MEASURE

2 pints = 1 quart
8 quarts = 1 peck
4 pecks = 1 bushel
2,150.42 cubic inches = 1 bushel
1.2445 cubic feet = 1 bushel

Common Metric Equivalents

1 pint = 0.550 liters
1 quart = 1.101 liters
1 peck = 8.809 liters
1 bushel = 35.239 liters

LIQUID MEASURE (CAPACITY)

4 gills = 1 pint
2 pints = 1 quart
4 quarts = 1 gallon
31.5 gallons = 1 barrel
2 barrels = 1 hogshead
1 gallon = 231 cubic inches
7.4805 gallons = 1 cubic foot
16 fluid ounces = 1 pint
1 fluid ounce = 1.805 cubic inches

Common Metric Equivalents

1 fluid ounce = 29.573 milliliters
1 gill = 118.291 milliliters
1 pint = 0.473 liters
1 quart = 0.946 liters
1 gallon = 3.785 liters

MARINERS' MEASURE

6 feet = 1 fathom
100 fathoms = 1 cable's length as applied to distances or intervals between
                    ships
120 fathoms = 1 cable's length as applied to marine wire cable
7.50 cable lengths = 1 mile
5,280 feet = 1 statute mile

6,080 feet = 1 nautical mile
1.15266 statute miles = 1 nautical or geographical mile
3 geographical miles = 1 league
60 geographical miles or 69.16 statute miles = 1 degree of longitude on the
$$\text{equator or 1 degree of meridian}$$
360 degrees = 1 circumference

Note: A *knot* is not a measure of distance but a measure of speed, about 1 nautical mile per hour.

U.S.-BRITISH WEIGHTS AND MEASURES

1 British bushel = 1.0326 U.S. (Winchester) bushels
1 U.S. bushel = 0.96894 British Imperial bushel
1 British quart = 1.03206 U.S. dry quarts
1 U.S. dry quart = 0.96894 British quart
1 British quart (or gallon) = 1.20095 U.S. liquid quarts (or gallons)
1 U.S. liquid quart (or gallon) = 0.83267 British quart (or gallon)

AVOIRDUPOIS MEASURE (WEIGHT)

27.343 grains = 1 dram
16 drams = 1 ounce
16 ounces = 1 pound
25 pounds = 1 quarter
4 quarts = 1 hundredweight
100 pounds = 1 hundredweight
20 hundredweight = 1 ton
2,000 pounds = 1 short ton
2,240 pounds = 1 long ton

Common Metric Equivalents

1 grain = 0.0648 grams
1 dram = 1.771 grams
1 ounce = 28.349 grams
1 pound = 0.453 kilograms
1 hundredweight (short) = 45.359 kilograms
1 hundredweight (long) = 50.802 kilograms
1 ton (short) = 0.907 metric ton
1 ton (long) = 1.016 metric tons

Note: The avoirdupois measure is used for weighing all ordinary substances except precious metals, jewels, and drugs.

TROY MEASURE (WEIGHT)

24 grains = 1 pennyweight
20 pennyweights = 1 ounce
12 ounces = 1 pound

Common Metric Equivalents
---

1 grain = 0.0648 grams
1 pennyweight = 1.555 grams
1 ounce = 31.103 grams
1 pound = 0.373 kilogrms

AVOIRDUPOIS-TROY MEASURE

1 pound troy = 5,760 grains
1 pound avoirdupois = 7,000 grains
1 ounce troy = 480 grains
1 ounce avoirdupois = 437.5 grains
1 carat or karat = 3.2 troy grains
24 carat gold = pure gold

APOTHECARIES' FLUID MEASURE (CAPACITY)

60 minims = 1 fluid dram
8 fluid drams = 1 fluid ounce
16 fluid ounces = 1 pint
8 pints = 1 gallon

APOTHECARIES' MEASURE (WEIGHT)

20 grains = 1 scruple
3 scruples = 1 dram
8 drams = 1 ounce
12 ounces = 1 pound

Common Metric Equivalents
---

1 grain = 0.0648 gram
1 scruple = 1.295 grams
1 dram = 3.887 grams
1 ounce = 31.103 grams
1 pound = 0.373 kilogram

PAPER MEASURE

24 sheets = 1 quire
20 quires = 1 ream
2 reams = 1 bundle
5 bundles = 1 bale

COUNTING

12 units or things = 1 dozen
12 dozen or 144 units = 1 gross
12 gross = 1 great gross
20 units = 1 score

Note: See also *Metric Tables and Common Equivalents* in this chapter.

BASIC SI UNITS AND SYMBOLS

UNITS

Quantity	Name	Symbol
amount of substance	mole	mol
electric current	ampere	A (*or* a)
length	meter	m
luminous intensity	candela	cd
mass	kilogram	kg
thermodynamic tempera- ture	Kelvin	K
time	second	S (*or* s)

PREFIXES

Prefix	Amount	Symbol
tera-	10^{12}	T
giga-	10^{9}	G
mega-	10^{6}	M
kilo-	10^{3}	k

Prefix	Amount	Symbol
hecto-	10^2	h
deka-	10^1	da
deci-	10^{-1}	d
centi-	10^{-2}	c
milli-	10^{-3}	m
micro-	10^{-6}	μ
nano-	10^{-9}	n
pico-	10^{-12}	p
femto-	10^{-15}	f
atto-	10^{-18}	a

Note: See also *Metric Prefixes and Multiplication Factors* in this chapter.

METRIC PREFIXES AND MULTIPLICATION FACTORS

WEIGHT

1 *kilo*gram = 1,000 grams   1 *deci*gram = 0.1 gram
1 *hecto*gram = 100 grams   1 *centi*gram = 0.01 gram
1 *deka*gram = 10 grams   1 *milli*gram = 0.001 gram
1 gram = 1 gram

LENGTH

1 *kilo*meter = 1,000 meters   1 *deci*meter = 0.1 meter
1 *hecto*meter = 100 meters   1 *centi*meter = 0.01 meter
1 *deka*meter = 10 meters   1 *milli*meter = 0.001 meter
1 meter = 1 meter

VOLUME

1 *hecto*liter = 100 liters   1 *centi*liter = 0.01 liter
1 *deka*liter = 10 liters   1 *milli*liter = 0.001 liter
1 liter = 1 liter

METRIC MEASUREMENT CONVERSIONS

When You Know	Multiply By	To Find

LENGTH

inches (in.)	2.54	centimeters (cm)
feet (ft.)	30.00	centimeters (cm)
yards (yd.)	0.90	meters (m)
miles (mi.)	1.60	kilometers (km)
millimeters (mm)	0.04	inches (in.)
centimeters (cm)	0.40	inches (in.)
meters (m)	3.30	feet (ft.)
meters (m)	1.10	yards (yd.)
kilometers (km)	0.60	miles (mi.)

AREA

square inches (in.^{2})	6.50	square centimeters (cm^2)
square feet (ft.^{2})	0.09	square meters (m^2)
square yards (yd.^{2})	0.80	square meters (m^2)
square miles (mi.^{2})	2.60	square kilometers (km^2)
acres	0.40	hectares (ha)
square centimeter (cm^2)	0.16	square inches (in.^{2})
square meters (m^2)	1.20	square yards (yd.^{2})
square kilometers (km^2)	0.40	square miles (mi.^{2})
hectares (ha) (10,000 m^2)	2.50	acres

WEIGHT

ounces (oz.)	28.00	grams (g)
pounds (lb.)	0.45	kilograms (kg)
short tons (2,000 lbs.)	0.90	tonnes (t)
long tons (2,240 lbs.)	1.01	tonnes (t)
grams (g)	0.035	ounce (oz.)
kilograms (kg)	2.20	pounds (lb.)
tonnes (1,000 kg)	1.10	short tons
tonnes (1,000 kg)	0.98	long tons

VOLUME

teaspoons (tsp.)	5.00	milliliters (ml)
tablespoons (tbsp.)	15.00	milliliters (ml)
fluid ounces (fl. oz.)	30.00	milliliters (ml)
cups (c)	0.24	liters (l)
pints (pt.)	0.47	liters (l)
quarts (qt.)	0.95	liters (l)
gallons, U.S. (gal.)	3.80	liters (l)
gallons, Imp. (gal.)	4.50	liters (l)
cubic feet (ft.^{3})	0.028	cubic meters (m^3)
cubic yards (yd.^{3})	0.76	cubic meters (m^3)
milliliters (ml)	0.03	fluid ounces (fl. oz.)
liters (l)	2.10	pints (pt.)
liters (l)	1.06	quarts (qt.)
liters (l)	0.26	gallons, U.S. (gal.)
liters (l)	0.22	gallons, Imp. (gal.)
cubic meters (m^3)	35.00	cubic feet (ft.^{3})
cubic meters (m^3)	1.30	cubic yards (yd.^{3})

TEMPERATURE

$$°C = (°F - 32) \times 0.555$$
$$°F = (°C \times 1.8) + 32$$

METRIC TABLES AND COMMON EQUIVALENTS

LINEAR MEASURE

1 centimeter = 0.3937 inch
1 inch = 2.54 centimeters
1 decimeter = 3.937 inches = 0.328 foot
1 foot = 3.048 decimeters
1 meter = 39.37 inches = 1.0936 yards
1 yard = 0.9144 meter
1 dekameter = 1.9884 rods
1 rod = 0.5029 dekameter
1 kilometer = 0.62137 mile
1 mile = 1.6093 kilometers

SQUARE MEASURE

1 square centimeter = 0.1550 square inch
1 square inch = 6.452 square centimeters
1 square decimeter = 0.1076 square foot
1 square foot = 9.2903 square decimeter
1 square meter = 1.196 square yards
1 square yard = 0.8361 square meter
1 acre = 160 square rods
1 square rod = 0.00625 acres
1 hectare = 2.47 acres
1 acre = 0.4047 hectare
1 square kilometer = 0.386 square mile
1 square mile = 2.59 square kilometers

VOLUME

1 cubic centimeter = 0.061 cubic inch
1 cubic inch = 16.39 cubic centimeters
1 cubic decimeter = 0.0353 cubic foot
1 cubic foot = 28.317 cubic yards
1 cubic yard = 0.7646 cubic meter
1 stere = 0.2759 cord
1 cord = 3.624 steres
1 liter = 0.908 quart dry = 1.0567 quarts liquid
1 quart dry = 1.101 liters
1 quart liquid = 0.9463 liter
1 dekaliter = 2.6417 gallons = 1.135 pecks
1 gallon = 0.3785 dekaliter
1 peck = 0.881 dekaliter
1 hectoliter = 2.8375 bushels
1 bushel = 0.3524 hectoliter

WEIGHTS

1 gram = 0.03527 ounce
1 ounce = 28.35 grams
1 kilogram = 2.2046 pounds
1 pound = 0.4536 kilogram
1 metric ton = 0.98421 English ton
1 English ton = 1.016 metric ton

APPROXIMATE METRIC EQUIVALENTS

1 decimeter = 4 inches
1 liter = 1.06 quarts liquid = 0.9 quarts dry
1 meter = 1.1 yards
1 kilometer = 0.625 mile
1 hectoliter = 2.625 bushels
1 hectare = 2.5 acres
1 kilogram = 2.20 pounds
1 stere or cubic meter = 0.25 cord
1 metric ton = 2,200 pounds

Note: See also *Tables of Weights, Measures, and Values* in this chapter.

LAND MEASUREMENTS

1 rod = 16½ feet
1 chain = 66 feet or rods
1 mile = 320 rods, 80 chains, or 5,280 feet
1 square mile = 272¼ square feet
1 acre = 160 square rods
1 acre = 208¾ square feet
1 acre = 8 rods × 20 rods or any two numbers (of rods) whose product is
        160
25 × 125 feet = 0.0717 acre
1 section = 640 acres

CENTIGRADE/FAHRENHEIT TEMPERATURES

Centigrade (degrees)	Fahrenheit (degrees)
0 (freezing)	32 (freezing)
10	50

20	68
30	86
40	104
50	122
60	140
70	158
80	176
90	194
100 (boiling)	212 (boiling)

Note: $°C \times 1.8 + 32 = °F$; $°F - 32 \div 1.8 = °C$.

Glossaries

Account. An **accounting** record of financial transactions for any one of a business' **assets** and **liabilities.**

Accounting. The systematic recording, analyzing, and reporting of financial transactions of a business consistent with accepted professional standards.

Accounting cycle. The period in which a business conducts a full set of **accounting** procedures.

Accounts payable. The amount a business or an individual owes a creditor for merchandise and services.

Accounts receivable. The amount customers owe a business or an individual for merchandise or services.

Accrual accounting. An **accounting** method whereby income and expenses are allocated to the period to which they apply, regardless of the actual date of receipt or payment.

Adjusting entry. A journal entry made at the end of an **accounting** period to make corrections and to assign income and expenses to the correct period.

Amortization. Gradual reduction of a debt by periodic payments until interest and principal are fully paid on the date of maturity.

Asset. Anything owed by a business or an individual that has commercial or exchange value.

Audit. A professional examination of **accounting** records and supporting documents to verify transactions and to determine their accuracy and propriety for a specified accounting period.

Balance sheet. A detailed statement that lists an organization's **assets, liabilities,** and **capital (net worth)** on a given date.

Blind entries. **Accounting** entries that show **debits** and **credits** but fail to record other essential information.

Book value. The worth of the **assets** of a business as reported in its **accounting** books and on its **financial statements.**

Bookkeeping. The practice of recording financial transactions systematically and consistent with the accepted **accounting** method.

Books of final entry. **Accounting** books, such as the **ledgers,** where information is transferred from the **books of original entry.**

Books of original entry. **Accounting** books, such as the **journals,** where transactions are first recorded.

Capital. The excess of **assets** over **liabilities;** the **net worth** of a business.

Capital account. An **account** that records the equity of an owner(s) in the business; an account that shows investments in a business.

Capital assets. Those **assets** of a business that are not readily converted into cash but are held for use over a long period. See **Fixed assets.**

Capital gains. The profit indicated by a higher selling price minus a lower purchase price of an **asset.**

Capital goods. Commodities, such as raw materials, that are used to produce other capital goods or consumer goods.

Capital liabilities. Obligations created to fund a project or to purchase **fixed assets.**

Capital loss. The loss indicated by a higher purchase price minus a lower selling price of an **asset.**

Capital stock. An **accounting** record that indicates the amount received from stock sales; evidence of ownership in a corporation.

Capitalization. The total **accounting** value of **capital stock, paid-in capital in excess of par value,** and borrowed **capital;** the total amount of a corporation's outstanding securities in the form of capital stock and long-term bonds.

Carry back. A tax computation that averages out gains and losses over a period of more than one year.

Carry forward. A step that moves a figure or item forward from one place to another.

Cash accounting. An **accounting** method whereby income and expense items are recorded when they are actually received and paid, regardless of any other period to which they apply.

Cash disbursements journal. An **accounting** book where payments are first recorded.

Cash journal. An **accounting** book where all transactions are first recorded.

Cash position. The percentage or ratio of cash to **net assets** in a business.

Cash receipts journal. An **accounting** book where receipts are first recorded.

Cash reserve. Cash and liquid **assets** kept for special purposes and emergencies.

Certified public accountant (CPA). A professional person certified by his or her state as qualified to practice accounting.

Closing entries. Final entries made at the end of an **accounting** period to transfer income and expense account balances to the **balance sheet** accounts.

Control account. An **account** in the **general ledger** that summarizes information in a **subsidiary ledger.**

Controller (or comptroller). An officer in charge of **bookkeeping** and **accounting** matters in a business.

Credit. An entry on the right-hand side in **double-entry bookkeeping** that records increases in **capital, income,** and **liability** accounts and decreases in **asset** accounts.

Cross-footing. Totaling the columns in books of account.

Current assets. All **assets** that will be realized or converted within an **accounting** period.

Current capital. See **Working capital.**

Current liabilities. Debts and obligations met within an **accounting** period by using **current assets** or incurring additional **liabilities.**

Debit. An entry on the left-hand side in **double-entry bookkeeping** that records increases in **asset** and expense accounts and decreases in **capital** and **liability** accounts.

Depreciation. The expiration of usefulness of **fixed assets** through physical or functional causes such as wear and tear with use, lapse of time, obsolescence, and inadequacy.

Double-entry bookkeeping. A record-keeping system whereby each transaction is recorded as both a **debit** and a **credit.**

Financial statement. A summary report of financial data, such as an **income statement** and a **balance sheet,** prepared periodically from the **accounting** records.

Fiscal year. A period of any 12 successive months of business operations.

Fixed assets. Permanent, tangible **assets** held for use, for example, land, buildings, and equipment.

Footing. See **Cross-footing.**

General ledger. An **accounting book of final entry** where financial transactions are summarized in separate **accounts.**

Gross income. Total income received by a business or an individual before deductions.

Gross profit. The excess of income over the cost of merchandise sold and the expense of doing business.

Imprest fund. See **Petty cash.**

Income statement. A financial summary that reports the income and expense of a business and shows the **net profit** or loss in a specified **accounting** period.

Intangible assets. Items of value, such as patents and franchises, other than tangible property or the direct right to tangible property.

Journal. An **accounting book of original entry** where financial transactions are first recorded.

Ledger. An **accounting book of final entry** where financial transactions are summarized in separate **accounts.**

Liabilities. The debts and obligations of a business.

Net assets. The excess of the **book value** of **assets** (the price reported on a **financial statement**) over **liabilities.**

Net income. Gross income less all operating expenses, maintenance, taxes, losses, and other expenses, except interest and financial charges on borrowed or other **capital.**

Net profit. Gross receipts less all costs of doing business and income taxes or, in the case of a single transaction, the price of goods or services less the cost of the goods or services used up in completing the transaction.

Net worth. The **book value** of the **assets** minus the **liabilities** of a business.

Notes payable. A **general ledger account** that shows the amount of promissory notes, or the liability of notes, given by the business.

Notes receivable. A **general ledger account** that shows the amount of negotiable promissory notes received from customers and other debtors.

Overhead. The ongoing general and administrative expenses of a business, for example, rent, maintenance, and insurance.

Paid-in capital in excess of par value. Contributions of **capital** by stockholders that are not credited to **capital stock.**

Payroll. The record of employees' wages, salaries, deductions, and net pay for a certain period; the total amount paid to employees in a certain period.

Payroll journal. A book where all **payroll** information is systematically recorded.

Petty cash. A small fund of money kept on hand for incidental expenses paid without writing a check.

Posting. The process of transferring entries from the **journals (books of original entry)** to individual **ledger accounts (books of final entry).**

Profit and loss statement. See **Income statement.**

Single-entry bookkeeping. An **accounting** method where transactions are recorded as a single entry rather than both a **debit** and a **credit** as in **double-entry bookkeeping.**

Subsidiary journal. A specialized **accounting** book, such as a sales **journal,** where similar transactions are recorded.

Subsidiary ledger. A specialized **accounting** book, such as an **accounts payable ledger,** where similar **journal** entries are summarized.

Trial balance. A means of checking the accuracy of **ledger accounts** by listing **debit** and **credit** balances and totaling them to prove that total debits equal total credits.

Working capital. The excess of **current assets** over **current liabilities;** the **capital** kept to pay daily operating expenses.

STATISTICS

Absolute value. The numerical value of a number, regardless of its plus or minus sign ($-14 = 14$).

Arithmetic mean. The sum of a set of terms divided by the number of terms.

Average. A value that represents a middle point or is typical of a group, class, or series. See **Arithmetic mean, Median, Mode,** and **Geometric mean.**

Axis. A reference line of a coordinate system.

Bias. A deviation in the expected value of an estimated quantity.

Boolean algebra. An algebraic system of notation and binary computation that is widely used in computer theory and analysis.

Breakdown charts. Graphic portrayals of profits or expenses, usually showing two or more alternatives with one or more intersections.

Causation. A related action or association between two things, whereby an act or agency produces some effect.

Census. A total survey of a finite **population.**

Central-tendency measures. Averages of which each represents the best single summary of a group of data. See **Arithmetic mean, Median, Mode,** and **Geometric mean.**

Chi-square. The sum of terms, with each term obtained by dividing the square of the difference between the observed and theoretical values of a quantity by the theoretical value.

Coefficient of correlation. A measure that shows the degree of **correlation** between two sets of data or random **variables** and is equal to their covariance divided by the product of their **standard deviations.**

Confidence level. A statistical calculation that expresses a degree of certainty about something.

Consumer price index. A measure of the change in the cost of significant, commonly purchased goods and services expressed as a percentage of their cost in a base period.

Continuous data. Those data found at any point along a continuous linear scale, for example, a thermometer.

Correlation. A relationship between things or **variables** not based on chance alone.

Correlation coefficient. See **Coefficient of correlation.**

Cyclical movement. A swing from prosperity to recession or depression and back again.

Data arrangement. The organization of items in a table (alphabetically, chronologically, geographically, by size, by category, and so on) to facilitate analysis and comparison and to accomplish the objective of the table.

Data gathering. The collection of data by some means and for some purpose, for example, observation, experimentation, graphic presentation, and tabular presentation.

Dependent variable. A mathematical **variable** plotted on the Y axis that is determined by one or more other variables.

Direct relationship. An association between values whereby an increase or decrease in the value of one **variable** is associated with an increase or decrease in the value of another variable.

Discrete data. Distinct or mathematically noncontinuous data that are always expressed in whole numbers, or integers.

Discrete series. A series where differences between successive observations are always finite, with no values falling between the observed values.

Domain. The set of elements to which a **variable** is limited.

Element. A single item in a **sample, set, population, universe, collection,** or **matrix.**

Extrapolate. To estimate a value from values in an already known range.

Forecasting. To calculate a future event or condition by logical, rational means using available data.

Frequency distribution. A table with statistical data arranged to show the number of occurrences of each value.

Functions. Variables with each one depending on and varying with another; a correspondence where one element of one **set** is assigned to each element of another set.

Gantt chart. A graphic indication of activity against time.

Geometric mean. The nth root of a product of n numbers.

Gradient. A change in the value of a quantity with a change in a given **variable;** a graded difference in some activity along an **axis.**

Heuristic. Exploratory problem solving by means of trial and error.

Hypothesis. A tentative question or assumption to be tested.

Increment. An added part or portion.

Independent variable. A mathematical **variable** plotted on the X **axis** whose value is indicated first and which determines other values.

Index number. A number that measures fluctuations or changes during intervals of time.

Integer. A whole number.

Intercept. The intersection of a line and a coordinate **axis.**

Interval. The range or set of real numbers between two given numbers.

Inverse relationship. An association where an increase in the value of one **variable** is accompanied by a decrease in the value of the other variable.

Law. A written or positive rule; a statement of an order, relation, or sequence of phenomena that are invariable under the same conditions.

Least-squares method. A method of fitting a curve to a set of points so that the total of the squares of the distances to the points from the curve is a minimum.

Linear programming. A mathematical technique for problem solving using linear functions when there are a number of **variables** and possible courses of action.

Logarithm. An exponent indicating the power to which a number is raised to produce a given number ($10^1 = 10$; $10^2 = 100$, etc.).

Mean. See **Arithmetic mean.**

Median. The value of the middle item in a group of items arranged by size.

Mode. The most frequent or the most common value in a group of items.

Multiple correlation. A measure of the relationship between a **dependent variable** and two or more **independent variables.**

Normal curve. A symmetrical, bell-shaped frequency curve of a **normal distribution.**

Normal distribution. A probability density function that is symmetrical about the **mean.**

Null hypothesis. A statistical hypothesis that no real difference exists between the true **means** of two **populations** and that any observed difference occurs by chance.

Parameter. The numerical property of the distribution of a statistical **population;** a value that describes the limits of a system.

Population. A group of persons or objects that have a common characteristic from which samples can be taken for statistical measurement.

Probability distribution. Tables that show the probability of a value falling within an interval; the relative frequency of occurrence for listed values.

Probable error. The error that will not exist in more than 50 percent of the cases.

Quartiles. Averages that divide a **population** into four parts (just as a **median** divides a population into two parts).

Random sample. A selection in which each item in the **population** has an equal chance of being included in the **sample.**

Range. The difference between maximum and minimum items, or high and low values, in a series.

Ratio. The relationship, proportion, or relative value of two items.

Regression coefficient. A number that represents a measure of some property or characteristic in a regression equation.

Sample. A selected number of items chosen from a larger population.

Sampling. The process of selecting **sample** items from a larger **population.**

Sets. A number of items that have a common characteristic(s).

Skewness. The lack of symmetry in a **frequency distribution.**

Standard deviation. A measure of the dispersion in a **frequency distribution.**

Standard error. The **standard deviation** that measures the variability of means in a sample distribution.

Statistics. A science that deals with the collection, analysis, interpretation, and presentation of masses of numerical data; a branch of mathematics.

Theory. Speculation, belief, or a plausible body of scientific principles used as an explanation of something.

Time series. A **frequency distribution** where time is the **independent variable.**

Universe. The whole **population** or **set.**

Variable. See **Dependent variable** and **Independent variable.**

Vector. A quantity that has magnitude and direction and is generally represented by an arrow where the line is the magnitude and the head is used to show direction.

BANKING

Amortization. Gradual reduction of a debt until it is eliminated by making periodic payments to the creditor.

Automated teller. A computerized teller machine, commonly located on the outside of the bank for use during nonbanking hours, capable of accepting transactions such as deposits and withdrawals made by customers.

Bank discount. The charge made by a bank for payment of a **note** or commercial paper before maturity, usually expressed as a percentage of the face amount.

Bank draft. A check drawn by one bank against funds deposited to its account in another bank that authorizes the second bank to make payment to the person named on the draft.

Bank note. A noninterest-bearing promissory **note** of a **Federal Reserve Bank** issued to serve as currency and payable to the bearer on demand.

Bank rate. The interest rate on loans set by a bank; the discount rate set by a central bank.

Bank statement. The periodic statement sent to customers summarizing transactions during the month and balance on hand at the end of the month.

Callable loan. A loan that must be repaid upon the creditor's demand.

Cancelled check. A check paid by the bank and returned to the payer with the monthly **bank statement,** which lists the amount of the check as a withdrawal.

Cashier's check. A check drawn by a bank against its own funds and signed by a cashier or other authorized officer.

Certificates of deposit. Written evidence of an investment, or deposit, with a bank that earns interest over a specified period; known as CDs.

Certified check. A check that has been certified by the bank and for which payment from the depositor's account has therefore been guaranteed by the bank.

Checking account. Any one of various types of accounts in which a customer may make deposits and withdrawals. See also **Interest-bearing checking account** and **Joint account.**

Clearinghouse. An association of banks established to exchange checks, drafts, and so on and settle balances among members.

Comaker. Someone who signs another's **note** and in so doing also assumes responsibility for payment, thereby strengthening the principal maker's credit.

Commercial bank. A bank that accepts deposits and provides **checking** and savings accounts, makes short-term loans, and may offer other services such as **trust** administration.

Commercial credit. The money a bank loans to business organizations for use in providing goods and services.

Commercial draft. A written order signed by one party that directs a second party to pay a specified sum to a third party.

Commercial letter of credit. A credit instrument provided by a bank authorizing a seller to receive money before goods are shipped and thereby enabling the customer to finance the purchase of the goods.

Correspondent bank. A bank that permits another, often smaller, bank to make deposits and establish a line of credit with it to help the bank handle its customer's needs.

Credit limit. The maximum amount a customer may borrow.

Days of grace. Additional days provided for a customer to make payment on a debt without penalty.

Deferred credit. A delayed credit to an account, for example, a deposit made after banking hours credited to the customer's account on the following business day.

Demand deposit. A **checking account** deposit that may be withdrawn at any time without prior notice.

Deposits. Checks, cash **notes,** and other items placed with a bank or other institution to be credited to the customer's account; money or something of value used as a down payment or to guarantee fulfillment of an agreement.

Direct deposit. The automatic deposit of funds, such as social security checks, by the issuer into the customer's account upon authorization by the customer.

Drawee. The party directed to pay the amount of a draft or check to the **drawer.**

Drawer. The party who draws the draft or check upon another party for payment of money.

Endorsement. A signature on the back of a negotiable instrument such as a check to effect its legal transfer.

Escrow. An account where funds or other securities are held until certain conditions are met before delivery to the specified party.

Exchange rate. The rate at which one country's currency is exchanged for another's currency; the price of one country's currency expressed as an equivalent amount of another's currency.

Federal Deposit Insurance Corporation (FDIC). A federal agency that insures the deposits in member banks up to a specified limit.

Federal Reserve Bank. One of 12 regional banks, plus branches, established by the Federal Reserve Act of 1913 to maintain reserves, issue bank **notes,** and lend money to other banks.

Federal Reserve Board. The seven-member Board of Governors that supervise **Federal Reserve Banks.**

Federal Reserve System. The central banking system of the United States established by the Federal Reserve Act of 1913, consisting of 12 **Federal Reserve Banks** plus branches, supervised by the 7-member Board of Governors, that controls credit and the flow of money in the United States.

Federal Savings and Loan Insurance Corporation (FSLIC). A federal agency that insures deposits in all federal savings and loan associations and in other member associations.

Fiat money. Money issued by a government as **legal tender** that is not redeemable or convertible.

Forgery. The illegal alteration of or reproduction of a signature, document, or negotiable instrument.

Frozen account. An account on which all activity has been suspended until court or other legal action permits resumption of activity.

Gold standard. A monetary system in a country that specifies the value of currency in terms of the weight of gold and redeems the currency for gold.

Individual retirement account. A retirement savings plan whereby individuals may deposit a specified amount of money annually that earns interest and of which the principal and interest are not taxed until funds are withdrawn any time after the age of 59.

Interest. The amount paid for the use of borrowed money or credit.

Interest-bearing checking. A checking account such as the NOW (negotiable order of withdrawal) accounts in which any funds that are in the account earn interest until they are withdrawn.

Investment bank. A firm that buys and then sells to the public corporate and government securities.

Investment trust. A trust fund established to produce income through investments; a company that invests in other companies.

Irrevocable trust. A trust fund that cannot be changed, controlled, or terminated by the grantor.

Joint account. A checking or savings account held in the names of two or more persons.

Kiting. Drawing against deposits before the checks have cleared; illegally drawing against an account before checks are presented to the bank for payment.

Legal reserve. The minimum amount that a bank is legally required to have on hand to meet the demands of depositors.

Legal tender. A country's coin and currency that by law must be accepted in payment of debts.

Letter of credit. An instrument issued by a bank on behalf of one party that guarantees payment to a third party.

Living trust. A trust established while the person is alive for the benefit of that person, other beneficiaries, or both.

Loan. The advance of money by one party to another, usually to be repaid with interest and secured by **note** or property.

Mint ratio. The ratio of the prices or weights of gold to silver in a country that uses a bimetal standard.

Monetary policy. The policy of a country in controlling its money supply and available credit; in the United States, the policy of the **Federal Reserve System.**

Money order. A negotiable instrument that can be purchased to make payments without writing a check against a **checking account.**

Money supply. The supply of currency a country has in circulation at any given time.

Mutual savings bank. A bank that has no capital stock but is owned by the depositors who share in its profits.

Note. A written promise to pay a specified amount of money on demand or at a future date.

Overdraft. The amount by which the withdrawal of money from an account exceeds the amount credited to the account.

Participation loan. A large loan in which two or more banks each lend a portion of the total amount.

Passbook. The small book in which a customer's savings account withdrawals, deposits, and interest are recorded.

Payee. The party to whom a promissory note or check is payable.

Payer. The party responsible for payment of the amount specified on a note or check.

Prime rate. The rate of interest on loans that banks charge their preferred customers.

Private bank. An unincorporated, privately owned **commercial bank.**

Revocable trust. A **trust** that can be terminated at any time or when specified in the agreement.

Safe deposit box. A locked metal container rented to customers that is safeguarded in the bank's vault as a secure place for customers to store their valuables.

Savings bank. A bank chartered by the state to receive deposits, pay interest on them, and invest deposited funds in bonds, mortgages, and other investments.

Savings bond. A U.S. Treasury bond that can be purchased in various amounts at a specified rate of interest and is redeemable at a specified future date.

Savings and loan associations. A federally or state-chartered financial institution that sells shares to individuals, invests in mortgages, and pays dividends to members.

Sight draft. A commercial draft payable on demand.

Stop payment. A customer's order to a bank not to honor payment on a check the customer wrote.

Straight loan. A short-term loan at a specified rate of interest, which is paid periodically, with the principal payable in full on maturity.

Time deposits. Deposits that are held for a specified time or for which advance notice must be given before withdrawal.

Time draft. A draft that is payable at a certain time, for example, 24 hours, after receipt and acceptance.

Traveler's checks. Special checks, widely accepted worldwide, that can be purchased in various denominations and used in place of currency and personal checks by travelers.

Trust. An arrangement whereby a trustee such as a bank holds the title to property and manages it for the benefit of the beneficiaries

Voucher check. A check that has a stub attached on which to record facts pertinent to the transaction.

Warrant. Evidence of a debt that will be redeemed for cash or check when presented to the drawee.

INVESTMENTS

American Stock Exchange (AMEX). The second largest stock exchange in the United States, located in New York City, where listed **stocks, bonds,** and **options** are traded.

Arbitrage. Buying and then selling securities in a different market to make a profit from the difference in market prices.

Arrears. Unpaid **dividends** on **cumulative preferred** stock.

Auction market. The system of trading securities through **brokers** or agents on one of the stock exchanges.

Averages. Measures of the trend of security prices. See **Dow Jones Averages.**

Averaging. See **Dollar cost averaging.**

Basis point. A means of expressing variations in **bond** yields, with one gradation on a 100-point scale equal to 1 percent.

Bear. A person who believes stock market prices will decline.

Bear market. A declining market.

Bearer bond. An unregistered **bond** on which interest and principal are payable to whoever holds it.

Bid and asked. A quotation, or **quote,** with *bid* being the highest price offered for a security at a given time and *asked* being the lowest price anyone will take at the same time.

Block. A large stock holding, for example, 10,000 or more shares.

Blue-chip stock. Stock with a good earnings record in a reputable company recognized for its quality product or service and stability.

Bond. Evidence of a debt in the form of an IOU or promissory note issued by a government of corporation in various denominations, with the promise to pay a specified amount of interest and repay the loan on the expiration date.

Book value. The value of **common stock** represented by total assets minus debts and other liabilities plus the liquidation price of any **preferred stock.**

Broker. The agent who, for a **commission,** buys and sells securities, **commodities,** and other property for the public; the intermediary between buyer and seller.

Bull. A person who believes stock market prices will rise.

Bull market. An advancing market.

Call. See **Option.**

Callable. Subject to redemption before maturity; **bond** issues or **preferred** shares of **stock** that may be redeemed in full or part by the issuing corporation before maturity.

Capital stock. All **common** and **preferred** shares of **stock** issued by a corporation, representing the ownership of the corporation.

Capitalization. The total amount of **preferred** and **common stocks, bonds,** and **debentures** issued by a corporation, representing its total capital funds.

Cash sale. A transaction on the floor of a stock exchange that specifies delivery of the purchased securities the same day.

Commission. The fee, often a percentage of the transaction, for a **broker's** services in buying or selling securities.

Commodities. See **Futures.**

Commodity Futures Trading Commission (CFTC). A U.S. commission created by Congress in 1974 to regulate the commodities exchanges.

Common stock. The shares of securities that represent ownership in a corporation and on which **dividends** are paid (after dividends on **preferred stock** have been paid).

Convertible. Preferred stock, bonds, or **debentures** that may be exchanged for **common stock** or another security, usually from the same corporation, according to the terms of the issue.

Coupon bond. A **bond** that has attached to it interest coupons that are removed when due and presented for payment of interest.

Cumulative preferred. Preferred stock on which unpaid **dividends** are due before they may be paid on **common stock.**

Day order. A buy or sell order that expires at the end of the trading day if not executed.

Debenture. A certificate, or promissory note, evidencing a debit that is not secured by collateral but is backed by a company's general credit.

Debit balance. The amount of the purchase price of **stocks, bonds,** or **commodities** covered by credit that is extended by the **broker** to a customer who has a **margin** account.

Delayed opening. The delay beyond the normal opening in trading an issue on a stock exchange when exchange officials deem that a postponement is warranted.

Depository trust company (DTC). A central securities certificate depository through which members make security deliveries among one another by computer without delivering the actual certificates.

Discount. The difference between the price of a security and its redemption value.

Discretionary account. An account in which the customer authorizes someone else in the investment firm to make decisions on his or her behalf.

Dividends. The earnings of a corporation designated by its board of directors to be distributed to shareholders according to holdings, or share of ownership.

Dollar-cost averaging. The method for determining the amount of periodic investment, or purchase of securities, by fixed dollar amount instead of number of shares.

Dow Jones averages. A measure of stock prices on the **New York Stock Exchange,** computed by Dow Jones & Co., that represents the sum of the prices of 30 widely held stocks divided by an adjusted denominator.

Down tick. See **Up tick.**

Equipment trust certificate. A **bond** issued in serial maturity form to finance the purchase of equipment to be used in the business.

Equity. The ownership interest in a corporation represented by **common** and **preferred stock;** the excess of the value of securities over the debit balance in a customer's **margin** account.

Ex-dividend. Without **dividend,** meaning that a customer purchasing stock will not receive the most recently declared dividend.

Ex-rights. Without rights, meaning that a customer purchasing stock is not entitled to the right to subscribe to additional or new shares at a discounted price.

Extra. Short for "extra dividend," one in addition to the regular **dividend.**

Face value. The value specified on the face of a **bond** certificate as the amount the issuer promises to pay at maturity.

Financial futures. **Futures** contracts on interest-sensitive financial instruments such as Treasury bonds and **certificates of deposit**. See **Futures.**

Flat income bond. A **bond** that trades without accrued interest, such as bonds in default and bonds where the seller retains all interest earned up to the settlement date.

Formula investing. A means of investing based on preestablished rules. See **Dollar-cost averaging.**

Free and open market. A market in which supply and demand operate freely and are reflected in the prices of securities.

Futures. Trading contracts that specify a future date for delivery or receipt of objects such as agricultural commodities, metals, and financial instruments.

General mortgage bond. A **bond** secured by a general, or blanket, mortgage on a company's property.

Gilt-edged. A descriptive term usually applied to high-quality **bonds** that have demonstrated their profitability and their ability to pay interest without interruption.

Gold fix. The worldwide price of gold bullion and products set by gold dealers.

Good delivery. A requirement that certain standards such as proper endorsement be met before a **broker** may deliver a security sold on the exchange.

Good 'til cancelled (GTC). An open order to buy or sell that remains in effect until the customer cancels it.

Government bonds. **Bonds** issued by the U.S. government.

Growth stock. Stock that is expected to increase in value at a rapid rate.

Hedging. A method of reducing risk by using two offsetting securities; in **commodities,** the practice of selling **futures** contracts for an amount equal to cash purchases.

Hypothecation. Pledging securities or other assets as collateral for a loan while retaining ownership.

Income bond. A **bond** that promises to pay interest only when and if earned.

Indenture. A written agreement between an issuer and bondholders specifying terms such as the rate of interest and the date of maturity.

Index. A measure of market trends expressed as a percentage of a base year(s).

Intermarket trading system (ITS). The electronic communications network that links the various exchanges and enables fast action on transactions involving **NYSE** and **AMEX** listings.

Issue. A class of securities; the process of distributing securities.

Limited order. A buy or sell order where the customer sets a maximum buying price or a minimum selling price.

Liquidation. The process of selling securities and other assets to generate cash.

Liquidity. The ability of the market in regard to a particular issue to absorb a reasonable amount of buying and selling at reasonable price changes.

Listed stock. Stock that has qualified for trading and is traded on a registered exchange.

Locked in. The position of investors who cannot sell a security because the sale would create a profit immediately subject to capital gains tax.

Long. Refers to ownership (long 20 shares means ownership of 20 shares).

Margin. The customer's portion of a payment, or the customer's equity, in transactions that include the credit of the **broker;** in **commodities,** the customer's deposit on a **futures** contract.

Margin call. A **broker's** notice to a customer to make payment in money or securities to satisfy the minimum percentage of equity required on **margin** transactions.

Market order. An order to buy or sell a specified number of shares at the best price after the order is received in the marketplace.

Market price. The last reported sale price of a stock or **bond.**

Maturity. The date when a loan or **bond** is due and payable.

Money-market fund. A mutual fund for individuals that invests in short-term, high-yield instruments such as **certificates of deposit** and federal securities.

Mortgage bond. A **bond** secured by property as collateral that promises to pay interest and repay the principal.

Municipal bond. A **bond** issued by a state, city, or other political subdivision that is authorized by legislation and on which interest is exempt from federal income tax and local tax where issued.

Net asset value. A computation of net asset value per share that is equal to the market value of securities less liabilities divided by the number of outstanding shares.

Net change. The point difference between a security's closing price one day and that of the next day, for example, +1 means up $1 a share, and −1 means down $1 a share.

New issue. A security offered for sale by the issuer for the first time.

New York Stock Exchange (NYSE). A nonprofit corporation and the oldest and largest securities market in the United States, founded in 1792 and governed by a Board of Governors, where stocks are traded, with prices determined by supply and demand.

Noncumulative stock. A **preferred stock** whose unpaid **dividends** do not accrue, or accumulate, when they are omitted at any time.

Odd lot. Exchange transactions for less than the common trading units of 100-share or 10-share lots.

Open order. See **Good 'til canceled order.**

Option. The right to buy (call) or sell (put) a fixed amount of stock at a fixed price within a specified time.

Over the counter. Transactions of unlisted securities that do not take place on an exchange but are handled by telephone or telex.

Par. The dollar value equivalent to the specified face value of a **bond** at the time of redemption; the dollar value designated for **common stock** by a corporation's charter; the dollar value on which **dividends** are computed for a corporation's **preferred stock.**

Participating preferred. **Preferred stock** on which a bonus **dividend** is paid when dividends paid on the **common stock** exceed a specified amount.

Penny stocks. Speculative, low-cost stocks often selling at less than $1 a share.

Point. In stocks, 1 point = $1; in **bonds,** which are quoted as a percentage of $1,000, 1 point = $10.

Portfolio. Assets, or securities holdings, of a person or organization.

Preferred stock. A class of stock with a fixed annual **dividend** that has priority over **common stock** in the distribution of dividends and assets when a company is dissolved.

Price-earnings ratio. A measure used to compare stock where the market price of a share of **common stock** is divided by earnings per share over a 12-month period.

Prospectus. A detailed, printed summary of a registration statement filed with the **SEC** and given to buyers and prospective buyers of the new security.

Puts and calls. See **Options.**

Pyramiding. Successively buying or selling more stock each time by using profits from previous transactions as collateral.

Quote. The buyer's highest bid to buy or the seller's lowest offer to sell a particular security at a particular time.

Registered bond. A **bond** registered with the issuer in the name of the onwer.

Regular-way delivery. For **bonds,** settlement on the following business day after the transaction; for securities sold on the **NYSE,** settlement on the fifth business day after the transaction.

Rights. The privilege offered to holders of **common stock** of purchasing additional securities in proportion to present holdings, usually at a price below the current market price, before the public is allowed to purchase shares.

Round lot. The generally accepted trading unit or multiple thereof; for active stocks on the **NYSE,** usually 100 shares; for inactive stocks, 10 shares; for **bonds,** $1,000 par-value units (**over-the-counter** units vary).

Securities and Exchange Commission (SEC). A federal agency established by the Securities Exchange Act of 1934, with five commissioners responsible for the interpretation, supervision, and enforcement of U.S. securities laws.

Serial bond. A **bond** of which portions mature at stated intervals.

Short position. Stocks, **options,** or **futures** sold short and not covered by a certain date; sale of borrowed securities that are owed to the **broker.**

Sinking fund. Money regularly set aside by a corporation to redeem its **preferred stocks, bonds,** or **debentures.**

Split. An increase (split up) or decrease (split down) in the number of outstanding shares of stock, with the proportionate equity remaining the same for each shareholder in spite of the change in the number of shares (up or down) held.

Stock dividend. A payment to shareholders in **dividends** rather than cash, with dividends from the issuing corporation or another company held by the issuer.

Stock ticker symbols. Abbreviations of corporate names (XRX = Xerox) that serve as identification symbols on the **NYSE** or **AMEX.**

Stop limit order. An instruction by a customer on a **stop order** to buy or sell at a certain price.

Stop order. An instruction by a customer to buy or sell once a stock reaches a certain price above or below the current market price.

Treasury stock. Outstanding company stock reacquired by the issuer to be retired or resold.

Unlisted stock. See **Over the counter.**

Up tick. A new transaction at a price higher than the preceding one, as opposed to a *down tick* for a new transaction at a lower price.

Volume. The total number of securities or **bonds** trading in a certain period such as a day or week.

Voting trust certificate. A negotiable receipt issued by a bank for **common stock** certificates delivered into a trust, which holds the voting rights on the shares.

Warrant. A certificate that enables the holder to buy securities at a specified price, with or without a time limit.

When issued. Short for "when and if issued"; refers to a transaction on a security not yet issued for which the settlement date is not yet established.

Yield. The percentage return on securities; **dividends** or interest in terms of a percentage of the current market price.

Zero coupon bonds. Noninterest-bearing **bonds** sold at a discount from the face value.

CREDIT AND COLLECTION

Accounts payable. The total amount a debtor owes a creditor on **open account.**

Accrued expenses. Expenses incurred during a certain accounting period for which payment is postponed until a later period.

Acid test ratio. A means of determining whether current liabilities can be met relatively quickly (in the near future) that is computed by dividing the sum of cash and receivables by current liabilities.

Actuarial method. A complicated means of computing the simple annual percentage rate on a declining debt balance that is based on a uniform periodic rate applied to a schedule of installment payments multiplied by the number of payments in the year.

Adjustment bureaus. Organizations formed to handle in behalf of creditors the affairs of embarrassed and bankrupt debtors.

Average collection period. The average time that receivables are outstanding, for example, 60 days.

Bad-check law. A state-enacted law indicating the type of crime (e.g., felony) and punishment that applies in the issuance of a worthless check within that particular state.

Bank credit. Generally, the **credit,** or borrowing capacity, provided by a bank in the form of a **cash loan** or a drawing account in the name of the borrower.

Bankruptcy. The legal process by which an insolvent debtor's assets are liquidated and distributed to creditors, after which the debtor is relieved of further liability.

Business credit. The **credit,** or borrowing capacity, extended to business by financial and mercantile institutions and other lenders such as **investment credit, mercantile credit, short-term cash credit, intermediate-term credit,** and real estate credit.

Business finance companies. Companies that lend money primarily to businesses.

Business loans. See **Business credit.**

Carrying charges. The charges a creditor imposes for lending money to a debtor (interest, **finance charges,** and so on).

Cash credit. **Credit** provided by financial and other lending institutions involving **cash loans** for various uses such as short-term business loans and personal cash to consumers.

Cash discount. A discount that represents a premium for paying a bill before a specified date, which falls before the remaining free or net credit period that is left after the discount expiration date.

Cash loans. See **Cash credit.**

Charge account. Any account established for a customer that enables the customer to make purchases on **credit** and pay for the goods and services later.

Chattel mortgage. A debt for which personal property is pledged as security, although the property remains in the hands of the debtor as long as payments on the loan are made as required.

Check credit. A **bank credit** plan in which customers are given checks to use—up to a specified line of credit—in writing themselves **cash loans** and to make purchases on **credit** from the bank.

Collateral. The security (e.g., personal property or real estate) pledged to a lender for a loan.

Collection. The process of securing settlement of accounts in which monies are owed by debtors.

Collection agency. An organization whose principal function is to collect delinquent accounts for clients.

Collection follow-up system. The means used to pursue the collection of a delinquent account until satisfactorily concluded, for example, with a series of planned statements, reminders, notices, telephone and wire messages, personal visits, registered letters, and lawsuits.

Collection index. A measure used to plot the general trend in **collections,** computed by dividing the collections made in a certain period by the receivables outstanding at the beginning of the period.

Collection-letter series. A succession of varied appeals to debtors for payment of delinquint accounts, usually ranging from a friendly notice to increasingly strong reminders and culminating in the threat of legal action.

Collection systems. The policies and records and files used in **collection** work, for example, the ledger system, the card-tickler system, and the duplicate-invoice system.

Commerical credit. **Credit,** or borrowing capacity, used by businesses to purchase or sell goods and services intended for resale or for use in the conduct of the business, with the promise of future payment.

Commercial finance companies. See **Business finance companies.**

Commercial letter of credit. A letter from a bank to a seller on behalf of a buyer that specifies the maximum amount of **credit** available to the buyer as well as other terms of the particular transaction.

Conditional sales contract. An installment contract that specifies the terms of a sale in which title to goods sold remains with the seller until the buyer has completed all payments.

Constant-ratio method. A means of converting **finance** or service **charges** into an annual rate whereby a constant percentage of each payment is assigned to the finance charge and the rest to repayment of the principal.

Consumer credit. **Credit,** or borrowing capacity, extended to consumers in purchasing consumer goods and services, with the promise of future payment.

Consumer Credit Protection Act. A law applied to consumer **installment credit** transactions that requires disclosure of credit terms and **finance charges** before a transaction is concluded.

Consumer finance companies. Organizations that make small loans primarily to individual consumers.

Consumer lending institutions. Organizations that lend money to consumers such as consumer **finance companies,** bank personal loan departments, pawnbrokers, credit unions, and various other loan companies.

Credit. See **Commercial credit** and **Consumer credit.**

Credit bureaus. An organization whose principal function is the collection of **credit** information about debtors and the exchange of this information among associated creditors.

Credit cards. Small, usually plastic, cards from issuers that enable buyers to purchase on **credit** and make payments later within the limits imposed by the issuer (for example, a retail credit card usable only in a certain retail store versus a multipurpose, universal card such as Visa).

Credit-checking service. Organizations such as **Dun & Bradstreet** that collect and evaluate **credit** information and make recommendations to subscribers concerning the advisability of extending credit to a prospective customer.

Credit departments. A department within an organization whose function is to manage the organization's **credit** activities, for example, credit-application processing, reference checking, accounts management, correspondence, billing, **collection follow-up,** and credit sales promotion.

Credit elasticity of demand. The effect that **credit** has on the expansion or contraction of demand for certain goods, for example, increasing the demand for installment goods such as household appliances.

Credit equation. Any formula a company employs to evaluate **consumer credit** risk by scoring or weighting factors such as occupational class, stability of income, business history, and the ratio of monthly mortgage obligations to income to identify excellent, good, fair, and doubtful credit risks.

Credit Exchange, Inc. An organization whose function is to provide a **credit-checking service** in the wearing apparel, sporting-goods, and gifts industries.

Credit history. The record of a person's or company's **credit** references, **credit limit,** promptness of making payments, credit rating, and so on.

Credit instruments. Written evidence of a debtor's obligation to a creditor such as a promissory note or an implicit promise to pay such as an **open book** of **account.**

Credit interchange bureaus. A network of organizations whose function is to collect information from creditors and distribute it to members in the form of reports.

Credit limit. The maximum amount of **credit** an organization will extend to a customer under specified terms and conditions.

Credit line. Usually, an annual arrangement between a bank and a customer in which the customer may borrow up to a maximum limit within the specified year before a **credit** recheck is conducted.

Credit period. The time over which **credit** is extended, for example, 30 days.

Credit reports. The information about debtors that a reporting agency provides to subscribing creditors, for example, information about a debtor's **credit** rating, financial resources, and previous payment record.

Credit sales index. The percentage of total sales accounted for by **credit** transactions computed by dividing total net sales into credit sales.

Cycle billing. A billing plan whereby alphabetical sections of the ledger files are billed each day, until all billing is completed within each one-month period.

Delinquency index. A measure of the proportion of total accounts that is past due computed by dividing the total of outstanding accounts into the total of past due accounts.

Direct-ratio method. A means of converting **finance** or **service charges** into an annual rate whereby the charge is allocated among the months in direct ratio to the total month-dollars in use by the customer.

Direct-reduction loans. Plans whereby a borrower repays a loan in fixed amounts at regular intervals, with part of each payment allocated to interest due and part to repayment of the principal, leaving a reduced outstanding loan balance with each payment.

Dun & Bradstreet. An organization whose function is to collect, evaluate, and publish **credit** ratings and other credit information for the use of subscribers, including the publication of directories, magazines, and other business and economic material.

Effective rate of charge. The rate of charge in installment transactions that is based on a declining balance due.

Extensions. The time that a creditor extends to a debtor to satisfy a delinquent account.

Factoring. The purchase of accounts receivable from a client and the assumption of all associated **credit** risks and **collection** activities.

Finance charges. The charges for installment transactions that includes interest and costs to the creditor pertaining to carrying the account such as insurance and investigator fees.

Finance companies. See **Business finance companies** and **Consumer finance companies.**

Industrial credit. See **Business credit.**

Insolvency. The state of a debtor who has temporarily stopped paying debts or who cannot pay them at a particular time, even though the debtor's total assets may exceed total liabilities; the state of a debtor who is temporarily financially embarrassed, because the assets cannot readily be converted into cash without substantial loss; the state of a debtor whose liabilities exceed assets.

Installment credit. A type of **consumer credit** whereby the purchaser pays the obligation in installments at regular intervals.

Intermediate-term credit. A classification of **credit** in which the payment of principal is usually due in one to ten years.

Investment credit. A form of long-term business **credit** used to purchase fixed assets such as machinery and buildings and to conduct minimum business activity.

Liabilities. The debts and obligations of a business.

Mechanics' lien. A claim against the title to property placed by contractors and others for labor and materials furnished on **credit** in improving the property.

Mercantile credit. See **Commercial credit.**

Mortgage credit. Real estate **credit** whereby the borrower pledges the property as security for the loan.

Notes payable. A debtor's liabilities, or borrowed money, in the form of notes payable to banks, merchandise creditors, and others.

Open-book account. A seller's means of extending **credit** by debiting the customer's account for each purchase and billing the customer later.

Overdraft plan. A bank **credit** plan whereby depositors may write checks, representing a loan, above the amount in their accounts and within an established line of credit, the amount to be repaid in full or in monthly installments, with a service charge on the unpaid loan balance each month.

Promissory note. The written promise of a debtor to pay a stated sum of money on demand or at a specified future time.

Ratios. Relationships studied as a means of determining creditworthiness, for example, net worth to debt ratio, sales to receivables ratio, sales to net worth ratio, and net profit to net worth ratio.

Revolving credit. A form of **installment credit** whereby users make fixed monthly payments on the outstanding balances of their loans.

Short-term cash credit. **Business credit** in which a borrower promises to repay the principal within a specified time of one year or less.

Trade credit bureaus. Organizations formed to provide a **credit**-information service to members of an association or to a particular industry.

Truth in lending. A congressional bill, which became part of the **Consumer Credit Protection Act,** that requires disclosure of **installment credit** terms, including **finance charges,** before the **credit** is extended.

DATA PROCESSING

Access. The ability to control a system or acquire data from it.

Active file. A computer file currently being used.

Address. A number or label that identifies the location of stored information in a computer.

Algorithm. A rule or set of rules for problem solving in a finite number of steps.

Alphanumeric. A combination of alphabetic and numeric, for example, alphabetical and numerical information.

Analog computer. One that transmits nondigital information in the form of waves, or output signals.

Arithmetic function. The computation operations in computer processing.

Arithmetic and logic unit. The part of a computer that performs the arithmetic and logic operations.

Artificial language. A computer language used in special applications for easy communication as opposed to a natural, spoken or written language.

Assembler. A **computer program** that converts higher-level symbolic language into a lower-level **machine language** that can be handled directly by computer.

Audio-response unit. A device that connects a computer to a telephone and provides voice response to inquiries.

Autocode. A method for converting symbolic code into a machine-coded **computer program.**

Automated data processing (ADP). The handling of data (clerical, arithmetic, etc.) with electronic devices (e.g., computer).

Automation. The process of making machine operations automatic, requiring a minimum of human intervention.

Batch processing. Collecting and processing separate groups of data in a computer as a single unit, or batch, instead of one at a time.

Baud. Transmission speed of digital signals numerically equal to **bits per second.**

Bead. A small **computer program** designed for a specific function.

Binary-coded decimal system. A system in which an individual decimal digit is represented by four binary digits, for example, $1 = 0001$ and $2 = 0010$, so $12 = 0001\ 0010$.

Binary number system. A system of writing numbers for a computer using the base 2, instead of our familiar base 10, in which 1 and 0 are the only digits.

Bit (binary digit). The smallest unit of computer information, 1 or 0, on or off.

Bits per second (bps). A measure of **bit** rate, or machine speed.

Block. Any group of information (e.g., **bits,** words) treated as a single unit.

Block diagram. A graphic representation of a system or **computer program** that uses labeled boxes and connecting lines to describe the parts or sequence of steps in computer operations.

Branch. A point in a **computer program** where the computer may move to a step other than the next step of a fixed program sequence.

Breakpoint. A point in a **computer program** where the sequence of steps may be interrupted manually or by a control routine to check or test something.

Buffer. An area where information is temporarily stored between two devices such as a high-speed computer and a slow printer to accommodate differences in speed or other factors.

Bug. An error in a **computer program;** a malfunction in equipment.

Byte. A unit of data consisting of a series of **bits;** one byte represents one letter or character.

Card punch. An **output** device that records data by punching holes in cards corresponding to the output from a computer.

Card reader. An **input** device that senses information on **punched cards** and translates it into **machine language** that can be transmitted to a computer.

Cassette. A container for film or magnetic tape; a method of storing information.

Cathode-ray tube (CRT). An electronic tube, like a television tube, that is used to display images from a computer (both words and graphics) on a video screen.

Cell. A computer storage unit for one unit of information such as a **byte,** character, or word.

Central processing unit (CPU). The main part of a computer that contains the **arithmetic** and logic **unit** and the **memory** and control unit and carries out instructions, controls the functioning of all peripheral units, and coordinates operations.

Character. A single number, letter, mark, or symbol.

Character reader. A device that converts **high-level language** characters (type fonts or scripts) into **machine language** for processing in a computer.

Cluster. A group of separate work stations each connected to a central control unit to enable them to operate together.

Common machine language. Information presented in a way that is common to a group of **data-processing** machines.

Compiler. A **computer program** that replaces **higher-level language** statements with **machine-language** instructions.

Computer code. The **machine** code, or **language,** used by a specific computer.

Computer program. The set of instructions prepared for a computer to use in solving a problem of accomplishing some other task.

Configuration. The layout of machines and devices that are interconnected to operate as an integrated system.

Console. The part of a **data-processing** system where operators communicate with the components of the system and monitor and control operations.

Control panel. The plugboard, or wiring panel, where the wires that control computer functions are inserted manually.

Control program/microcomputer (CP/M). An operating system for **micro-computers,** used on business-oriented and home computers.

Conversational mode. A computer-user interaction in which the user and the machine each responds to the information or response of the other.

Critical-path method. A management technique where large-scale, long-term projects are controlled by monitoring and acting upon each critical step leading to completion.

Cybernetics. A science of communications and control theory that compares the control systems of humans and machines.

Cycle. A full sequence of operations.

Daisy-wheel printer. A printer that uses a circular print element (typehead) with the characters on the end of spokes, commonly used in **word-processing** systems.

Data processing. The manual or electronic processing of data by a sequence of steps leading to a desired result.

Data reduction. Converting raw data into a simplified, condensed form that can be used in **data processing.**

Databank. In a strict sense, a collection of numerical data. For the general sense, see **Database.**

Database. A collection, or store, of reference material on files designed for retrieval by computer.

Debug. Finding and correcting errors in a **computer program** on a computer system.

Decode. The process of interpreting coded instructions and information.

Diagnostic routine. The procedure used to find a machine malfunction.

Digital computer. A computer that processes information by manipulating digital data (numbers).

Disk. A device with a magnetic surface for storing data in a computer, containing tracks and sectors that can each be addressed, allowing for random access.

Disk drive. The electromechanical device that moves the disk or diskette to read from or write to it.

Diskette, floppy disk, mini floppy. A soft, flexible disk, usually 5¼, 3½, or 8 inches, with a magnetic surface for storing data, providing for random access but with more restricted storage than a hard disk.

Downtime. The period when equipment is not being used.

Editor. Software that can check characters and correct and change the form of data; a routine that performs editing operations in the course of a program.

Electronic data processing (EDP). Processing information with electronic machines (e.g., by computer).

End of file (EOF). Indication that the end of a particular collection of information is reached in computer processing.

End of message (EOM). Indication that the end of a message is reached in teletypewriter transmission.

Error-detection system. A system that uses a code to determine whether and where an error has occurred in data transmission and to delete it or indicate that it was detected.

Execution time. The time required to carry out an instruction in **data processing.**

Field. That part of a computer record where specific information is stored.

Flowchart. A diagram that represents the flow of data, or sequence of steps, by symbols and interconnecting lines.

Garbage in, garbage out (GIGO). Incorrect computer **output** resulting from incorrect **input.**

General-purpose language. A computer language suitable for use on a wide variety of computers.

Hard copy. Computer **output** printed on paper.

Hardware. A computer's electronic, magnetic, and mechanical equipment.

Heuristic. Problem solving by trial and error.

High-level programming language. A computer language that uses familiar terms for signals and instructions.

Housekeeping routine. An operation that is not part of the actual **data processing** such as setup and maintenance.

Information-processing system. The total equipment and procedures used to receive, process, and output information.

Information-retrieval system. A system designed to search for and make available selected items from stored data.

Input. The information fed into a computer.

Integrated data processing (IDP). The use of a system that links various **data-processing** steps and activities to create a more unified and efficient overall operation.

Interface. The link between two or more systems, pieces of equipment, or programs that allows the compatible items to communicate or function together.

Internal storage. An area of addressable storage in a computer where programs and data are retained.

Keyboard. An **input** device consisting of keys, like a typewriter keyboard, for manually recording characters or encoding data.

Keypunch. A **card-punch** device that perforates cards under computer control or manually with a **keyboard.**

Language. See **Machine language.**

Language translator. A **computer program** designed to convert information in other programs from one **machine language** to another.

Letter-quality printer. A printer capable of producing printed copy of a quality comparable to that of a typed letter.

Linear program. A program that follows a succession of increasingly complex steps.

Loading routine. A routine designed to enter information, or a program, into a computer.

Logic function. A computer operation that involves a decision(s) such as testing data.

Lines per minute (lpm). A measure of composition speed.

Loop. A sequence of program instructions that can be repeated until specified conditions are met.

Machine language. The code used by a computer; a low-level computer language designed for direct interpretation by machines.

Magnetic tape. A reel of magnetically coated plastic tape on which data can be stored in a code of magnetized spots.

Mainframe computer. A very large computer with extensive capabilities.

Matrix printer. A line or character printer that produces printed copy where each character is a series of dots.

Megabyte (mb). A measure of storage capacity equal to one million bytes.

Memory. The part of a computer where information is stored.

Menu. A list of options (e.g., EDIT, PRINT) in computer processing displayed on a video screen, with selection made on a **keyboard** or by pointing a special device at the item listed on the screen.

Microcomputer. A small computer, often sold in retail stores for home as well as business use.

Minicomputer. An intermediate size, general-purpose computer (between a **microcomputer** and a **mainframe computer**).

Modem. Short for modulator-demodulator; a device that converts digital (e.g., computer) signals into analog or audio information and vice versa, which enables users to transmit and receive material using regular telephone circuits.

Nanosecond. One billionth of a second.

Numeric code. A code in which data and instructions consist solely of digits.

Numerical control. The automatic control of machine tools through numerically coded instructions.

Off-line equipment. Peripheral equipment that does not interact directly with a computer's central processor.

On-line processing. Data processing conducted by entering data directly into a computer and receiving the **output** directly from the computer.

Optical character recognition (OCR). The ability of a light-sensitive, optical-scanning device to sense characters in **hard copy,** or printed copy, and to convert them into digital form for electronic processing or transmission.

Optical scanner. A device that scans both written text and graphics and converts them into digital information suitable for electronic processing or transmission.

Output. The information transmitted by a computer into a storage device, onto a screen, or in the form of printed paper or **punched cards** or **tape**

Peripheral equipment. Separate units or devices connected to a computer.

Postmortem routine. A routine used to analyze the cause of a problem, coding error, or other failure; a routine used to analyze an operation after its completion.

Printout. Hard copy; the printed roll or pages of information transmitted by the computer.

Program. A sequential set of instructions prepared in a language acceptable by a computer to direct its operations.

Program evaluation and review (PERT). See **Critical-path method.**

Punch card. A stiff card in which holes are punched in a coded pattern to represent data.

Punch tape. A continuous strip of paper in which holes are punched in a coded pattern to represent data.

Random-access memory (RAM). Also known as read/write memory; the area in a computer where data can be stored (written to) randomly and retrieved (read from) directly from any **address** (location).

Raw data. Unprocessed data.

Read-only memory (ROM). A machine memory that can be read but not changed or moved.

Readout. Soft copy; computer **output** displayed on a video screen.

Real time. Computer processing of information as each transaction occurs.

Routine. A sequence of computer operations.

Scanner. A device that senses printed text or graphics and converts the information to electrical signals.

Sequential operation. The processing of items in a data file according to the order in which they are stored; operations that are performed one after another.

Serial programming. Computer programming in which **arithmetic** and logic **functions** are completed one at a time.

Software. The programs that are prepared to direct the operations of a computer.

Sorter. A device that puts information or records into a preselected order.

Statement. A computer instruction.

Subroutine. A portion of a routine, or program, that can be compiled and executed independently.

Tape. See **Punch tape** and **Magnetic tape.**

Telecommunications. Transmitting or receiving information by way of electromagnetic signals (e.g., telephone, telegraph).

Time sharing. Simultaneous use of a computer by two or more users.

Turnaround time. The time it takes to begin and end a project; the time it takes to reverse the direction of a transmission.

Word processing. Handling text electronically (e.g., by computer); a system of processing communications by using equipment with electronic intelligence and memory and an automated printer.

BUSINESS MANAGEMENT

Affiliated companies. Companies that are associated with one another by a community of interest or through a parent company's ownership of their **stock.**

Affirmative action. Company policies intended to counteract discrimination, for example, by employing minorities.

Agency. An organization that functions on behalf of another person or organization.

Agribusiness. A large business that deals in agricultural products and services.

Alien corporation. A business organization incorporated outside the United States and its territories.

American Federation of Labor-Congress of Industrial Organizations (AFL-CIO). A national labor organization consisting of local, national, and international unions, formed by the merger of the AFL and the CIO in 1955.

Annual report. A **corporation** report prepared at the close of the fiscal year containing audited financial information and other information about the company and its operation.

Arbitration. The process of hearing and reaching a settlement in a controversy by means of negotiations between representatives of the opposing bodies.

Articles of incorporation. Also known as certificate of incorporation and charter; a document that creates a private **corporation** and states what the organization is authorized to do.

Backlog. Work not completed or orders not processed and filled.

Bankruptcy. The state of a business in which its property is taken over by a receiver or trustee for the benefit of creditors, thereby relieving the business of its debts.

Barter. Exchange of a product or service for another without the use of money.

Bill of exchange. A written order used in business transactions that is signed by the issuer and that requires the addressee to pay a specified sum of money to a third party.

Bill of lading. A document that sets forth the terms of a contract between a shipper and a carrier for the transport and delivery of goods.

Bill of sale. A legal document that conveys from seller to buyer the title to or right or interest in certain personal property.

Black market. The market where illegal transactions are conducted.

Blue-collar workers. Industrial and maintenance employees.

Board of directors. The persons elected by **stockholders in a corporation** to set policy and manage operations.

Budget. A plan for business operations in a future fiscal period based upon an estimate of income and expenditures in that period.

Bureaucracy. An operation characterized by red tape, excessive adherence to regulations, and rapid and excessive growth.

Business corporation. A **corporation** organized to conduct business for profit.

Bylaws. An organization's official rules and regulations enacted to regulate the conduct of its affairs.

Capital. The total of a **corporation's stock** accounts, surplus, undivided profits, and so on, that is, its net worth; ownership interest in a business.

Capital goods. Commodities such as raw materials used to produce consumer goods or other capital goods.

Cartel. A close association—syndicate, combine, or trust—of companies formed to conduct a similar business.

Chamber of commerce. An association of business people organized to advance the interests of its members.

Charitable corporation. Also known as an eleemosynary corporation; a **corporation** organized for charitable or nonprofit purposes.

Charter. See **Certificate of incorporation.**

Close corporation. A **corporation** in which a limited group holds its **capital stock,** and shares are not sold to the general public.

Collection agency. A business organization whose chief function is to collect the debts of its clients.

Commerce. Trade, for example, buying and selling goods and services, particularly among states and nations.

Common carrier. A business that provides a transportation service for hire, charges uniform rates, and makes its service available to the public.

Conditional sale. An installment sale in which title to the goods remains with the seller until all payments have been made.

Conglomerate. A **corporation** that consists of companies in different industries.

Consignment. The transfer of goods for shipment or sale to another party while retaining title to the goods.

Consolidation. Combining separate organizations into a single company.

Consortium. An association or society; a group formed to undertake a venture beyond the capabilities of an individual member.

Consultant. A person who provides professional advice and services as an expert.

Consumer goods. Goods produced for consumption rather than for the production of other goods.

Corporation. A legally chartered organization created to conduct specified business operations in which owners are liable only for the amount of their investment in the corporation.

Corporation service company. An organization that provides services for **corporations** that they cannot or do not want to provide for themselves.

De facto corporation. A company that exists "in fact" but is not legally chartered to conduct business.

De jure corporation. A company that is a legal **corporation** and is legally entitled to carry on its business.

Direct mail. Marketing goods and services to prospective customers through the mail.

Dummy incorporators. The persons who initially set up a **corporation** to meet a state's corporation laws but then drop out.

Economy of scale. Efficiency in production, where average or per-piece costs decline as output increases.

Eleemosynary corporation. See **Charitable corporation.**

Employment agency. A business whose chief function is to find available positions for job seekers and to find prospects for available positions.

Entrepreneur. Someone who assumes the risks of starting, managing, and operating an enterprise.

Equal-opportunity employer. An employer who does not discriminate because of race, color, religion, sex, nationality, age, or physical handicap.

Ergonomics. Also known as human engineering; the science of efficient, effective, and safe worker-machine interaction.

Fair-market value. An obtainable price that is fair and reasonable in terms of current conditions.

Featherbedding. The illegal practice of paying for services or work that has not been or will not be performed.

Feedback. Returning a portion of the output of a machine, system, or process to the input stage; returning to the point of origin; loosely, any information provided about someone or something.

Finance company. A business whose chief function is to lend money to individuals and/or other businesses.

First in-first out (FIFO). A method of valuing goods where those acquired first are sold first.

Foreign corporation. A **corporation** doing business in a state other than the one in which it was incorporated.

Franchise. A right that one business gives to another to market its goods or services in a particular territory in return for some compensation.

Free trade. Foreign commerce that is free from import-export duties and other government restrictions.

General contractor. A person or business that assumes complete responsibility for an entire construction project but may hire **subcontractors** to perform certain tasks.

Goodwill. An intangible asset that represents the difference between the market value of a business and its net assets.

Gross national product. The total value of a nation's goods and services produced in a specified period.

Holding company. A company that controls other companies by owning and holding their **stock.**

Honorarium. A nominal payment in recognition of and gratitude for services performed when traditional compensation is inappropriate.

Incorporate. To form a legal corporation.

Interlocking directorates. **Boards of directors** of two or more **corporations** that have one or more directors in common.

Interstate commerce. Trade in which shipments cross state borders.

Intrastate commerce. Trade carried on within one state.

Inventory. A detailed list of property and goods on hand at a given time; the assets of a business.

Investment company. A company that invests in other companies' securities and sells its own shares to the public.

Job lot. An odd, or mixed, assortment of goods; a contract for something less than the usual contract.

Joint stock company. A company similar to a **corporation** except that each of the owners has unlimited liability.

Joint venture. A business association of two or more parties for a specific purpose without the usual requirements of a formal **partnership.**

Last in-first out (LIFO). A method of valuing goods in which the ones acquired last are sold first.

Limited partnership. A **partnership** where a partner's liability is limited to the amount of his or her investment.

Liquidation. The distribution of assets in a dissolved **corporation** to the **stockholders** after paying all corporate debts.

Management by objectives. A management technique whereby goals are set for a specified period and management and labor jointly direct their efforts toward meeting those goals.

Markdown. The amount by which a price is reduced below the original retail price.

Markup. The amount by which a price is raised above the original retail price.

Massachusetts trust. A business organized like a trust, with permanent trustees similar to directors and beneficiaries similar to **stockholders.**

Merchandising. Buying, controlling, and reselling merchandise.

Merger. The union of two or more **corporations** where one retains its identity and the other(s) becomes a part of it.

Merit rating. The change in state unemployment insurance tax according to a company's stabilization of employment, with lower rates available to companies that avoid a high labor turnover.

Moneyed corporation. A **corporation** that deals in money or lending it.

Moonlight. To hold another job in addition to one's regular, principal source of employment.

Nonprofit corporation. Also known as not-for-profit corporation; a **corporation** organized for some purpose other than making a profit.

Nonstock corporation. A **corporation** such as an educational institution that does not have **capital stock.**

Palletization. Shipping goods on lightweight wooden platforms so that several units can be sent as one large unit.

Parent corporation. A business that owns the majority of another company's stock and fully controls that company.

Partnership. An association of two or more persons conducting business for profit, with each partner fully liable for all partnership debts.

Preemptive right. The right or privilege extended to **stockholders** to buy additional shares of new **stock** in proportion to their current holdings before the stock is offered to others.

Promoters. Persons who form a **corporation** and occupy a position of trust until **stockholders** elect a **board of directors.**

Proprietorship, sole. A business with one owner.

Public corporation. A **corporation** formed by a state or federal agency to serve the public.

Public service corporation. Also known as public utility company; a **corporation,** regulated by a public service commission, that provides public services.

Public utility corporation. See **Public service corporation.**

Pyramiding. The process by which one or more **holding companies** purchase **stock** in other holding or operating companies to control them or speculate for profit.

Quasi-public corporation. See Public service corporation.

Registered office. An office set up by a **corporation** in another state to meet that state's requirements for doing business there.

Resident agent. Someone who resides in another state where a **corporation** does business to satisfy that state's requirements.

Retailing. See Merchandising.

Rights. A privilege extended to **stockholders** to purchase additional shares of **stock** at a specified price before a specified date.

Seniority. The status of an employee who because of long service in a company has a position of preference in matters such as job security and promotions.

Silent partner. A partner who has no voice in management affairs but is nevertheless fully liable for the **partnership's** debts.

Shareholder. See Stockholder.

Stock. Units, or shares, of ownership in a corporation.

Stock corporation. A **corporation** that has its ownership divided into shares of **stock** and that distributes its net profits in the form of dividends to **shareholders.**

Stock insurance company. An insurance company that has its ownership divided into shares of **stock,** with net earnings distributed to the **shareholders.**

Stock ledger. A book, or record, containing information about each **stockholder's stock** ownership in a **corporation** and any changes in those holdings.

Stockholder. Also known as shareholder; someone who owns shares of **stock** in a **corporation.**

Subcontractor. A person or business that agrees to perform part or all of the work specified in another party's contract.

Subsidiary. A business controlled by a **holding** or **parent company** that owns a majority of its **stock.**

Trademark. A symbol, mark, or design that legally identifies a business or its product.

Transfer agent. A person, bank, or trust company that oversees the transfer of a **corporation's stock** and insures that all requirements are properly fulfilled.

Vetoing stock. A class of **stock** that carries no right to vote in the election of directors but does carry voting rights on certain other matters.

Voting trust. An agreement whereby **stockholders** transfer their **stock** and voting rights to a small group of people for a specified period.

White-collar workers. Personnel in clerical, office, and professional positions.

BUSINESS LAW

Abrogation. The repeal or annulment of a law by an authoritative act.

Acceleration clause. A contract statement that makes an entire debt immediately due and payable when some condition of the contract is breached.

Acknowledgment. A declaration that something is genuine; signing a legal instrument before an authorized official such as a notary public and swearing that you executed the instrument.

Affidavit. A written statement sworn to by the maker before someone officially authorized to administer an oath.

Agreement. A contract; an understanding between two or more persons.

Allegation. A statement that is claimed to be true but has not yet been proved true.

Allonge. A piece of paper attached to a **negotiable instrument** to allow space for writing **endorsements.**

Amendment. A change or revision in a formal document.

Amicus curiae. "Friend of the court"; someone permitted to appear in a lawsuit even though not a party to the suit.

Answer. A **defendant's** formal written response to a **plaintiff's** charges.

Antitrust laws. Laws to protect trade from monopolies and to prohibit conspiracies and trusts that restrain interstate commerce.

Assignment. The transfer of property or rights to property to another party.

Attachment. The act of taking or seizing a debtor's property to place it under the court's control.

Attestation. The act of witnessing the signing of a written instrument and signing it to so signify.

Bailment. Delivery of property by the owner to another party for temporary care.

Binder. A temporary agreement that is binding until a formal contract takes effect, especially common in arrangements for insurance coverage.

Blue law. A state law prohibiting Sunday business activity.

Blue-sky laws. Laws that regulate and supervise stock sales and other investment activities to protect the public from fraudulent stock deals.

Bona fide. Honest or real; in good faith.

Breach of contract. Failure, without legal justification, to carry out one or more terms of a contract.

Breach of warranty. Failure of a seller to provide what a warranty promises.

Caveat emptor. "Let the buyer beware"; a common-law doctrine that customers buy goods at their own risk.

Cease and desist order. An order from an administrative agency, similar to a court order, to refrain from some practice deemed unfair.

Certiorari. "To make sure"; a writ from a superior court to an inferior court to send the records of a particular case.

Citation. A summons to appear in court; a notice of legal violation; a reference to legal authority in printed material.

Civil law. Law handed down from the Romans.

Class-action suit. A lawsuit brought by one party on behalf of others in the same situation.

Codicil. An addition to a will that modifies the previous version.

Collusion. Secret action undertaken by two or more persons to commit fraud or to cheat another party.

Common law. Law based upon custom and tradition as opposed to statutory enactment.

Complaint. A formal written statement by the **plaintiff** in a civil lawsuit charging the **defendant** with some wrongful action.

Confiscate. The government's act of seizing private property without payment.

Construction warranty. The promise of a contractor that the construction work is free from defects.

Constructive. That which is legally if not factually true.

Default. Failure to fulfill a legal obligation.

Defendant. The person or organization against whom a civil or criminal legal action is brought.

Defraud. To cheat or to deprive of something rightfully due to a person or organization.

Del credere. An agent who sells goods for another party and guarantees that the buyer will pay for the goods.

Disaffirmance. The repudiation of something or withdrawal of prior consent.

Eminent domain. Government's right to take private property for public use upon payment for it.

Endorsement. The writing of one's signature, with or without additional words, on a **negotiable instrument** or **allonge.**

Equity. Fairness, or fair dealing, in a particular situation.

Estoppel. A bar that prevents someone from taking a certain position that is contrary to or inconsistent with a prior act or statement.

Ex parte. Done by or for one party; done with only one side present.

Felony. A serious crime, usually carrying a minimum prison sentence of one year or more.

Garnishment. A legal proceeding by a creditor, following judgment against a debtor, to compel a third party to pay money to the creditor instead of the debtor; a court order that attaches a person's wages or property.

Guaranty. A promise to fulfill an obligation if another party fails to do so.

Holder in due course. Someone who acquires a **negotiable instrument** in good faith, unaware of any claims against it or other problems.

Indemnity. An express or implied contract to compensate or reimburse someone for possible or actual loss or damage.

Indenture. A formal written instrument that defines reciprocal rights and duties.

Joint and several. Both together and individually; for example, one or all parties may be responsible for something depending on the option of another party.

Jurisdiction. The geographical area within which a court or other official body has the power and right to exercise authority.

Libel. Written or published defamation or injury to someone's reputation.

Lien. A claim against property where the property serves as collateral until a debt is paid.

Liquidated damages. The amount decided by parties to a contract, or fixed by the court, to satisfy the loss resulting from a **breach of contract.**

Malpractice. Injurious or improper conduct by someone acting in a professional or official capacity.

Mechanic's lien. A worker's legal claim to property until the owner pays money due to the worker.

Misfeasance. The improper performance of an otherwise legal act.

Mistrial. A trial that a judge declares void because of a major defect in procedure.

Negotiable instrument. A signed document, which promises to pay a specified sum of money on demand or at a future date, that can be transferred by **endorsement** and/or delivery.

Nonfeasance. Failure to perform a required legal duty.

Nonnegotiable instrument. A financial document that cannot be transferred to another party by **endorsement.**

Notarize. To witness and certify the validity and authenticity of a signed document.

Novation. The substitution, by agreement, of a new contract for an old one.

Null and void. No longer having legal force or validity.

Obligation. Any duty, debt, or formal written promise.

Option. The right to buy or sell something at a certain price by a certain date.

Patent. A right given by the federal government to make, use, and sell an invention during a specified period.

Personal property. A legal right to or interest in something movable (not land or anything permanently attached to it).

Plaintiff. The party that brings a lawsuit against another party.

Pledge. The personal property that is offered to a lender as security for a debt until the debt is paid.

Power of attorney. A document signed by one party that authorizes another party to act in the first party's behalf.

Price fixing. Setting prices artificially instead of letting them respond to free-market operations; the illegal setting of prices by private firms.

Privity. Private or inside knowledge; a close or successive relationship among persons who have a legal interest in the same right or property.

Probate. The process of proving the validity of a will.

Protest. A written statement that expresses disagreement with a payment being made and reserves the right to recover it later; a formal certificate to liable parties giving notice that an instrument has been dishonored by refusal to make (or accept) payment.

Quasi contract. An obligation based on a relationship between parties instead of a formal written agreement.

Quiet title, action to. Proceedings to establish clear title to land.

Quo warranto. "With what authority"; a court proceeding that questions someone's right to do something or to hold a particular office.

Rescission. Court action to annul or cancel a contract.

Referendum. Submission of a law to the direct vote of the people.

Restraining order. A court order to prevent someone from taking certain action until a hearing has been held.

Restrictive covenant. A clause in an agreement that limits one party's action.

Search warrant. Written permission from a judge or magistrate for the police to search some person or place.

Slander. Oral defamation of another person in the presence of a third party.

Statute of frauds. State laws requiring that certain contracts be signed and in writing to be valid and enforceable in court.

Statute of limitations. State laws setting a time limit within which legal action must be brought.

Statutory law. Laws enacted by legislative action.

Stipulation. A formal agreement, usually in writing, between opposing lawyers in a lawsuit; a condition stated in a contract or agreement.

Subpoena. A court order requiring a person to be in court to testify at a specified time and date.

Substantive law. Law pertaining to rights and duties (e.g., contract law) as opposed to procedural law (e.g., law of pleading).

Succession. The legal transfer of a deceased person's property and rights to the heirs.

Summary proceeding. An abbreviated form of legal proceeding available in certain situations.

Tort. A civil wrong done to another person other than a **breach of contract.**

Trespass. Wrongful entry onto another person's property.

Trust. An arrangement whereby one party holds property for the use and benefit of another person(s).

Ultra vires. "Without power"; outside the scope of or in excess of something.

Unfair labor practices. Illegal action by a union or employer.

Uniform Commercial Code. A set of laws covering major types of business law that have been adopted in whole or in part by most states.

Unilateral contract. A contract in which one side agrees to do something.

Usury. The practice of charging an illegally high interest rate.

Waiver. The act of giving up a right voluntarily.

Warranty. A promise or affirmation made by a seller to a buyer as part of a transaction.

Without recourse. The phrase used by an endorser of a **negotiable instrument** to indicate that he or she will not be liable if the other party refuses to accept payment.

REAL ESTATE

Abandonment. The act of voluntarily giving up the rights of ownership or other interest in property.

Abeyance. The suspension of title to **real property** until correct ownership has been determined.

Abstract of title. An abbreviated history, or compilation, of the documents that record the succession of ownerships pertaining to a parcel of land.

Accession. The right of a property owner to own something that becomes part of his or her property through an act of nature or by improvements to the property.

Appraise. To analyze and place a value on **real estate.**

Appurtenance. A right (e.g., a **right of way**) that is accessory or incidental to the other rights of property ownership.

Assessment. The estimation of property value for tax purposes.

Blanket mortgage. A general **mortgage** that covers all of the **mortgagor's real property.**

Broker. Someone licensed by the state to deal in **real estate** who brings buyers and sellers together for a commission or fee.

Cloud on the title. A claim against or an **encumbrance** on property that affects its **title.**

Commercial property. Property zoned for business use.

Community property. Property owned in common by husband and wife, with both persons owning all of the property.

Condemn. To take private property for public use without the consent of the owner but with just compensation.

Condominium. A residential complex in which the interior living space is privately owned by each resident and the rest of the complex, including the land, is owned in common with all other residents.

Cooperative. A residential complex in which residents buy stock in the corporation owning the complex in order to secure the right to occupy a unit.

Deed. A document that represents the transfer of **real property** ownership from one person to another.

Deed of release. A **deed** that is evidence of the release of property from a lien after the debt is paid.

Deed of surrender. A **deed** that temporarily transfers **real property** to another party.

Documentary stamps. Stamps affixed to a **deed** or a stamped notation on a deed that shows the amount of transfer tax paid in the sale of **real property.**

Domicile. A person's permanent place of residence.

Dominion. Ownership of or power over something.

Earnest money. The deposit a buyer pays to a seller to show good faith and intention to purchase the property at an agreed-upon price.

Easement. The right of others to use a portion of someone's land for specified purposes.

Eminent domain. The government's right to take private property for public use with just compensation to the property owner.

Encroachment. Construction of something that intrudes onto another party's property.

Encumbrance. A claim against property such as a **mortgage.**

Equitable mortgage. A lien against **real property** that is enforceable in court but does not constitute a legal **mortgage.**

Equitable ownership. Also known as equitable title; ownership of **real property** by someone who does not have legal **title.**

Equity. The market value of **real property** minus any liens or **mortgages** on the property.

Escheat. The reversion of property to the government when there are no legal owners or heirs.

Escrow. A deposit (**deed,** money, etc.) with a third party such as a real estate broker until certain obligations are met.

Estate. Interest in or **title** to **real property.**

Eviction. Court action to remove someone such as a **tenant** from possession of **real property.**

Fee simple. Ownership of property whereby the owner has unrestricted power and rights in disposing of it.

First mortgage. A **mortgage** on **real property** that takes priority over all other voluntary claims against the property.

Foreclosure. Legal proceedings to terminate a **mortgagor's** rights to property and to sell the property to pay off the **mortgage.**

Graduated lease. A lease under which the rental charge will vary with subsequent appraisal or passage of time.

Homestead. The house, adjacent buildings, and contiguous land of the head of a family.

Investment property. Property purchased and sold or used primarily to produce a profit.

Joint estate. Ownership of **real property** by two or more persons whereby the remaining owners inherit the share of any owner who dies.

Joint tenancy. The undivided interest in **real property** of two or more **tenants** with interest passing to the survivors when one tenant dies.

Judicial partition. The legal process by which a coowner relinquishes his or her interest in **real** or personal **property.**

Judicial sale. A sale ordered by the court.

Land grant. A gift of land from the government to a person or an organization, usually with certain provisions.

Landlord. The owner of land or buildings that are leased to **tenants.**

Lease-purchase agreement. A **lease** with an option that enables the **lessee** to purchase the property being rented.

Leaseback. The sale of land by someone who then leases it from the buyer.

Leasehold. Land or buildings held by lease.

Lessee. The party (tenant) that leases land and/or property from someone else.

Lessor. The party that owns land and/or property and leases it to a **tenant.**

Life estate. A right to property that exists during the life of someone and then reverts to the grantor or a third party but cannot be inherited.

Life tenant. Someone who has possession of land during his or her lifetime.

Mortgage. An instrument by which a **mortgagor** pledges property as security in return for a loan from the **mortgagee.**

Mortgagee. The party that lends money to a **mortgagor** and receives a **mortgage.**

Mortgagor. The party that borrows money from a **mortgagee** and gives the **mortgage.**

Multiple listing. A listing with one **realtor** that is then submitted by that **realtor** to all other members of an association.

Ninety-nine-year lease. The longest-term lease available to a **tenant** in many states.

Nonnegotiable title. A **title** to **real property** that cannot be transferred to another party by endorsement.

Open-end mortgage. An agreement whereby the **mortgagor** may borrow money paid on the principal under the same **mortgage.**

Open listing. A nonexclusive listing of **real property** with any real estate agent(s) of the seller's choosing.

Property tax. A tax on both personal and **real property.**

Purchase and leaseback. The purchase of **real property** from an owner who then leases the property back from the buyer.

Purchase-money mortgage. A **mortgage** on property that a buyer gives to a seller as security to finance part of the purchase.

Purchase and sale agreement. The contract between a buyer and a seller.

Quiet enjoyment. A covenant in a lease or conveyance that promises a **tenant** or grantee the right to enjoy and use the premises without disturbance or interference.

Quiet title action. Court action that establishes ownership of **real property.**

Quitclaim deed. A **deed** that releases someone's **title,** interest, or claim to property rights or ownership.

Real estate. Synonymous with **real property** in many states; land and anything permanently attached to it such as a building.

Real property. Synonymous with **real estate** in many states; land and anything permanently attached to it such as a building.

Realtor. A **real estate broker** who is a member of the National Association of Realtors.

Realty. See **Real estate.**

Right of way. The right that a property owner grants to another party to pass over the property, for example, an **easement;** a strip of land used by the general public, a railroad, or a public utility for a roadbed, a sidewalk, power lines, sewer pipes, and so on.

Sale and leaseback. The sale of **real property** by someone who then leases it back from the buyer.

Seasoned mortgage. A **mortgage** on which payments have been made regularly over a relatively long period.

Sheriff's deed. A document to indicate property ownership rights that is given to a buyer at a **sheriff's sale** held in **foreclosure** of **mortgage.**

Sheriff's sale. A court-ordered sale of property to satisfy a judgment against a debtor's property.

Special warranty deed. A **deed** that includes the seller's promise to protect the buyer against claims of ownership involving the seller and his or her heirs.

Standby mortgage. A **mortgage** on which regular interest payments are made and the principal is repaid upon maturity.

Sublease. An agreement whereby a **lessee** in turn leases part or all of the leased premises to another party.

Tenancy in common. Undivided ownership of an **estate** by two or more persons in which the separate interest of a person who dies passes to the heirs and not the surviving coowners.

Tenancy by the entirety. Joint ownership of an **estate** by husband and wife in which each owns the entire property so that when one dies the survivor automatically owns the property without probate.

Tenancy at will. Possession of premises by permission of the owner or **landlord** without a formal lease.

Tenant. A **lessee,** or renter, of **real property.**

Title. Evidence of ownership.

Title defect. See **Cloud on the title.**

Title search. The process of reviewing all recorded documents pertaining to certain **real estate** to determine if any defects or problems exist that might affect the condition of the **title.**

Unencumbered property. **Real property** that is clear and free of liens and other **encumbrances.**

Warranty deed. A **deed** used in many states that promises that the **title** to **real property** is good, complete, and free of defects.

INSURANCE

Absolute liability. A classification of liability where a negligent person is considered liable regardless of fault.

Actual cash value. Replacement cost of property minus depreciation; a fair cash price for something on the open market.

Actuarial rates. Rates calculated using mathematical formulas in conjunction with loss history and pertinent loss projections.

Agent. A representative of an **insurance company.**

All-risk insurance. Coverage for all perils except those excluded or restricted in the contract.

Annuity. A contract that pays benefits from a predetermined date for a specified period or during the **insured's** lifetime.

Assumed liability. A contract in which one party assumes liability that another party may incur.

Assumption-of-risk rule. A common-law doctrine, superceded by **workmen's compensation laws** in some states, that employees are paid for assuming risks associated with their work and hence cannot recover for work-related injuries.

Automatic coverage. A policy feature by which coverage is automatically extended under certain circumstances.

Average-loss clause. See **General-average loss** and **Particular-average loss.**

Beneficiary. The party designated to receive the benefits of a life insurance contract.

Binder. A temporary agreement to provide insurance coverage until the formal policy is ready.

Blanket bond. Coverage for all employees in an insured organization.

Blanket coverage. Coverage in one policy for several locations or shipments.

Block limit. The maximum amount of insurance that one company will provide within a city block or area.

Blue Cross-Blue Shield plans. State-authorized plans providing health-care coverage by nonprofit associations.

Broker. Someone who sells insurance and represents the client rather than the **insurance company.**

Business interruption insurance. Property insurance coverage for loss of profit resulting from loss of building and/or contents.

Cash value. The dollar value of the reserve of an individual life insurance policy.

Clause. A statement, section, or part of a policy or **endorsement** that qualifies the policy provisions.

Coinsurance. Insurance where the **insured** pays a percentage of the cost in all losses, according to the terms of the policy; joint insurance provided by more than one insurer.

Commercial blanket bond. A **fidelity bond** with a single limit per loss regardless of the number of employees involved.

Commercial policy. A policy with high **indemnity** limits for certain risks.

Comprehensive. A type of coverage including all perils except those identified in the agreement as restricted or excluded.

Contingent liability. A liability dependent upon a future event or some condition.

Contributory negligence. A situation where a negligent person is harmed by another's negligence as well as his or her own failure to be careful.

Cosurety. One of two or more persons who signs a bond as a guarantor.

Declarations. The part of an insurance contract that identifies the parties to and states the terms of the contract.

Deductible. The specified amount that the **insured** must pay in the case of losses, with the insurer paying the balance.

Deposit premium. The **premium** paid for a provisional amount of insurance on something that will fluctuate during the period covered requiring an adjustment at the expiration date.

Direct loss. The amount of damages to property directly resulting from some insured peril.

Divided coverage. A different amount of coverage for each category within a general form of coverage such as personal property; coverage usually included in one policy that is divided between two or more companies.

Domestic insurer. An insurer that maintains a legal residence in one state and is licensed to do business in that state.

Earned premium. The dollar portion of a policy **premium** that represents the time portion of the policy period that has passed; for example, the dollar amount of an annual $100 premium that applies to the first six months' protection is $50.

Effective date. The date on which a policy goes into effect.

Effective time. The time that a policy goes into effect on the **effective date.**

Endorsement. An attachment to a policy that qualifies, or amends, the original coverage.

Endowment policy. A life policy with a savings feature that provides a face amount if the **insured** dies or will repay a specified amount to the insured later as a lump sum or in periodic payments.

Equity. The value of a life policy minus liens or other claims against the policy.

Exceptions. Provisions in a health insurance contract that restrict or eliminate coverage.

Exclusion. Provisions in any insurance contract that restrict or eliminate coverage.

Face value. The dollar amount of coverage specified in an insurance contract.

Federal Deposit Insurance Corporation (FDIC). A federally authorized corporation that provides insurance for deposits in participating banks and other financial institutions up to $100,000 per account.

Federal Savings and Loan Insurance Corporation (FSLIC). A federally authorized corporation that provides insurance for deposits in participating federal savings and loan associations and other financial institutions up to $100,000 per account.

Fidelity bond. A form of suretyship secured by an employer to provide protection against the loss of money or property caused by the dishonest acts of employees.

Flat rate. An insurance rate that is not related to value.

Floater. A policy that provides coverage for goods at any location within a specified area.

General agent. Someone who represents an insurer in a specified territory.

General-average loss. In ocean marine coverage, a requirement that all parties having cargo on a vessel help pay for any loss by one of the parties that occurred as a result of attempts to rescue the vessel from an insured peril.

Graded policy. A policy with premiums based on size, where the greater the amount of insurance, the lower the per-unit cost.

Gross premium. An amount consisting of a charge for estimated losses, costs, and profit without consideration for loss experience.

Group insurance. Coverage provided through employers and associations to their employees and members, usually at a rate lower than individual policy rates.

Hazard. A potentially threatening or dangerous condition that may increase the probability of loss or injury.

Health perils. Conditions such as accidents, sickness, and disabilities that may cause loss or injury.

Hold-harmless agreement. A promise by one party to pay claims that might be brought against another party.

Indemnity. A provision for compensation or reimbursement in case of a particular type of loss.

Independent agent. Someone who arranges **contracts with insurance companies** of his or her choosing.

Indirect loss. An economic loss that results from another direct loss to property caused by an insured peril.

Insurance company. An organization whose function is to insure individuals and/or firms.

Insured. The party that purchases insurance protection from an **insurance company.**

Joint life policy. A life insurance policy that covers more than one person, with the **face value** payable upon the death of one of the **insured.**

Legal liability. Liability that can be enforced by the courts.

Liability insurance. Any form of coverage (e.g., general, automobile, employers' liability) for liability loss incurred by individuals and businesses.

Lloyd's of London. An insurance exchange where individual **underwriters** gather together to arrange to insure all sorts of risks.

Loans. Money advanced by the insurer to the holders of **endowment** and similar life insurance **policies** from their **premium** payments at a rate of interest specified in the contract.

Manual rates. Insurance rates established by combining large groups of similar exposures, or losses, into classes, with the same rate applied to all exposures in a particular class.

Medicaid. A federally funded, state-administered medical-care program for the needy.

Medicare. A medical-care program for retired persons, disabled workers, widows, children, and certain other cases funded by the Social Security Administration and consisting of both compulsory basic hospital insurance and voluntary supplemental medical insurance.

Modified no-fault automobile insurance. A common no-fault plan that permits tort actions in cases of loss exceeding a preestablished ceiling. See also **No-fault automobile insurance.**

Multiple-line insurance. Coverage that combines several lines of property and casualty insurance (e.g., fire, liability, crime) into a single contract.

Multiple-peril coverage. Property insurance that combines more than one property peril into a single contract.

Mutual insurance company. A corporation without capital stock owned by and operated for the benefit of the policyholders.

Net line limit. The maximum amount of insurance available on a single exposure, or loss.

No-fault automobile insurance. Coverage in some states where each operator or owner's **insurance company** pays for injury in or damage to his or her vehicle up to a specified limit no matter who caused the accident.

Noncancellable policy. A policy with a provision that the insurer may not cancel the policy before the insured reaches a specified age provided that premiums are paid as required.

Off-premises coverage. Protection for personal property while it is away from the premises named in a policy.

Old age, survivors', disability, and health insurance. A federally authorized plan (OASDHI) operated by the Social Security Administration for the benefit of retired persons, disabled persons, and certain other persons in need, with funds provided by mandatory employer-employee and self-employed contributions.

Overinsurance. Carrying so much insurance that benefits would provide more income than circumstances would otherwise provide, for example, more income from disability payments while not working than one would ordinarily receive from wages or salary if working.

Participating policy. An insurance policy that provides a dividend to the holder.

Particular-average loss. In ocean marine coverage, a partial loss to the cargo of one party that does not require contributions from the other parties as would be the case with a **general-average loss.**

Policy limit. The dollar amount of coverage specified in a contract.

Premium. The dollar amount that the **insured** pays to an **insurance company** for particular coverage.

Principal. The person who designates someone else **(agent)** to act on his or her behalf; the **surety** who insures or guarantees something.

Reinsurance. The protection one **insurance company** receives against all or part of its risk by in turn insuring itself with another insurance company (the reinsurer).

Replacement cost. The valuation of new property that would be purchased to replace the old that was damaged, destroyed, or lost.

Scheduled coverage. A list of property covered in a policy and the amount of coverage per item.

Self-insurance. The practice of predicting losses and setting aside funds (rather than purchasing insurance coverage) to pay for those losses if and when they occur.

Short-term policy. A policy that is in effect less than one year.

Standard policy. A basic contract form that is used by many **insurance companies.**

Stock insurance company. An **insurance company** that issues shares of stock and is owned by the shareholders and whose profits are paid to the owners as dividends.

Straight deductible. A specified amount that the **insured** pays in any loss (e.g., 20 percent), with the insurer paying the balance.

Surety. The party that guarantees someone else's performance and must answer to a third party in event of default.

Term policy. Life insurance that provides protection for a limited time and will make payment of the established amount if the **insured** dies within the specified period.

Underwriter. The party that decides whether to accept particular insurance risks and on what terms.

Valued policy. A contract that sets the value of insured items when the policy is written.

Waiver of premium. A provision in a policy that premiums need not be paid during a specified period of disability, but the policy will nevertheless remain in full force during that time.

Warranty. A promise by an applicant for insurance that certain conditions will be met in order for the coverage to be in effect.

Workers' compensation laws. Laws in effect in most states that require businesses to pay into a fund from which payments are made to workers injured on the job regardless of negligence or fault.

PRINTING AND PUBLISHING

Acetate overlay. A clear, transparent sheet placed over original **copy** or art to show separations of color and of **line drawings** and **halftones.**

Agate line. A measurement used by newspapers and with advertisements (14 agate lines = 1 **column inch**).

Air brush. A device used for artistic effect and to retouch photographs that functions like a small spray gun.

Artype. Various **typefaces** printed on transparent sheets that can be transferred to artwork.

Ascender. The part of a **lowercase** (small) letter that extends above the main body of letters such as b, d, f, h, k, l, and t.

Backbone. The bound edge of a book.

Backing up. Printing on the reverse side of a printed sheet.

Basis weight. The designation of paper based on the weight of 500 sheets in the standard size for the particular grade of paper.

Ben day. A process of creating special effects and tone variations in **printing** and **engraving** by using various special screens, or shading patterns.

Binding. A process of attaching loose pages together, usually by one of the six common types of binding: gluing, saddle stitching, side stitching, perfect binding, plastic binding, and spiral binding.

Bleed. **Printing** that is run off the edges of a sheet so that no white margin shows.

Blowup. An enlargement of a drawing, a photograph, or typography.

Boldface. A **typeface** that is dark and heavy **such as this.**

Bourges. Colors, whites, and grays printed in various tones on transparent sheets that are used with artwork as **acetate overlays.**

Bristol. Paper of various finishes in postcard weight or heavier that is used for announcements, posters, paperback book covers, etc.

Broadside. A large sheet of paper, printed on one or both sides, that is folded to a smaller size.

Burnishing. Rubbing over something such as **Artype** to make it adhere to another surface.

Caps. Also known as **uppercase;** capital letters.

Caption. The description accompanying an illustration.

Caret. A mark (^) used in copyediting and proofreading to indicate where a word(s) is to be inserted.

Center spread. The two pages in the center of a publication that are placed side by side, facing each other.

Character count. The number of characters (letters, figures, spaces) in a line of typed **copy.**

Cold type. A method of preparing **copy** for reproduction using paper, film, plastic, or any means other than **hot type.**

Column inch. A measure of space common in newspaper work that is the equivalent of one inch deep and one column wide.

Combination plate. An **engraving** plate that has both a **halftone** and a **line drawing** or type.

Complementary colors. Any one of the **primary colors** yellow, red, and blue in association with the other two primary colors combined (e.g., yellow alone with red and blue combined = yellow and violet).

Compositor. Also known as typesetter; someone who sets type by hand or machine.

Comprehensive. An elaborate, hand-prepared facsimile of the proposed finished (printed) job.

Copy. Manuscript material prepared for submission to a **compositor** or printer.

Copyediting. Correcting and improving drafts of written material in preparation for the **compositor.**

Copyfitting. The process of selecting type styles and sizes for **copy** to fit into the available space on each page.

Copyright. The legal protection of and exclusive rights to a literary, musical, or artistic work for a specified period.

Copywriting. Writing the text and heads for an ad or brochure.

Cropping. Marking on an overlay or on the edges the portions of a photograph to be used in reproduction.

Cut. A zinc **engraving** used in letterpress printing; any photoengraving; loosely, any **halftone** (halftone cut) or **line drawing** (line cut).

Dead. A **printing** job ready for disposal or distribution.

Descender. The part of a **lowercase** (small letter that extends below the base line of letters such as g, j, p, q, and y.

Direct mail. Advertising by mailing sales material such as letters, cards, and brochures directly to customers.

Dropout negative. A **halftone** negative with highlight dots that do not appear on an **engraving** or offset plate.

Dry brush. The technique of preparing a drawing by using a dry brush moistened only slightly with India ink.

Dry mount. A method of affixing photographs and other reproductions to another, usually heavier, surface by using a heated press and a tissue between the reproduction and its backing that melts under heat, binding the reproduction to the backing board.

Dummy. A complete, page-by-page drawing of the job to be printed that blocks off and labels the space for columns of type, headings, photographs, and so on, with all items drawn in the exact size they will appear in on the printed version. See also **Pasteup dummy.**

Duotone. A black and white photograph reproduced by making two plates, one for **printing** in a color and the other for printing in black, thereby creating an effect different from the usual photograph in black and white.

Editing. See **Copyediting.**

Em. The square of any size of type (1 em space in 12-**point** type = 12 points square).

En. One-half of the square of any size of type (1 en space in 12-**point** type = 6 points square).

Engraving. A zinc **cut;** a **printing** process (intaglio) where an image is etched into a plate and the depressions filled with ink to leave an impression on paper.

Etching. The process of using acid to eat away the unwanted parts of an **engraving,** or metal plate; an impression made from an etched plate.

Fake process. A means of full-color reproduction by making color separations with overlays on the original artwork for each color desired.

Flat. A large sheet of yellow or orange paper used in offset **printing,** with windows cut into it for taping negatives into position.

Flop. An instruction to the printer to turn a picture the opposite way it appears in a **proof.**

Flush. An instruction to a **compositor** or printer to set type, artwork, and so on against (flush with) the right or left margin.

Folder. A printed sheet folded to make separate pages.

Folio. The page number.

Font. An assortment of all characters in a particular size and style of type.

Format. The size, shape, style, and overall appearance of a typed or printed piece.

Four-color process. A full-color **printing** process in which the **primary colors** and black are printed together to achieve the effect of a full range of colors.

Freelancer. Someone who is self-employed and provices a service for other companies and individuals, for example, a freelance writer, copyeditor, and artist.

French fold. A sheet printed on one side and folded to make four pages.

Full color. See **Four-color process.**

Full measure. Type set the full width of a page or column, flush with the left and right margins.

Galley proof. A **proof** of type set in a galley (metal drawer or tray); generally, any first proof of typeset material.

Gang printing. Combining two or more jobs on one press run.

Gate fold. A double-size page in a publication, folded in half, that makes two facing, attached pages when opened and folded out.

Glossy. A photographic print on shiny, coated paper preferred for better tonal range in reproduction.

Gothic. See **Sans serif.**

Grain. The direction of the fibers in paper, which determines the way paper should be printed and folded.

Gutter. The inside margins in a book.

Hairline. An extremely thin line.

Halftone. Artwork with intermediate tones such as a photograph; a reproduction process that uses a pattern of dots of different thickness.

Hickey. A blemish.

Hot type. Type that is set using metal characters or lines of type, for example, linotype, as opposed to **cold type.**

Imprint. The name and address of a firm imprinted on a previously printed catalog, Christmas card, brochure, or other publication.

Indicia. A special permit notice authorized by the U.S. Postal Service that is printed on envelopes or mailers instead of metering the mail or applying postage stamps.

Initial letter. The first letter of text **copy** sometimes set in a size larger than the rest of the text.

Insert. An addition to a publication that is usually printed separately and placed in the publication before **binding.**

Italic type. A **typeface** with slanting lines *such as this.*

Justify. Setting type so that both the right and left sides of a typeset page or column are even, or in a straight line.

Kill. An instruction to the printer to delete certain material.

Layout. An artist's drawing of a proposed piece that blocks off and identifies type and illustrations in the size and position they will occupy on the final, printed version. See also **Comprehensive.**

Leading. The spacing between lines of type measured in **points;** inserting thin metal strips to separate lines of type in composition methods such as linotype.

Line drawing. Artwork consisting of black lines with no tonal values such as you would find in a **halftone.**

Logotype. A symbol used to identify a particular firm that appears on its stationery, products, and other material.

Lowercase (lc). Small letters such as *a, b,* and *c.*

Makeready. Preparing a press for **printing.**

Makeup. Preparing each page for reproduction by arranging the final typeset copy and finished illustrations in their proper position, often using a **dummy** or **pasteup dummy** as a guide.

Mask. A protective cover placed over portions of artwork to avoid having them blemished with unwanted ink and paint.

Mat. Short for "matrix"; a paper mold, commonly used by newspapers in letterpress **printing,** from which a **stereotype** is made.

Mechanical. A finished piece of artwork and type ready for the camera.

Montage. An arrangement of type, artwork, photographs, or anything else grouped together to depict something by way of a composite picture.

Negative. Photographic film made from **line drawings,** type **halftones,** and other material and used to make a **positive** image on an offset plate.

Overlay. See **Acetate overlay.**

Overrun. The excess of printed copies over the number ordered.

Page proof. A **proof,** or copy, of typeset material that has been divided into pages.

Pasteup. A **mechanical.** See also **Pasteup dummy.**

Pasteup dummy. A **dummy** that shows the desired arrangement of material to be printed with copies of the type, and sometimes of the illustrations, pasted down on sheets of the same size as the proposed final product. See also **Dummy.**

Perforating. The process of cutting through a dashed or dotted line on printed material so that a portion of the material can easily be torn off by readers.

Pica. A basic unit of measure in **printing** (1 pica = 12 **points** = ⅙ inch).

Point. A measure of type size (1 point = 1/12 **pica** = 1/72 inch).

Positive. A photographic image on paper, glass, film, or other surface that corresponds to the original in terms of tonal values, as opposed to a negative, which reverses the values.

Primary colors. Yellow, red, and blue; the three basic colors that can be combined to create all other colors and, when used with black, to accomplish **four-color process work.**

Printing. Often, the three stages of composition (typesetting), printing (duplicating type and illustrations on paper), and **binding** (attaching the printed pages together); the process of duplicating images on paper or some other surface as, for example, in *offset printing* (where negatives of original copy are made and, in turn, offset plates are made from the negatives) and *letterpress* (which uses a **relief** principle whereby raised surfaces are inked to create an impression on paper).

Proof. A copy of typeset material such as a **galley proof, page proof,** or **press proof,** used to check for errors and defects before final copies are photographed and printed.

Rate card. A card (or sheet of paper) on which a magazine or newspaper lists its advertising rates and its requirements for preparing and placing ads.

Ream. A measure in the paper industry, usually 500 sheets of any size. See also **Basic weight.**

Relief. A **printing** process (e.g., letterpress) that uses a raised surface such as an **engraving,** which is inked to create an impression on paper.

Roman type. An ordinary **typeface** such as the one used generally throughout this book unlike *italic* and **boldface.**

Rough. A **layout** without the elaborate detail of a **comprehensive.**

Sans serif. Modern, gothic **typefaces** without **serifs,** or without strokes along the tops and bottoms of letters.

Scaling. Computing the correct proportionate size (width and height) to which a photograph should be reduced to fit precisely in the space indicated on a **layout.**

Scoring. Creasing heavy paper for folding.

Screen. A cross-ruled sheet used to break up a photograph into dots for reproduction; a **Ben day** pattern used by engravers and offset printers to create a special effect; a transparent film with a pattern placed over a **mechanical** to create a special effect.

Self-cover. A cover on a publication of the same paper as the inside pages.

Self-mailer. A printed piece that can be mailed without an envelope.

Serif. A short line or stroke crossing the ends (bottoms and top) of a letter; the opposite of **sans serif.**

Signature. A large sheet of paper on which a number of pages (e.g., 8, 16, 32) are printed that is then folded so that the pages fall into sequence, ready for **binding.**

Silk screen. A stencil **printing** process that presses ink through a fabric screen to transfer the image onto another surface.

Small caps (sc). Small capital letters, or letters smaller than the regular **caps** in a piece of material, SUCH AS THIS.

Spine. See **Backbone.**

Stereotype. A duplicate **printing** plate made from a paper **mat.**

Stripping. Placing negatives in **flats** to use in making offset plates.

Substance. See **Basis weight.**

Tone. Color variation.

Trademark. A symbol or name that identifies the origin of a product, or the organization that makes it.

Transfer letters. See **Artype.**

Transparency. A color print placed on transparent film from which paper prints and **printing** plates can be made.

Trim size. The final size of printed material.

Typeface. A particular type design such as Times Roman available in various sizes (e.g., 10 **point**) and weights (e.g., **italic**).

Typemark. Writing on a manuscript next to the various sections and elements of **copy** (text, headlines, and so on) the desired **typefaces,** sizes, weights, **leading,** column widths, and so on in order that the typeset page will have the appearance and arrangement of copy that you want.

Typesetter. See **Compositor.**

Upper-lowercase (ulc). Capital and small letters as in the *Office Sourcebook*

Uppercase (uc). Capital letters such as *A, B,* and *C.*

Wash drawings. An artist's drawing using lamp black paint diluted to various **tones** of gray to create the effect of a **halftone.**

Watermark. A manufacturer's design lightly pressed into paper so that it can be seen when held up to the light.

White space. The blank area, or open space, around illustrations and type in printed material.

Widow. An undesirable short line at the end of a paragraph that falls at the top of a page.

Wrong font (wf). A **typeface,** accidentally inserted, that is different from the others where it appears

Index